TCP/IP For Dummies
5th Edition

S0-BCP-502

Sheet

Favorite RFCs

- RFC 3271 "The Internet is for Everyone," by V. Cerf
- RFC 2664 "FYI on Questions and Answers — Answers to Commonly Asked New Internet User Questions," by R. Plzak, A. Wells, E. Krol
- RFC 2151 "A Primer on Internet and TCP/IP Tools and Utilities," by G. Kessler, S. Shepard
- RFC 2504 "Users' Security Handbook," by E. Guttman, L. Leong, G. Malkin
- RFC 1244 "Site Security Handbook," by J.P. Holbrook, J.K. Reynolds; still useful after many years

And for laughs, some April Fools' Day RFCs:

- RFC 3251 "Electricity over IP," by B. Rajagopalan
- RFC 1925 "The Twelve Networking Truths," R. Callon, Editor
- RFC 2100 "The Naming of Hosts," by J. Ashworth; we love the poetry
- RFC 2549 "IP over Avian Carriers with Quality of Service," by D. Waitzman

Network Security Terms and Tips

- **Encryption:** Protecting network data by applying a secret code that makes the data indecipherable to anyone who doesn't have the key.
- **Public key/private key:** An encryption scheme that uses two keys to encrypt and decrypt data. Anyone can use a public key to encrypt data before it goes across the Internet. Only the receiver has the private key needed to read the data. PGP (Pretty Good Privacy) and DES (data encryption standard) use public key/private key encryption methods.
- **Authentication:** Proving that you are who you say you are. The simplest form of authentication, an unencrypted username/password challenge, is often not reliable enough for the Internet. On the Internet, where crackers can fake or steal more than your username and password, requiring authentication for computers and IP addresses is a good idea.
- **Digital certificate:** A special secure file that guarantees your online identity. A digital certificate contains security information, including your name and e-mail address, your encryption key, the name of the Certificate Authority, and length of the certificate's validity. Digital certificates are a popular way to perform authentication on the Internet.
- **TLS (Transport Layer Security):** A TCP/IP protocol that guarantees privacy on a network by providing authentication and encryption.
- **IPSec (IP Security):** Another TCP/IP protocol that provides authentication and encryption services, but on a lower layer than TLS.
- **Computer Security Information:** This site (www.alw.nih.gov/Security) covers security issues and advisories, and offers programs, patches, and a directory of other security sites.
- **Computer Security Resource Center at the U.S. National Institute of Standards and Technology Computer Security Resource Clearinghouse:** At www.csrc.nist.gov, you'll find security publications, alerts, and news, including documents from the U.S. Department of Defense on security architecture and trusted systems.

For Dummies: Bestselling Book Series for Beginners

TCP/IP For Dummies, 5th Edition

Cheat Sheet

TCP/IP Definitions

- **Protocol:** A formal description of the rules that computers on a network must follow to communicate. Protocols define communication rules that range from the order of bits and bytes to how two programs transfer files across an internet.

- **TCP/IP (Transmission Control Protocol/Internet Protocol):** A set of protocols, services, and applications for linking computers of all kinds. Intranets, private internets, and the Internet are built on TCP/IP.

- **IP address:** The 32-bit (IPv4) or 128-bit (IPv6) numeric address for a computer. You must have an IP address to be connected to the Internet. An IP address consists of two parts: the network piece and the host piece. An IPv4 example: 127.0.0.1; an IPv6 example: 0:0:0:0:0:0:0:1 (::1 for short).

- **Loopback address:** A special IP address (127.0.0.1) that isn't physically connected to any network hardware. You use it to test TCP/IP services and applications without worrying about hardware problems.

- **An internet:** Any network of networks connected by TCP/IP.

- **The Internet:** The largest international network of networks connected by TCP/IP. The Internet includes the World Wide Web.

- **Intranet:** An organization's private network. If your intranet is built on TCP/IP protocols, applications, and services, it's also an internet.

- **Extranet:** A private/public hybrid network that uses TCP/IP to share part of an intranet with an outside organization. An extranet is the part of an intranet that outsiders can access via the Internet. Be sure to have good security practices if you have an extranet.

- **Subnetting:** Dividing one large internet into smaller networks (subnets) where all share the same network portion of an IP address.

- **NAT (Network Address Translation):** Helps the Internet not run out of IP addresses by translating an IP address (perhaps not unique) on one network to another IP address on a different network, usually the Internet. Microsoft ICS (Internet Connection Sharing) software includes NAT.

- **CIDR (Classless InterDomain Routing):** Another way to conserve on IP addresses. An IP addressing design that replaces the traditional Class A, B, C structure. CIDR allows one IP address to represent many IP addresses. A CIDR address looks like a regular IP address with a "suffix" on the end, such as 192.200.0.0/12. The "suffix" is called an *IP prefix*.

- **Virtual private network (VPN):** A private network that runs over the public Internet. You can build a VPN at low cost by using the Internet (rather than your own system of private — and expensive — lines) with special security checks and a tunneling protocol. Companies today are beginning to use a private virtual network for both extranets and wide-area intranets.

Acronym challenged? If you don't know what a particular acronym means, try www.ucc.ie/info/net/acronyms, the World Wide Web Acronym Database. You may get a laugh out of some of the translations.

Copyright © 2003 Wiley Publishing, Inc. All rights reserved.

Item 1760-0.

For more information about Wiley Publishing, call 1-800-762-2974.

For Dummies: Bestselling Book Series for Beginners

TCP/IP

FOR

DUMMIES®

5TH EDITION

by Candace Leiden and Marshall Wilensky

Foreword by Scott Bradner

Wiley Publishing, Inc.

TCP/IP For Dummies®, 5th Edition

Published by
Wiley Publishing, Inc.
909 Third Avenue
New York, NY 10022
www.wiley.com

Copyright © 2003 by Wiley Publishing, Inc., Indianapolis, Indiana

Published by Wiley Publishing, Inc., Indianapolis, Indiana

Published simultaneously in Canada

For general information on our other products and services or to obtain technical support, please contact our Customer Care Department within the U.S. at 800-762-2974, outside the U.S. at 317-572-3993, or fax 317-572-4002.

Wiley also publishes its books in a variety of electronic formats. Some content that appears in print may not be available in electronic books.

Library of Congress Control Number: 2002110300

ISBN: 0-7645-1760-0

Manufactured in the United States of America

10 9 8 7 6 5 4 3 2 1

5O/RX/RS/QS/IN

About the Authors

Forced to learn about computers because she was afraid of slide rules, **Candace Leiden** has worked as a software developer, system administrator, and database designer and administrator. Formerly the president of Cardinal Consulting, Inc., Candace is currently a systems and database performance consultant and instructional design consultant for international courseware in those areas. Her customers have included Cardinal Consulting, Compaq Computer, Digital Equipment Corporation, the United Nations, several major pharmaceutical corporations, Oracle Corporation, and Hewlett Packard. Candace is an internationally recognized speaker on relational databases and the Linux/UNIX operating systems. Candace is also the author of the *Linux Bible*, published by Wiley Publishing, Inc. Candace met Marshall Wilensky in 1981 when they both worked at the same company. She taught him everything he knows.

Marshall Wilensky has been working with computers for more than 25 years (and still has fewer wrinkles than Candace and less gray hair). He has been a consultant, a programmer, a system administrator, and network manager for large multivendor and multiprotocol networks, including those at Harvard University's Graduate School of Business Administration. At IBM, he is a senior member of the team that created IBM Lotus LearningSpace - Virtual Classroom and the Lotus Hosting Management System. He is in demand worldwide as a speaker on Lotus Domino and Notes, Linux/UNIX, Windows, and networking. Marshall met Candace Leiden in 1981 when they both worked at the same company. He taught her everything she knows.

Candace and Marshall are both members-at-large of ICANN (Internet Corporation for Assigned Names and Numbers). They are also, most importantly, married (to each other).

Dedication

Candace dedicates this book to Emily Duncan, who is wise beyond her years. Even though she has been through some tough times, Emily rules!

Marshall dedicates this edition of the book to Roxcy Platte, who helps him with the toughest subject he has ever tackled.

Authors' Acknowledgments

We continue to be surprised at how many people it takes to create a book. We'd like to thank the team at Wiley for putting up with us. Thanks also go to Mary Bednarek for convincing us to update the 1st Edition (and also for that long ago lunch) and to Tiffany Franklin, our acquisitions editor. Thanks to all the people behind the scenes at Wiley who helped make our documents a real book, especially the graphics department, who had to deal with screen shots from the many diverse computers on our network.

Thanks also to our project editor, Kevin Kirschner for his patience, gentleness, and commitment. We'd also like to thank Nicole Haims at Wiley. When we started this fifth edition, Nicole encouraged us to reorganize the book and aim it at a new target audience. The new structure of this book is the result of Nicole's careful thought and hard work.

We'd like to thank the people who helped us out with software for the examples in this book. Nick Rohrlach of the University Computer Club at the University of Western Australia helped us get permission to use a picture of their soda machine. Thanks also to the UCC's technical skill and creativity for configuring and stocking such an interesting machine. When we next get to Australia, we're going to try Kole Beer (it's not what you think). Bob Watson, formerly from Compaq Computer at the Centre Technique Europe in Sophia Antipolis, France, was extremely generous in providing examples from an IPv6 server running Compaq TRU64 UNIX. When IPv6 was an infant, Bob was already an expert. Finally, thank you to Monte VanDeusen who allowed us to use his beautiful photographic Web page as an example.

Publisher's Acknowledgments

We're proud of this book; please send us your comments through our online registration form located at www.dummies.com/register/.

Some of the people who helped bring this book to market include the following:

Acquisitions, Editorial, and Media Development

Project Editor: Kevin Kirschner

Acquisitions Editor: Tiffany Franklin

Copy Editor: Nicole Sholly

Technical Editor: Joseph Phillips

Editorial Manager: Kevin Kirschner

Permissions Editor: Carmen Krikorian

Media Development Specialist: Megan Decraene

Media Development Manager: Laura VanWinkle

Media Development Supervisor: Richard Graves

Editorial Assistant: Amanda Foxworth

Cartoons: Rich Tennant (www.the5thwave.com)

Production

Project Coordinator: Dale White

Layout and Graphics: Joyce Haughey, Stephanie D. Jumper, Jacque Schneider, Jeremey Unger

Proofreaders: Laura Albert, John Greenough, TECHBOOKS Production Services

Indexer: TECHBOOKS Production Services

Publishing and Editorial for Technology Dummies

Richard Swadley, Vice President and Executive Group Publisher

Andy Cummings, Vice President and Publisher

Mary C. Corder, Editorial Director

Publishing for Consumer Dummies

Diane Graves Steele, Vice President and Publisher

Joyce Pepple, Acquisitions Director

Composition Services

Gerry Fahey, Vice President of Production Services

Debbie Stailey, Director of Composition Services

Table of Contents

Foreword

. . . .

*F*or both good and ill, modern society around the world has been trans-formed by the Internet. But the Internet was not the first data communi-cations network, not by a long shot. So what was it about the Internet that enabled the revolution? In a very basic way, it was the use of TCP/IP. TCP/IP enabled the Internet to be the first data network where the use could be driven by the users and not controlled by the carriers. TCP/IP is an end-to-end protocol. The network is there to carry the bits from any device at the edge of the network to any other device. This stands in stark contrast to X.25, frame relay, ATM, and other carrier-managed data networks, where the carrier determined who you could talk to, and in an even starker contrast to the phone network, where the carrier determined what you could do.

This end-to-end architecture has resulted in an amazing proliferation of appli-cations because the network does not get in the way of individual entrepre-neurs developing the next great thing and running it over the Internet. It also did not get in the way of millions of people putting up their own Web pages, or, with somewhat more controversy, swapping music and movie files. Even if you take into account the Internet boom and subsequent bust, the Internet, and TCP/IP, is here to stay. And, while here, they will continue to radically change the way we interact with employers, service providers, each other, and the world at large.

You can easily go through life without having to understand how this Internet thing works because it will continue to work even if you do not understand it. I do not have any meaningful understanding of the Theory of Relativity yet make use of its implications every day.

TCP/IP For Dummies, 5th Edition, is for those of you who aren't just curious about how things work, but who want to actually understand what's behind the curtain. (Hint: It's not the Wizard of Oz.)

Scott Bradner
Senior Technical Consultant, Harvard University

Introduction

*T*CP/IP is always a hot topic because it is and always will be the glue that holds the Internet and the World Wide Web together. To be well connected (network-wise, that is), sooner or later you have to become familiar with TCP/IP. So if you want to understand what it is, what it does, what it's for, why you need it, and what to do with it, but you just don't know where to start — this book is for you. If you have to install and set up TCP/IP on your computer at home or on lots of computers for your company, we give you lots of Hands-On sections that take you through the process step by step.

We've taken the mystery out of TCP/IP by giving you down-to-earth explanations for all the buzzwords and technical jargon that TCP/IP loves.

This isn't a formal tutorial; skip around and read as much or as little as you want. If you need to impress your boss and colleagues with buzzwords, you can find out just enough to toss them around intelligently at meetings and cocktail parties. On the other hand, you can go further and discover the most important features and tools, as well as the role that TCP/IP plays in the Internet. It's all right here in your hands.

About This Book

TCP/IP For Dummies, 5th Edition, is both an introduction to the basics and a reference to help you use TCP/IP applications and tools on all kinds of computers connected to networks. Here are some of the subjects that we cover:

- ✔ Uncovering the relationships among TCP/IP, the Net, and the Web
- ✔ Exploring client/server and how it is the foundation of TCP/IP
- ✔ Installing and configuring TCP/IP and its applications on clients and servers
- ✔ Understanding intranets, extranets, and virtual private networks (VPNs)
- ✔ Building and enforcing security
- ✔ Boldly going to the next generation: IPv6

This book is loaded with information. But don't try to read it cover to cover in one sitting. You may hurt yourself. If your head explodes, don't use Internet telephony or send e-mail for at least an hour.

Conventions Used in This Book

All commands that you need to enter yourself appear like this:

COMMAND to type

To enter this command, you type **COMMAND to type** exactly as you see it here and then press the Enter key.

When you type commands, be careful to use the same upper- and lowercase letters that we show (some computer systems are fussy about this).

Whenever we show you something that's displayed on-screen (such as an error message or a response to your input), it looks like this:

```
A TCP/IP message on your screen
```

Foolish Assumptions

In writing this book, we've tried not to make any assumptions about you. Our only assumption is that you're not really a dummy. You're just trying something new. Good for you!

How This Book Is Organized

This book contains five parts, each of which contains several chapters. Following is the layout and a quick look at what you can find in each major part.

Part 1: TCP/IP Basics and Buzzwords

In this part, we explain why TCP/IP is and will continue to be a hot topic. You read about the relationship between TCP/IP and the Internet, how TCP/IP got started, and where TCP/IP is going. You also find out that contrary to its name TCP/IP is a lot more than just two protocols, and you get a look at many of the most commonly used protocols. We also include some important background information about networks in case you don't have a clue about network terminology. You find out about all the major buzzwords that should take you far into the 21st century, "where no one has gone before . . . ."

Part II: Getting Technical with Protocols and Addresses

This part is especially helpful for system and network administrators. It contains some heavy-duty technical information about the protocols that make up the TCP/IP suite. Depending on how deeply you want to get into theory, you may want to skip over some of the topics here. But don't skip this whole part! We show you how IP addresses are constructed, including IPv6 addresses for those of you on the cutting edge. You find out how to assign an address the hard way, that is, manually. If you don't like the hard way (and who does if there's a choice?), we also show you how to let a very handy protocol and service, the Dynamic Host Configuration Protocol (DHCP), lease you an address automatically just for the asking.

And if you're worried that the Internet is getting low on addresses, Part II is where we clue you in on three different ways to make IP addresses go farther: subnetting, CIDR, and NAT. Watch for the Hands-On sections that help you install and configure TCP/IP on different operating systems.

Part III: Using and Configuring TCP/IP Services

TCP/IP is a big set of protocols, services, and applications. Whether you're aware of it or not, you use TCP/IP applications and services to do everything from reading news to exchanging e-mail and online conversations with your friends to copying good stuff like games, technical articles, and even TCP/IP itself. This section explains how these applications and services work behind the scenes with client/server technology. The many Hands-On sections help you configure popular applications and services for both clients and servers.

By the way, is your computer underpowered? In this part, we show you how TCP/IP services let you "borrow" processing power from across the network.

Part IV: Network Hardware and Security

Part IV gets into some advanced topics. If you're a system or network administrator, you may need to know more than just the basics about network hardware. This part describes how TCP/IP messages travel along cables and on routers, hubs, and modems. We give you a few pointers about how to choose the right hardware for your TCP/IP and Internet needs. After you've picked the hardware and installed and configured TCP/IP and your network applications, we hope nothing ever goes wrong for you, but stuff happens. Part IV steps you through a basic troubleshooting procedure so that you can figure out what went wrong and where. Then you can fix it.

The rest of Part IV is devoted to security. You get practical security tips including a Quick Start Security Guide. If you want to delve deeper, you can read about advanced security topics, including the security protocols that are part of TCP/IP. You also find out how to use encryption, authentication, digital certificates, and signatures. You get hands-on advice on setting up a software firewall and the Kerberos authentication server. If you're interested in e-commerce, walk through a secure Internet credit card transaction. Finally, get started with virtual private networks in this part.

Part V: The Part of Tens

You may already know that every *For Dummies* book has one of these parts. Here, you can find security tips, some silly-but-true TCP/IP factoids, places to go and things to do (even if you never leave your computer), and pointers on finding Requests for Comments (RFCs). And all this happens roughly in sets of ten.

Icons Used in This Book

 This icon highlights step-by-step procedures to follow to set up and configure the TCP/IP protocols themselves, as well as services, applications, and security features. We've provided Hands-On sections for different operating systems, including Microsoft Windows XP/2000/NT/98/Me, Linux, UNIX, and Mac OS X. Whew! That covers most of the operating systems you'll be using to access private networks and the Internet.

 This icon highlights buzzwords in the text so that you can find them more easily. You can even build your own Cheat Sheet from these pointers.

 This icon signals nerdy techno-facts that you can easily skip without hurting your TCP/IP education. But if you're a techie, you probably love this stuff.

This icon invites you to check out the software on the CD-ROM.

This icon indicates nifty shortcuts that make your life easier.

This icon lets you know that there's a loaded gun pointed directly at your foot. Watch out!

This icon marks important TCP/IP security issues.

Each time that we use this icon, we're highlighting a Request for Comments (RFC). RFCs are the documentation for the Internet and include standards for the protocols (STD), for your information reference materials (FYI), best current practices (BCPs), and even some humorous articles, such as "The Twelve Days of Technology Before Christmas" (RFC 1882) and "The Infinite Monkey Protocol Suite" (RFC 2795).

Where to Go from Here

Check out the Table of Contents or the index and decide where you want to start. If you're an Information Technology manager, you're probably interested in the buzzwords and why everyone seems to be getting on the TCP/IP bandwagon. If you have no idea what a network is, you may want to start with Chapter 2, just to get a little background. If you're a system or network administrator, you might like to leap to Chapter 5, where we list the major protocols and what they do. Chapters 18 and 20 are about security — a topic that's for everyone who is concerned that his or her data is at risk.

Or, you can just turn the pages one by one. We don't mind. Really.

Part I
TCP/IP Basics and Buzzwords

The 5th Wave — By Rich Tennant

"This part of the test tells us whether you're personally suited to the job of network administrator."

In this part . . .

You can't play the game if you don't know the rules. And TCP/IP is the set of rules — called protocols — for networks. Protocols are the software underpinnings of networks, and the TCP/IP protocols are the software underpinnings of all internet technology, including the Internet and its World Wide Web. TCP/IP also includes services and applications that work with the protocols. Before we get into the hairy details of the protocols themselves, we give you some background about the Internet and the Web, the absolute minimum you need to know about networks in general, and TCP/IP's relationship to them. We also discuss some often used buzzwords in the networking business.

Bear in mind that TCP/IP stays alive by morphing regularly — at times, daily. So in this part, we describe briefly how TCP/IP got to where it is today and what you should expect in the years to come.

Chapter 1

Understanding TCP/IP Basics

*Y*ou bought this book (or maybe you're just flipping through it) to find out about TCP/IP. TCP/IP stands for

Transmission Control Protocol / Internet Protocol

As you work through this book, you discover all kinds of cool stuff about TCP/IP — including what the terms *Transmission Control Protocol* and *Internet Protocol* mean. Let's start with something simple: pronouncing it!

Pronunciation Guide

Pronouncing this acronym correctly is easy — you just say the name of each letter. Oh yeah, ignore the slash (/). Ready? Go. Say

    T C P I P

Try to refrain from making any silly jokes. Please. As you find out in later chapters, sometimes it's technically correct to say just "TCP" or just "IP."

Dear Emily Post: What's a Protocol?

A protocol is a set of rules for behavior that people accept and obey. For example, in the 1970s, when friends met on the street they gave each other the peace sign and said, "Right on!" When Siamese citizens met their King (at least in *The King and I*), everyone kneeled and bowed, and they spoke Siamese (but only when spoken to).

Where do these behavior rules come from? How is it that they are so well known and understood? They aren't always written down, yet society standardizes on certain acceptable behaviors. You can find some minor differences due to circumstances and cultures, but here are some examples of situations when certain behavior is expected:

- When a commoner meets royalty
- When people meet and greet, as in *"Enchanté de faire votre conaissance"* or "Hey dude!"
- On the *Titanic,* as in "Women and children first" (or is it "Everyone for himself" nowadays?)

These examples are part of the formality of connected communication.

Sometimes the rules *are* written down — the rules for driving, for example. Still, they vary from country to country and region to region. In the United States, a yellow traffic light means "Caution, prepare to stop," but in Germany that same yellow light means "Get ready — the light is going to turn green." Similarly, for two or more computers to connect and communicate, they need rules of behavior and conventions. ("After you." "No, after you.")

Common behaviors regarding the connection aren't enough. You also need a common language. At any time, you can dial a telephone and connect with a person halfway around the world. But you can only communicate if you have a common language. (*"Ça va?"* Uh-oh. *"Parlez-vous anglais?"*) To communicate, computers need to speak the same language, and the one they use most often is TCP/IP.

So in the world of computers, a *protocol* is the collection of designated practices, policies, and procedures — sometimes unwritten but agreed upon by the users — and the language that facilitates electronic communication. If network computers are the basis of the Information Superhighway, the TCP/IP protocols are the rules of the road.

TCP/IP Protocols — Rules for the Internet

Although TCP/IP sounds like it's just one or two protocols, it's really a whole set of protocols for connecting computers into the Internet. This set of protocols is called the TCP/IP *stack* or *protocol suite*. We describe the most well-known protocols in the TCP/IP stack in Chapter 5.

Does anyone *not* know what the Internet is?

Talking about TCP/IP without talking about the Internet — and vice versa — is almost impossible. You probably have your own idea of what the Internet is, and in Chapter 4, we describe the Internet thoroughly, but here's a quick definition for now. The *Internet* is millions of computers around the world connected by TCP/IP. The World Wide Web runs on the Internet.

Remember the scene in *Jurassic Park* when Lex realizes she's on a UNIX system? "I know this!" she hollers, starting to press some keys. It's the beginning of the end for the raptors. Thank goodness it was a UNIX system. Otherwise, Lex would be lunch. Some form of Linux or UNIX exists for every hardware platform. A UNIX user can move from a PC to a mainframe and get around with ease because the basic commands are the same. UNIX is like the McDonald's of operating systems — wherever you are, you know what you're going to get.

When you extend this concept of portability and standardization to network protocols, you can understand why TCP/IP is the industry standard. With TCP/IP networks, users perform the Big Four network tasks — electronic mail (e-mail), file transfer, signing on to remote computers, and surfing the Web — in the same way, regardless of the computer hardware. If your company gets a brand-new computer system that you've never even heard of, the e-mail, file transfer, Web browsing, and remote logon all still work in familiar ways, compliments of TCP/IP.

The fact that TCP/IP is an internationally accepted standard for networking makes it an excellent choice for building the Internet.

Checking Out RFCs: The Written Rules

TCP/IP protocols are written down in special documents called RFCs (Requests for Comments). These RFCs are available for everyone to read and comment on — it's part of the democracy of the Internet.

Who writes RFCs?

Maybe you do. When someone comes up with an idea for a new or improved capability for TCP/IP, he or she writes the proposal as an RFC (pronounced R F C) and publishes it on the Internet. You can depend on one thing about RFCs: As long as we have TCP/IP and the Internet, people will write new RFCs.

RFC authors are volunteers and aren't compensated for their creations. Each RFC is assigned a number by which it is known forever after. Reviewers (more volunteers) respond with comments and constructive criticism. RFC authors then revise and update the documents. If everything goes smoothly, the RFC becomes a *draft standard.* Programmers use the draft standard as they design and build software that implements the functionality described by the RFC. Until there is real working code, the RFC isn't considered documentation of an official standard.

Understanding RFC categories

Three categories of RFCs are on the standards track:

- ✔ *STD (Standard):* Approved technical standard
- ✔ *Draft standard:* RFCs that are on the way to being adopted as standards
- ✔ *Proposed standards:* RFCs that are on the way to being adopted as draft standards

Other RFC categories include

- ✔ *EXP (Experimental):* Part of a research or development project, such as RFC 3283 ("Guide to Internet Calendaring").
- ✔ *Historic:* Most historic RFCs are former standards that are now obsolete and have been replaced by more current RFCs.
- ✔ *BCP (Best Current Practice):* Guidelines and recommendations, such as RFC 2350 ("Expectations for Computer Security Incident Response").
- ✔ *Informational and FYI (For Your Information):* Provide general information, such as RFC 2196 ("Site Security Handbook").

In Chapter 23, we describe various ways to get RFCs if you're interested in looking at the technical documentation for the Internet and its protocols.

What's a Transport?

When you need to travel from Boston to New York for a business meeting, how you travel doesn't really matter, as long as you get there on time. You may choose to go by car, taxi, bus, plane, train, bicycle, foot, or snowmobile. Certainly, there are differences in the length of the trip, the cost, your comfort level, and the exact route. But you really just want to get there, and for that, you need transportation.

Depending on your destination and your personal requirements, some transportation choices may be unwise, illegal, or impossible. If you need to get to the moon, would you ride your bicycle? If you had 1 million Euros and a hot date on the observation level of the Eiffel Tower in 30 minutes, how would you proceed? Now, consider transporting information. For example, how many different ways can you tell your mother that you'll be home for the holidays?

✔ Telephone call, telegram, or fax

✔ Postcard or letter

✔ E-mail

✔ Pager

✔ Tell your father and let him tell her

✔ Tie a note to a rock and throw it through the front window

Did you think of others? Does the method matter as long as she gets the message? Maybe not.

You may be used to thinking of a *transport* as the way you move yourself or your things around. But computer networks move information from one place to another. Many times you don't care exactly how the data gets where it's going, as long as it arrives

✔ On time

✔ Affordably

✔ Intact, intelligibly, and uncorrupted

TCP/IP is both a transport for carrying your data and a protocol with rules for how your data should move. And there's one more piece: TCP/IP also has a set of applications, or programs, for chatting with other people on a network, for sharing files, for signing on to other computers, and more. The chapters in Part III explore these services and applications.

The TCP/IP Declaration of Independence

When in the course of network events . . . to form a more perfect union. . . .

You can find many different kinds of network designs and hardware technologies, ranging from circles to stars, from telephone wire to signals bounced off satellites. And new technologies are emerging to enhance or replace the existing ones. One of the biggest strengths of TCP/IP is that it's independent of all the available alternatives:

✔ **The network design:** Circles or stars — TCP/IP doesn't care.

✔ **The transmission medium:** Wire or wireless — no problem.

✔ **Specific vendors:** Take your choice.

✔ **The operating system and computer hardware:** Pick your favorite.

TCP/IP ties networks and the Internet together, regardless of the hardware and software used to build those networks. TCP/IP runs on and connects just about everything. You may have heard about other network protocols, such as IBM's SNA or Novell's SPX/IPX. But no protocol connects as many different hardware and software platforms as TCP/IP. This versatility is the reason that TCP/IP is the world's most popular network protocol.

Dedicated to the proposition that all vendors are created equal

From the beginning, TCP/IP was designed to link computers from different vendors, such as IBM and Hewlett Packard, to name just two. Other network protocols aren't this flexible. With TCP/IP, you can buy the computer that you want or need and know that it can communicate with all of the others.

All implementations of TCP/IP must work together, or *interoperate,* regardless of who created those implementations.

Dedicated to the proposition that all operating systems are created equal

Over 162 million computers run TCP/IP. Many of these computers are capable of running several operating systems. For example, you can install any and all of the following operating systems on the same network:

✔ Microsoft — Windows 95/98/2000/XP

✔ Linux

✔ UNIX

✔ Mac OS

✔ z/OS and other IBM mainframe operating systems

✔ Compaq OpenVMS

✔ Many more

Not to worry — you can run any or all of these operating systems and still have TCP/IP working for you — just use the operating system that best meets your needs. In fact, although the UNIX operating system was the first to come with TCP/IP built in, most operating systems come with TCP/IP these days.

We don't recommend installing all these operating systems on the same computer.

This widespread incorporation of TCP/IP is one indication of its popularity. Other vendors' TCP/IP implementations are still important, though, because they may have features that the bundled implementations don't have. For example, the TCP/IP that Microsoft includes in Windows 95 and Windows 98 only contains network client capabilities. If you need server capabilities for these operating systems, you must get a TCP/IP product with more features. (See Chapter 3 for definitions of client and server.)

TCP/IP takes operating systems back to the future

TCP/IP works with over 20 years' worth of computers and operating systems. It's amazing how you can use TCP/IP with both very ancient computers and very new devices. For example, we saw in the news that someone has installed TCP/IP into a Lego Mindstorm Robot. This is about as futuristic as you can get. Even the latest gaming systems, such as the Nintendo GameCube, have developer kits available for TCP/IP networking. How about browsing the Web from your Sony Playstation2? On the other hand, we also read in the news that someone has used TCP/IP to turn the Commodore 64 (first introduced in 1982) into a Web server.

Chapter 2

What You Need to Know about Networks

etworks are a combination of hardware and software. The TCP/IP protocols are the software that glue the hardware into a working network. So before you get into the software, you need to understand some basic network hardware concepts and terminology, as well as the relationship between networking hardware and software. If you already know basic networking hardware, skip to Chapter 3 and read about client/server computing and where TCP/IP fits into that technology.

TCP/IP provides connectivity for networked computers. (*Connectivity* is just a fancy way of saying *communication*.) Because it's hard to describe just the TCP/IP piece without introducing how the machines are organized and cabled together in the network, we discuss just that in this chapter.

What's a Network?

A *network* is a combination of computers (and other devices) along with the cabling, the network interface cards (NICs) that are inside the computer, and the network software (such as TCP/IP protocols). Figure 2-1 illustrates some of the pieces that make up a network. (We're not kidding. Lots of refrigerators and home appliances are on the Internet. You can find out more about unusual networked appliances in The Part of Tens.)

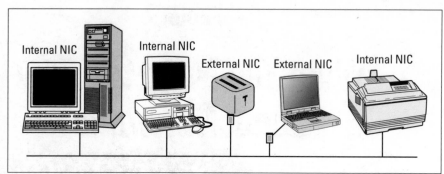

Figure 2-1:
A network
and a few
of its
components.

The protocol software governs how information moves around on the network hardware. TCP/IP is the most widely used protocol on the largest variety of hardware.

Network devices

Any device that sends or receives data can be part of a network, including

- **Computers:** This category includes PCs, palmtops, personal digital assistants (PDAs), workstations, computers running client software, and computers running server software. In Chapter 3, we tell you more about clients and servers. The computer category also includes devices where the computer is hidden inside, such as cars, gaming systems, and global positioning systems (GPSs). POS (point of sale) devices, such as price scanners in modern supermarkets, also fit into the computer category.

- **Printers:** Most people are familiar with printers attached to computers, which are then connected to a network. Instead of connecting a printer to a computer, you can hook certain printers directly to the network wiring.

- **Communications devices:** Anything and everything related to communication gets connected to the network these days — cellular telephones, and even radio and television stations.

- **Things you may not expect to find on a network:** Would you believe vending machines, toilets, and even piranhas? Read Chapter 21 if you're interested in weird and wild things that people have turned into network devices.

Connection media

You need something to connect all your networked devices. Connection media and devices include cables and wires, fiber optics, microwaves, infrared signals, and signals beamed to and from satellites, as well as the modems, hubs, switches, and routers that help hook everything together.

The most important device is a network interface card (NIC) — a computer circuit board, called a card for short, that allows your computer to be connected to a network. A NIC is sometimes called a network adapter. It allows your computer to be connected full time to a network without dialing in. Most office computers use NICs to connect to the corporate network. At home, you may or may not need a NIC. If you connect to the Internet by dialing a telephone number, you need a device called a modem. If you want a permanent always-on connection to the Internet, you need a NIC.

If you have a desktop computer, your NIC is usually inside the computer. If you have a laptop or notebook computer, your NIC is usually a small PC card, which goes in a thin slot on the side of your computer. If you're lucky, the NIC is built-in and simply plug the cable into the appropriate jack. Figure 2-1 shows some computers and their NICs.

If you use a NIC to maintain a "permanent" network connection, consider also adding a modem as a backup connection. Take nothing for granted in the networking world. For example, if you maintain an Internet connection through your cable company and they have an outage, your network connection goes away until the cable company finishes its repairs. But if you have a modem, don't worry. You may not be able to watch your favorite TV show, but you can still connect to the Internet with your modem. You can find more information about these devices in Chapter 16.

Protocols

With all these hardware possibilities for a network, you can see why you need a set of rules for how data should be transmitted across the connection media among all those components. These rules are the network protocols, such as TCP/IP. Some of the other network protocols available are SPX/IPX from Novell and SNA from IBM.

Networks and protocols are inseparable: Without networks, protocols have no reason to exist. Without protocols, a network would be a useless collection of expensive machinery. And without TCP/IP, the Internet would be an idea in search of an implementation. We describe the pieces of the TCP/IP protocol suite in more techie detail in Chapter 5.

Packets, Protocols, and TCP/IP

Protocols aren't really tangible "things" on the network. Instead, they specify how tangible things (the network devices and computers) talk to one another. TCP/IP tells the network devices what to do with your data. Each time a network device handles your data, it obeys the rules set down by TCP/IP.

What do we mean by network data?

We know you know what data is. Now we need you to understand exactly what we mean when we talk about data in a networking context. In this book, we use the term *data* (here short for *network data*) when referring to anything you want to send or receive across a network, such as

✔ An e-mail message

✔ A request to transfer a file

✔ A request to see a Web page

The importance of packets

An important rule says that your data should be moved in small chunks called *packets*. TCP/IP makes sure that your data doesn't get ruined in the process of getting split up and put back together again. TCP/IP determines the format for each packet. Each packet holds

✔ One or more headers containing control information, which tells the network what to do with the packets, including

• The IP address of the destination

• The number of packets that hold your data

• The packet's sequence number

✔ The data that it has to transmit

After the packets are sent, they may not arrive at their destination in order. In fact, the individual packets for one message may travel different routes across a network. In Figure 2-2, an e-mail message is split into packets. At the destination, TCP/IP reassembles the data so that it makes sense.

Breaking your data into packets keeps any network (including the Internet) working efficiently for four main reasons:

Figure 2-2:
TCP/IP
sequences
packets
correctly.

- ✔ **Network efficiency:** The network can balance traffic, including the separate packets of your data, across its hardware. This load balancing makes for faster delivery across a network.

- ✔ **Network sharing:** Your packets can slip onto the network in between someone else's. This means that no one can hog the network by sending out a long stream of data, such as a big picture or an outrageously long e-mail message.

- ✔ **Network availability:** Packetizing network data means that your data is likely to arrive at its destination even if a problem arises with the network hardware. If a piece of network hardware breaks while your data is in transit, the packets can be rerouted to avoid the hardware problem. Your message might take longer to deliver, but the packets will arrive, ensuring the completeness of your data.

- ✔ **Data reliability:** TCP error checks each packet. If a packet becomes damaged while traveling across the network, TCP resends an uncorrupted version of the packet, so that all of your data remains ungarbled and readable.

Packets travel over many different kinds of networks ranging from local area networks (LANs) to wide area networks (WANs). TCP/IP doesn't care much about the network type — just the fact that your data gets where it's going. The following section explains the different types of networks.

How Ethernet Works

Ethernet is by far the most often used local area network architecture. Ethernet allows any device on the network, from a corporate mainframe computer to a cash register in the local delicatessen, to send packetized data to any other location on the network, at any time. Often, lots of devices are on a network, perhaps sending data simultaneously. If the packets collide, Ethernet tells the devices to stop transmitting, wait a little while, and then try again. The wait interval is random and is different every time. The original Ethernet can move information across a network at a *theoretical* rate of 10 Mbps (mega, or million, bits per second). Each character you type is usually 8 or 16 bits. Do the math — 10,000,000 ÷ 8 — and that seems like a lot of data speeding over your network. If that's not fast enough for you, check out the section "Ethernet, how fast can it go?"

The Ethernet architecture is called *CSMA/CD* (Carrier Sense Multiple Access/ Collision Detection), meaning that the devices realize when a collision has occurred, so they know when to wait and retry. With Ethernet, the data from the small deli's cash register is just as important as anything that the headquarters' mainframe has to send. All the devices on the network are equal. Figure 2-3 illustrates a very basic LAN connected by Ethernet. Each device on the network, including the printer, has a NIC and TCP/IP software running.

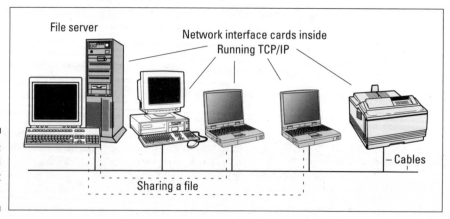

Figure 2-3:
A small
Ethernet
LAN.

How Token Ring Works

In contrast to Ethernet, token ring architecture is more controlled and organized. The network devices are connected in a circle (ring), and a token is passed among the devices on the ring. When a device has data to send, it must first wait to get the token. Possession of the token ensures that the sending device will not compete with any other device. If a device has nothing to send, or when it is finished sending, it passes the token. In a token ring, everyone gets an equal turn, unimpeded. Figure 2-4 shows a token ring LAN. Token ring networks usually run at 16 Mbps, although some older, small ones still run at 4 Mbps. While this may seem slow compared to Ethernet, token ring saves time by not having to manage collisions. In the following section, we describe some faster token ring solutions.

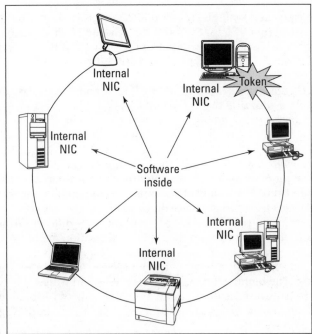

Figure 2-4:
A token
ring LAN.

Getting More Speed

So you want more speed. You have lots of choices — the more money you have, the more choices you have. Both Ethernet and token ring have evolved new technologies that let your data go fast, faster, and fastest.

Fast token ring

No matter how fast data moves across a network, people always seem to need to transmit faster. For token ring users with greed for speed, High-Speed Token Ring (HSTR) runs at 100 Mbps. FDDI (Fiber Distributed Data Interface) technology runs over a pair of fiber-optic rings that pass a token in opposite directions.

Don't expect token ring to go faster than it does today. While there are lots of token rings running, research into higher speed token ring is at a standstill.

Ethernet: How fast can it go?

Fast Ethernet (specified by IEEE standard 802.3aa-1998), moves data at a rate of 100 Mbps — ten times faster than regular Ethernet! Still, collisions, acting like electronic friction, keep your data from reaching top theoretical speed. At 100 Mbps, even slowed down, your data still burns rubber.

Then there's *Gigabit Ethernet* (specified by IEEE standard 802.3z-1998). Imagine your data whizzing by on the network at 1 billion bits per second — 1 Gbps. Be prepared to spend giga-units of money if you need this kind of speed.

Wow! *10GbE* is even faster! An IEEE (The Institute of Electrical and Electronics Engineers) task force developed the standard for an even faster Ethernet informally called 10GbE, running at 10 Gbps. Ten billion bits per second! That's 10,000 times faster than what you probably use every day. The official name for the standard 10GbE is IEEE 802.3ae. 10GbE is different from "regular" Ethernet. It only works over optical fiber connection media.

Also, 10GbE has some bells and whistles built in so that Ethernet doesn't have collisions. The technical name for these bells and whistles is full duplex mode. If you're truly interested in the technical details of 10GbE, have a look at some of the technical white papers at www.10gea.org, the 10 Gigabit Ethernet Alliance Web site.

By the way, don't expect to wire your house or your office for 10-Gigabit Ethernet. This kind of speed is more useful for very large corporate networks and the Internet's backbone connections between networks.

Choosing between Ethernet and Token Ring

Whether your network runs on token ring or Ethernet technology, your data goes where it's supposed to go. Ethernet keeps evolving to satisfy large networks' need for speed. The evolution of token ring, on the other hand, seems to be crawling to a halt. An advantage of token ring is that Ethernet-style collisions don't occur, no matter how busy the network gets. On the other hand, all devices must take a turn with the token, even if they have nothing to send. So on a not-so-busy network, the devices with data to send have to wait for devices that aren't doing much besides taking the token and passing it on. When you're trying to choose between Ethernet and token ring, here are some more factors to consider:

- ✔ **Availability of network interface cards for the particular computers you're using:** In general, Ethernet cards are more common, come from more manufacturers, and are cheaper, but for the most popular computers, both Ethernet and token ring cards are available.

- ✔ **How fast you need to go:** If you need to speed your data across your network, both Ethernet and token ring can go at 100 Mbps. If you need to go even faster, only Ethernet provides Gigabit (and more) speed.

- ✔ **Amount of traffic on your network:** How big is your network? In a high-traffic network, unless you're using 10GbE, collisions may slow down your Ethernet considerably.

- ✔ **Geographical area spanned by the network:** How BIG is your network? Token ring has fewer distance limitations than Ethernet.

- ✔ **Likelihood of network failures, such as broken cables:** When an Ethernet cable is cut, you may still have other working networks in place of the original network. When a token ring cable is cut, you probably just have one disabled token curve.

Geographical Types of Networks

Packets travel over many different kinds of geographical distances, ranging from local to global and beyond to space. TCP/IP doesn't care much about the network geography — just the fact that your data gets where it's going.

LAN versus WAN: Which one for TCP/IP?

It doesn't matter — TCP/IP works for both. TCP/IP is the protocol that connects various computers on LANs as well as WANs. Your choice of network depends on the distance between the computers that you want to network, not on which protocol you want to use. Remember, the Internet comprises gazillions of interconnected networks, and the individual networks can be WANs, LANs, or a combination.

Networks come in different shapes and sizes. The two main geographies for networks, LANs (Local Area Networks) and WANs (Wide Area Networks), are based on how much distance the network covers. The main LAN/WAN categories break down into subcategories, based on a variety of factors, including

- Architecture and connection media

- Speed

- Purpose; for example, does the network connect a city, a campus, or just a bunch of storage devices?

What's a LAN?

LAN stands for *local area network*. (It's usually pronounced as a word, LAN, not as the letters L A N.) The computers and other devices in a LAN communicate over small geographical areas, such as the following:

- Your home office — or even the whole house

- One wing of one floor in a building

- Maybe the whole floor, if it's a small building

- Several buildings on a small campus

LANs can run over various network architectures, such as Ethernet (specified by IEEE standard 802.3) connected by cables and wires, wireless Ethernet (IEEE standard 802.11), and the declining token ring (specified by IEEE standard 802.5). The Institute of Electrical and Electronics Engineers (IEEE) is a group that designs and champions standards. These standardized *network architectures* are ways for data to move across wires, cables, and through the air. We use Ethernet, both wired and wireless, for the examples in this book because it is by far the most popular network architecture.

What's a WAN?

What if your company has several buildings in different towns and states, or even in different countries? Does that mean that all the people who work in the company can't be on the same network because a LAN is limited by distance? Of course not. The Internet is worldwide, so you can even space out with your network by bouncing data off satellites in outer space and create a WAN.

A WAN (*wide area network*) spans geographical distances that are too large for LANs. LANs can be joined together by special-purpose hardware, such as routers, hubs, and gateways (see Chapter 16), to form a WAN. Figure 2-5 shows how you can connect two LANs to form a WAN.

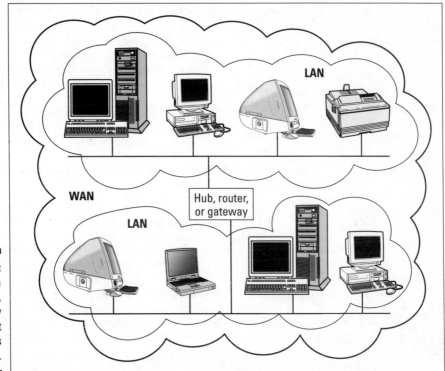

Figure 2-5:
Using a router, hub, or gateway to connect two LANs into a WAN.

Even more "ANs" (area networks)

LANs and WANs are the most common types of networks in the TCP/IP world. The Internet is the largest and best known WAN. The network in your office building is probably a LAN. But let's not stop here. There are also MANs, CANs, and HANs. *CAN*s (campus area networks) connect buildings spread across a college campus, small office park, or a military base. *MAN*s (metropolitan area networks) connect buildings, LANs, and CANs spread across a city. A *HAN* (home area network) connects the devices within a home. Regardless of the network hardware and distances, these networks have one element in common — TCP/IP.

Don't take these "AN" definitions too literally. They refer more to geographic size than to the kind of buildings they connect. For example, for a really large college campus widely spread out, the network type will probably be a MAN instead of a CAN. If your HAN includes your garage, maybe it's really better defined as a LAN. And just to get even more connected, if a university with campuses in two cities connects its two CANs, the end result is a WAN.

A *VAN* (vehicle area network) contrary to what you might think, doesn't let your car talk to your neighbor's truck. A VAN links the electronics and microprocessors in a single vehicle. For example, the ten microprocessors in the Segway Human Transporter (a scooter with a brain) can be called a VAN.

A *PAN* (personal area network) is a tiny network. Only about six feet separate its pieces. If you have a cell phone hooked onto your belt, you could wear an earpiece with a microphone. This is a simple wireless PAN. The geeks at MIT (the Massachusetts Institute of Technology) use more complex PANs. They wear their computers around their waist with a keypad on their arm or leg. The monitor is a pair of goggles. And all these pieces form another wireless PAN. And to get even more geeky, the MIT PANs usually have a wireless connection to the MIT CAN.

What's a SAN (storage area network)?

A *SAN* (storage area network) is a high-volume, high-speed network made up of lots of different storage devices. These storage devices are attached directly to a network, usually through a very fast, expensive connection called Fibrechannel. Figure 2-6 shows a small SAN.

TCP/IP lets you get the benefits of a SAN without the cost of Fibrechannel. First, you need to understand some terminology:

- ✔ SCSI (Small Computer System Interface) is a common interface for connecting peripheral devices, such as disks and tapes, to a computer. SCSI works at the hardware level of your computer.

- ✔ iSCSI (Internet SCSI) is a new Internet Protocol that describes how to connect storage devices into a SAN by putting SCSI commands into IP packets.

Connecting islands of SANs with IP

If you already have Fibrechannel SANs, you may be interested to know that FCIP (Fibrechannel Over TCP/IP) describes a way to use TCP/IP to connect multiple Fibrechannel SANs. In other words, you can build a very large SAN across LANs and WANS by using TCP/IP to connect your individual Fibrechannel SANS.

Because TCP/IP is basically free, that's a SAN that's a whole lot cheaper than the traditional Fibrechannel SAN. The packets then travel across good old Ethernet, and you can use your fancy storage management software to administer your SAN as if it were a Fibrechannel-based SAN.

RFC 2143 describes the protocol for using IP with SCSI.

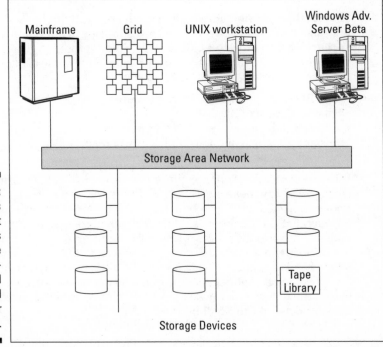

Figure 2-6:
A SAN lets different computers share network-attached disks and other storage.

What's a VLAN (virtual area network)?

So far, all the "ANs" we've described are based on geography, from someone's body to an office building to across a city. A VLAN is a network that has nothing to do with geography. For example, instead of networking a university by CANs, a VLAN lets you network a university by things like departments or type of user.

SOHO Is Not Just a London Neighborhood

Do you have a SOHO — a Small Office Home Office — in which you work, telecommute, or telework? As the number of computers in homes around the world has increased, so have the types of LANs designed for in-home use. You can use Ethernet or token ring or you can choose from the following connection technologies:

- ✔ **Electrical power line networks:** With the right adapters, your computers can exchange data over the electrical wiring in your home. Network speeds range from 10 to 14 Mbps. While older products generally provide only 1 Mbps, that's often plenty of speed for home or for offices that use networking for simple tasks such as file transfers.

- ✔ **Phoneline networks:** With the right adapters, your computers can exchange data over the telephone wiring in your home or office — without tying up the phone. Today's adapters give you network speeds of 1 Mbps and 10 Mbps, but newer devices will reach 100 Mbps. Visit www.homepna.org for more information.

- ✔ **Wireless networks:** Your computers can exchange data by using an *RF (radio frequency) network*. This is similar to the way a cordless telephone transmits to its matching base station, but quite different from the way that cellular phones work. With adapters that comply with the IEEE 802.11b standard, network speeds can reach 11 Mbps. For office use in North America and Europe, fast wireless, IEEE 802.11a, runs at 45 Mbps. 802.11a is not available on other continents as of this writing. Everyone on all continents interested in faster wireless should keep an eye on the progress of the 802.11g research, which will turbocharge wireless networks to 54 Mbps.

Chapter 3

Internetworking Technologies: Client/Server, P2P, and Grid

• •

In This Chapter

▶ Defining clients and servers

▶ Exploring how TCP/IP enables client/server computing and takes advantage of it

▶ Finding out how an old technology — Peer-to-Peer — became new again

▶ Moving towards pervasive collaboration with grid computing

• •

*C*lient/server solutions are the foundation of most TCP/IP services and applications. As you take a look at what client/server means to a network computer user, you see that TCP/IP is an excellent protocol choice for client/server computing. Why? Because TCP/IP allows so many different computers and network devices to communicate as both clients *and* servers.

What Exactly Is Client/Server, Anyway?

Client/server is a distributed style of computing. This distributed approach spreads computing from the central data center to desktops, laptops, and even handheld devices, regardless of where people are located.

Contrary to popular belief, software — not hardware — defines client/server. In the client/server game, a client application on one computer requests services from another computer running server software. The client and server software can run on any kind of hardware. You may even use a gigantic supercomputer running client software to request services from a tiny little PC via some network protocol, such as TCP/IP.

The Server Part of Client/Server

In the preceding section, we write that client/server is defined by software. While that's technically correct, you're going to hear most people refer to computer hardware as clients and servers. So in this section, we extend the definition to more informal definitions of clients and servers. Even though the word *client* comes first in client/server, we need to start with the definition of the server.

What is a server?

A server is software that provides a resource or a service to share with clients. People often call the computer that is running the software "the server." Specialized servers include

- ✔ **Web servers — spun across the Internet:** A *Web server* is software that accepts requests from browser clients to deliver Web objects, such as home pages, documents, graphics, and applets. A Web server finds the requested information on the Internet and ships it back to the browser for you to see. Flip to Chapter 12 for more on how Web servers work. (Note that a Web server on a private intranet is called an *internal information server.*)

- ✔ **Web application servers — collaboration across space and time:** Most Web servers simply deliver information and files to browsers. But there's more to life than just raw information. A *Web application server*, such as Lotus Domino, enables groups of users to interact through browsers to generate collaborative results that aren't possible otherwise. These Web services extend to all kinds of industries, including banking and financial services, healthcare, customer service, advertising, and entertainment. Read Chapter 12 for more information on Web services.

- ✔ **Commerce servers — may I please have your credit card information?** A *commerce server* is a type of Web application server that enables you to conduct business over the Web. The server software includes security features, such as the Secure Sockets Layer (SSL), so that you can use your credit card without worrying. You still have to worry about your bills, though. Check out Chapter 20 for information on commerce servers and SSL.

- ✔ **File servers — from Timbuktu to Kalamazoo:** A *file server* runs applications and services, such as FTP, to share its disk space with other computers. One advantage of having a file server, besides being able to borrow another computer's disk space, is that the shared files still look like they're on your own computer. You don't have to do anything special or different to use the files stored on a file server in your network — even if that file server is thousands of miles away in Timbuktu. Most users don't even realize that they use files that aren't on their own computers. The system administrator usually sets up file sharing for network users.

The computers that borrow the file server's disk space are the clients. These clients may use an operating system that's different from the server's and from one another's. And when you have various operating systems, you have various file formats. The server's job is to hide those format differences from the clients.

✔ **Print servers — closer to home:** Of course, you can print without worrying about networking or client/server if you have your own personal printer connected to your computer. But in a multiple-computer environment, giving each computer its own printer is expensive. Instead, connect one printer to one computer, and let everyone in the office share that one printer. The computer with the printer connected to it is called the *print server* because it runs TCP/IP-based print-sharing software.

✔ **Compute servers — both near and far:** A *compute server* is a computer that runs a program for you and sends the results back to you. For example, analyzing weather patterns requires enormous amounts of computer power. The meteorologists' client workstations often aren't capable of solving the complex mathematics involved, so they send the problem from their workstations over to a supercomputer, which does the calculations and sends the results back. That supercomputer is the compute server. See Chapter 14 for more information on compute servers and cycle stealing.

Dedicating servers to tasks

Usually you dedicate a server computer to one task only. For example, you don't usually run a file server together with an e-commerce server. Reasons to use dedicated servers include

✔ **Performance:** Running different server programs on a single computer may slow down all the servers.

✔ **Management:** Different servers require different system administration tasks. For example, a file server may require a large disk farm and nightly backups, while a compute server, which needs only weekly backups, may require more fine-tuning and a more powerful CPU.

✔ **Security:** Some of the tasks involved in protecting the servers are very different. For example, protecting an e-commerce server requires that you set up secure transactions, something you don't need to do on a file server.

File servers and all those formats — how do they do it?

Software is what makes it all work. Suppose you're on a PC, where your files are in the FAT32 (32 bit file allocation table) format, and you want to use some files on a UNIX server that uses the UNIX File System. If your PC doesn't understand UNIX, how can you make any sense of the files over on the server? Easy! Software on the server translates the files from the server's UNIX file format to your PC's (the client) FAT32 format. And you never see it happen. As far as you, the client, are concerned, your file is automatically in the appropriate format for you to use. This translation is part of what's called *transparent file access* in a client/server environment.

The Client Part of Client/Server

If you've read the previous section about servers, you know that a client/server network relies on specialized central points, namely servers, to provide services. Having all these services available unless something *needs* service, however, doesn't make sense. That needy something is the client. A network contains many, many more clients than servers because a single server can satisfy hundreds (sometimes thousands) of client requests.

What is a client?

It's this simple: A *client* is software that asks for and receives a resource or service from a server. Clients do all sorts of work — anything they want. We could write a whole book just on the types of clients that are out there.

People often call a computer that runs client software *the client*.

Clients, clients everywhere

For each of the servers that we describe in the previous section, you have a choice of many different clients. Consider these examples:

- ✓ **E-mail clients:** If you and your spouse are both accessing the same e-mail server, one of you may use Outlook Express for your e-mail client and the other may use Eudora. The e-mail client you choose is a matter of personal preference.

- ✓ **Browsers:** Probably the most used clients on the Internet, *browsers* are client software that receive services from a Web server. For a full-function browser, you need a graphical browser. Text-based browsers, however, usually work faster than graphical ones and provide access to Web data for people who don't have a graphical interface. Many cell phones contain a *microbrowser* that knows how to display information on the phone's tiny screen.

✔ **Mobile clients:** Mobile, wireless communication devices, including smart cellular telephones, two-way alphanumeric pagers, and PDAs (personal digital assistants, such as the Palm handheld companions), are examples of *mobile clients*. Many organizations are interconnecting their e-mail and voice messaging (also known as voice mail or phone mail) systems together with inbound and outbound FAX services to create *unified messaging* solutions. When companies want employees to be able to work anywhere, at any time, they make their mission-critical applications accessible via WAP, the Wireless Application Protocol.

Client/Server/Server?

Many client/server applications consist of just those two parts: the clients and the server. When a slightly more sophisticated application requires connecting to an additional server, you have a *3-tier application;* the middle piece is often called *middleware.* The accompanying figure shows a 3-tier client/server architecture in which the browser requests information from the application server, and the application server retrieves the data from the database server.

When an application increases in complexity and connects to even more servers, you stop counting the pieces. Anything more complicated than three pieces is called *n-tier* or *multi-tier* client/server computing.

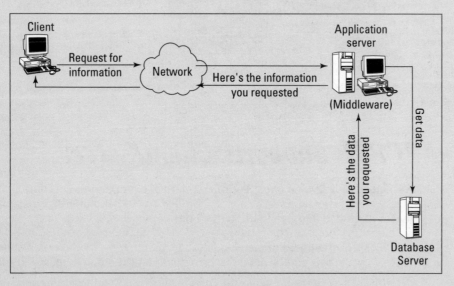

Are You Being Served?

Because of the software it's running (or not running), any computer can be

- ✔ Either a client or a server
- ✔ Both a client and a server
- ✔ Neither a client nor a server

and can change as often as necessary to provide and access any number of services.

Figure 3-1 shows an example of multiple roles: One computer provides a shared printer and is thus a print server, the same computer also shares some of its disk space and files and is thus a file server, and that same computer accesses some files from another computer and, therefore, is also a client of a file server.

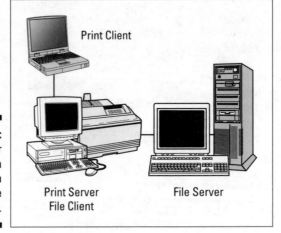

Print Client

Figure 3-1:
A computer
can be a
client and a
server at the
same time.

Print Server
File Client

File Server

How TCP/IP Supports Client/Server

Not only is TCP/IP one of the major enablers of client/server computing, it is also one of the biggest users of it. TCP/IP's layered and modular design makes it easy to design and implement new network services.

TCP/IP is a key element of many, but not all, client/server solutions. Other network protocols can be used on the network at the same time as TCP/IP.

TCP/IP is accepted as *the* protocol that links computers not just to each other but also to all of the different computers and servers in the world, from the smallest palmtop to the mightiest mainframe. TCP/IP makes all of them candidates for clients or servers.

Recognizing Other Internetworking Styles

While TCP/IP itself is built on a client/server architecture and enables most client/server computing, other internetworking architectures also run across TCP/IP networks. Peer-to-Peer (P2P) is an older networking style that has become new again as the Internet has become accessible to so much of the world's population. Grid computing is a different style of internetworking that allows huge numbers of computers to network and collaborate on a single problem.

P2P (Peer-to-Peer): Everything old is new again

Years ago, in the days of yore (yore being Windows for Workgroups), peer-to-peer networks were everywhere. They provided an easy way for cooperating users to share files and other computer resources. In a *peer-to-peer network*, no computer is better than any other or different from any other, at least not until the system managers and users make them different. A peer-to-peer network doesn't require dedicated servers.

Peer-to-Peer workgroups today — still handy?

Small workgroups consisting of Microsoft Windows NT Workstation, Windows 2000 Professional, and Windows 98/Me are still useful today in informal settings. But this convenient network sharing has its downsides:

- Peer-to-peer slows down when too many users (more than 15) try to share.

- Access to resources can be unreliable. For example, imagine that your colleague's computer has a file that many people share. And then suppose that one day your colleague's computer has a disk failure! The end result — a critical file resource is lost to many users.

✔ When resources in a workgroup are limited, the workgroup may disintegrate into a collection of separate computers. Suppose members of your workgroup use so much of your computer's shared disk space that there's no space left for your files. Do you turn off disk sharing or disconnect the network cable?

In the days before Windows 95, many Microsoft-based workgroups ran over a proprietary protocol, NetBEUI. Today's workgroups run across local TCP/IP networks.

Exploring a new use for P2P

The dear departed Napster application brought a new style of P2P computing to the Internet. Napster allowed Internet users to connect to each other's computers to share music. The recording industry sued Napster for copyright infringement, and while Napster is now dead, its application of P2P across the Internet has been adopted by other applications, such as Gnutella. Gnutella allows users to share any type of files over the Internet directly without going through a Web site.

How do the new P2P systems work?

To do P2P file sharing across the Internet, you need a P2P program. The P2P program functions as both a client and a server in one easy-to-use application. In this section, we describe the steps you need to use Gnutella:

1. **Download a free Gnutella P2P program.**

   The Gnutella Web site (`www.gnutella.com/connect/`) maintains a list of clients. So select a client, and begin your download.

2. **Install the P2P software.**

   When you download the software, it is in compressed format, such as a Zip file. The client site tells you how to install the software. Many clients, such as LimeWire from LimeWire LLC (`www.limewire.com`) set up an install wizard for you. Just follow the wizard's instructions.

3. **Run the P2P program.**

4. **Use the search function to find the kind of files you want, such as audio, documents, images, or programs.**

5. **Select the file(s) you want to download and begin downloading.**

Network administrators can use applications to manage network traffic, such as PacketHound from Palisade Systems, Inc. (`www.palisadesystems.com`) to block Gnutella traffic from a network. Reasons to do this might include the following:

 ✔ An effective but brute force way for an organization to protect against employees possibly violating copyright laws is to block all unauthorized P2P sharing.

 ✔ Over-enthusiastic file sharers can clog an organization's network bandwidth. Blocking P2P downloading activity relieves network stress.

Depending on the P2P program you use, security may be extremely lax. For tips on improving P2P security, see Chapter 18.

Exploring grid computing

Grid computing is a networking style that uses many of the computers in a network to work on the same problem at the same time. SETI (Search for Extraterrestrial Intelligence) is a public grid that runs over the Internet. Thousands of computers share unused CPU power to analyze radio telescope signals from outer space. The European Union (EU) is sponsoring research into a grid for high-energy physics, earth observation, and biology applications. In the United States, the National Technology Grid is prototyping various grid applications. The advantages of grid computing to the owners and users include

 ✔ Saving money by utilizing unused CPU power

 ✔ Solving problems that require huge amounts of computing power without using supercomputers

Purdue University and Indiana University have linked their IBM supercomputers into a grid called the Indiana Virtual Machine Room. The grid consists of more than 900 processors. Each supercomputer contains hundreds of separate processors. When a computer program consists of many small parts, those small parts can run on the separate processors of the grid.

The grid is connected by a new super-high-performance fiber-optic cable that enables data to travel at the speed of light. The grid can perform over 1 trillion (1 teraflop) calculations per second.

Chapter 4

TCP/IP and Internets, Intranets, and Extranets

*I*n this chapter, we explain the difference between the Internet and internets, intranets, and extranets. You also get a peek at some high-performance Internet technologies, and you find out who's in charge of the Internet and TCP/IP and how to join them.

The Internet versus an internet

Yes, we know that you already know what the Internet is. But just so that we're all using the same definition: The *Internet* is the worldwide collection of inter-connected computer networks that use the TCP/IP protocol. These networks reach every continent — even Antarctica — and nearly every country.

The Internet is also much more than its network connections. It's all of the individual computers connected to those individual networks, plus all of the users of those computers, all of the information accessible to those users, and all of the knowledge those people possess. The Internet is just as much about people and information as it is about computers and computer networks.

The term *Information Superhighway* is an oft-used synonym for the Internet. If the Internet is a superhighway, the network hardware is the road surface itself. The rules of the road are TCP/IP. And just as on a motorway, issues such as safety, traffic control, detours, vandalism, and accidents must be dealt with to keep traffic flowing smoothly.

When you look up the word *internet* in the dictionary, you find that

✔ *inter* means between, among, or in the midst of

✔ *net* is a group of communications stations operating under unified control

So an internet is what goes on between, among, and within communications stations that are on a network.

While *The* Internet is public, many organizations (companies, universities, and so on) have their own private internets. *An* internet is also how you link one network to another — for example, to extend a local area network (LAN) so that it becomes a wide area network (WAN); see Chapter 2.

In this book, we distinguish "the Internet" from "an internet" by capitalizing the "I" in "Internet."

Is the Internet free?

Yes, the Internet is free, in the sense that you don't pay any of the Internet committees to access the Internet. (See the "Who's in Charge of TCP/IP and the Internet, Anyway?" section for more information on Internet committees.) If you want to register an organization or a private citizen for an Internet address, such as a .com address, however, you must pay a fee. Your Internet Service Provider (ISP) — the company that supplies you with access to the Internet — can take care of the registration for you. The fees and service charges vary.

TCP/IP — child of the Cold War

In the 1960s, the United States government agency DARPA (Defense Advanced Research Projects Agency) funded research on how to connect computers in order to exchange data among them. The purpose of this research was to build command and control functions that would survive a nuclear "incident."

This first network was called the ARPANET, and it connected academic and military research centers. As the ARPANET continued to grow, people began to use it for purposes quite different from the original military uses. The major users were still universities and military and government installations, but they began using the network to share all kinds of nonmilitary information, files, and documents.

DARPA funded the development of a whole set of protocols for communication on the ARPANET. These internetworking protocols are known by two of its parts, TCP and IP, yielding TCP/IP. In the early 1980s, the Secretary of Defense mandated that all computers connected to the ARPANET had to use TCP/IP. That's when the Internet came into being.

You can often find free Internet services, such as free Web site hosting, if you're willing to allow the provider to put advertising on your site.

Is TCP/IP free?

No one group or company "owns" TCP/IP. With the TCP/IP specs conveniently at hand on the Internet, anyone can take them and implement TCP/IP. In fact, many people have. Some of those people and their companies sell their implementations. Most operating systems come with TCP/IP built in. Although hardware vendors usually include some form of TCP/IP with the operating systems installed on their computers, your free version of TCP/IP may not include all the features you need. For example, the TCP/IP bundled with Windows 98 includes a File Transfer client (FTP client) software but no File Transfer server program. This means you can use the FTP application on Windows 98 to copy files to or from an FTP server, but you can't use FTP on another computer to copy files from your Windows 98 computer. To do that, you need to install Windows 98 FTP server software.

If no one owns TCP/IP, who keeps house for it? Today, TCP/IP is an international standard, watched over by the Internet Society, which we describe in the following section.

Who's in Charge of TCP/IP and the Internet, Anyway?

No one and everyone. No one person, organization, corporation, or government owns or controls the TCP/IP protocols or the Internet. Moreover, no one person, organization, corporation, or government finances the TCP/IP protocols or the Internet. "The only thing constant is change," as the saying goes, and TCP/IP is no exception. New capabilities are regularly added and additional organizations connect every day, bringing more users online every minute.

To say that no one controls TCP/IP and the Internet doesn't mean, however, that protocols take effect randomly or that the Internet just does whatever it wants. Here are a few important organizations that influence TCP/IP and Internet policies:

- **The Internet Corporation for Assigned Names and Numbers (ICANN):** ICANN (www.icann.org), pronounced by saying the letters I C A N N or as "eye can," is a nonprofit corporation run by an international board of directors and funded by the Internet community. ICANN is in charge of giving out Internet addresses. The ICANN home page is www.icann.org.

✔ **The Internet Society (ISOC):** The Internet Society (www.isoc.org) guides the future of the Internet by overseeing Internet standards, public policy, education, and training. The members of ISOC include corporations, international and governmental organizations, and individuals. The Internet Activities Board, the Internet Engineering Task Force, and the Internet Research Task Force are all part of the ISOC.

✔ **Internet Activities Board (IAB):** IAB (www.iab.org), pronounced by saying the letters I A B, defines the architecture for the Internet backbone and all the networks that attach to the backbone. The IAB also oversees the Internet's protocols (TCP/IP). The IAB contains subcommittees of volunteers who set standards and work on new solutions to Internet growth problems and works with the IETF, the IRTF, and the IESG to set the direction for research and development of the Internet.

✔ **Internet Engineering Task Force (IETF):** IETF (www.ietf.org), pronounced simply as I E T F, is responsible for keeping the Internet up and running every day. The IAB supervises the IETF. Over 70 working groups make up the IETF. Members of these groups draft and develop standards for TCP/IP protocols.

IETF meetings are open to anyone. If you want to participate in guiding the Internet and TCP/IP, this is the place to start. You don't formally "join" the IETF; you simply participate in a working group or subscribe to one of the many IETF mailing lists. For information about how to join an IETF working group, browse the IETF home page at www.ietf.org.

Check out RFC 3160, "The Tao of the IETF — A Guide for New Attendees of the IETF."

✔ **Internet Research Task Force (IRTF):** The IRTF (www.irtf.org) researches new network technology and experimental protocols. (This group's name, too, is pronounced by saying the letters I R T F.) The IRTF does the theoretical design work, and IETF moves the theory into the practical world of TCP/IP and the Internet.

✔ **Internet Engineering Steering Group (IESG):** The IESG (www.ietf.org/iesg.html), pronounced by saying the letters I E S G, manages how a possible protocol becomes an Internet standard.

✔ **The World Wide Web Consortium (W3C):** A separate standards group just for Web protocols and issues (because the Web is such a huge part of the Internet), the W3C (www.w3c.org) decides which standards to adopt for the Web and its protocols.

What's in store for the Internet?

Governments and universities around the world sponsor various research on super-high-speed Internet technology. Two of these high-speed Internet projects are backbones for the Internet2 in the U.S. and GEANT in Europe. The common goals for both Internet2 and GEANT include boosting the speed, reliability, and security of the Internet. Before we describe these nifty projects, we should tell you a little about the Internet backbone and network backbones in general.

The backbone's connected to the Internet backbone

Your spine is not a single bone, but a collection of connected vertebrae with ligaments, muscles, and nerves spreading from it. Like your spine, a networking backbone is not a single entity. A network backbone is the central connection medium that other lines or even other networks connect to. For example, a corporate network backbone in a small office building would be a trunk of cables (or other connection media) that runs up the building, and other cables, maybe one per floor, would extend from it, kind of like a river with tributaries. From those tributary cables on each floor, there would be other cables that run to each office. Figure 4-1 shows a small corporate network with its backbone.

The corporate backbone in Figure 4-1 connects to an ISP's backbone. The ISP connects our corporate backbone as well as many other organizations' backbone. The ISP's backbone connects to a regional backbone, which is the central connection core for other ISPs. You may have noticed in Figure 4-1 that the backbone no longer looks like a single cable trunk. As you move from your office building's LAN, the "backbones" are made up of many servers and lots of connection media.

On the Internet, the backbone is a set of paths that regional networks connect to for long-distance interconnection. By the time you get out to the Internet in Figure 4-1, the backbone is a set of very large, very fast networks, owned by a few telecommunications companies. For example, America Online, MCI, Sprint, WorldCom, and others provide America's Internet backbone. We think the most amazing thing about the Internet backbone is how it works even though no one controlling network is "in charge."

For maps of many U.S. backbones, check out `www.nthelp.com/maps.htm`. `www.cybergeography.org/atlas/isp_maps.html` includes backbone maps for Europe and Japan.

What is Internet2 (I2)?

Internet2 (I2 for short) connects universities, government organizations, and some corporations that are working on Internet research. Internet2 runs on a very speedy backbone named Abilene.

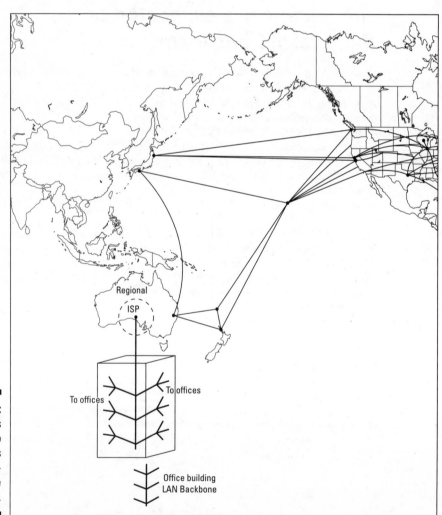

Figure 4-1: Backbones connect to backbones to interconnect the world.

What is Abilene?

Abilene is a super-high-speed backbone for the Internet2 (see Figure 4-2). The fiber-optic backbone is over 10,000 miles long and moves data at rates of 2.4 and 9.6 gigabits per second. Users of Abilene connect not through PoPs, but through GigaPoPs — *Giga* meaning bigger, faster, better.

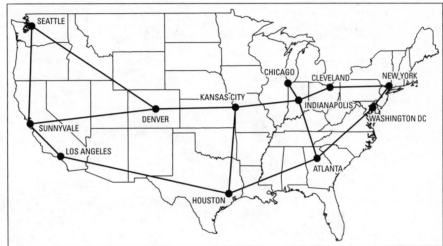

Figure 4-2:
The Abilene backbone crosses the United States.

What is GEANT?

GEANT is another warp-speed research network. GEANT connects 31 countries in Europe for research into advanced Internetworking technologies. The backbone runs at 2.5 and 10 Gbps and connects to other research nets, such as Abilene. Figure 4-3 shows GEANT speeding across Europe. (Want to see it in full, living color? Go to `www.dante.net/geant/AccessSpeedsAug2002.jpg`.)

What do I2 and GEANT mean for me?

The new technologies and capabilities of I2 and GEANT will trickle down to the Internet. Eventually we will all share in the technologies developed for I2 and Abilene as they eventually wind up on the Internet.

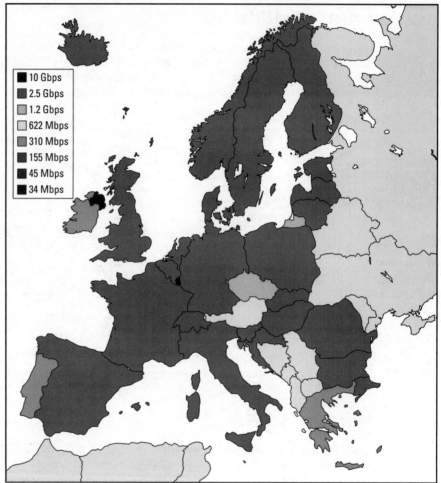

■	10 Gbps
■	2.5 Gbps
■	1.2 Gbps
■	622 Mbps
■	310 Mbps
■	155 Mbps
■	45 Mbps
■	34 Mbps

Figure 4-3:
GEANT's
warp-speed
network
runs across
Europe.

What Is an Intranet?

An *intranet* is a private network within an organization or department —
a university on the East Coast, for example, may have one intranet for its
medical school, another intranet for its college of liberal arts, and a third
intranet for the business school. That university may also network those
intranets together into an even bigger intranet. Then, so that the university
community can reach the rest of the world, the university intranet needs to
be connected to the Internet.

When that university needs to share data with a different university on the
West Coast, the two universities can link their respective internets together
to create an *extranet*.

Virtual private networks are used for both intranets and extranets.

What's the difference between an internet and an intranet?

That's easy. An internet and an intranet are the same if they both use TCP/IP protocols. If a network functions like an internet, but uses some other network protocol suite, it's an intranet.

The Internet consists of both internets and intranets.

How many internets make an extranet?

As many as you need. Internets are the building blocks of extranets. If part of your intranet is available to people outside your organization (such as customers and suppliers), that part you share with the outside world is called an *extranet*. An extranet is

- Multiple, interconnected intranets and internets
- An organization's extended family of business partners, vendors, suppliers, customers, and research partners that all collaborate electronically
- Something that may not exist physically — it's a virtual network

Suppose writers from three companies work together to write a large series of books. They need to share information, but they don't want to open their corporate intranets completely to each other. The solution for these writers is to build an extranet by connecting pieces of their intranets to each other over a telephone line or the public Internet. The writers' extranet may include private discussion groups (in which they work out ideas and share technical knowledge), some shared document files, and multimedia programs and data.

What's a Virtual Private Network (VPN)?

A VPN is a private network that runs over public facilities, such as the Internet. While it may seem like a contradiction to run a private network over the very public Internet, it works. A VPN

- Is safe and secure because it scrambles (encrypts) data before sending on the public lines

✔ Uses a special tunneling protocol on the public network — see Chapter 20 for more information

✔ Is a money-saver for a large organization's networks because sharing public telecommunications lines is usually cheaper than leasing private lines

✔ Is used for both intranets and extranets

The most common use of VPNs is to let an organization's members work as if they were on-site when they're not. Each remote user runs VPN client software to establish a secure connection over the Internet to the organization's network. It's just like being in the office, but a bit slower.

A few words about virtual

In computing terms, *virtual* means something that you think is there, but really isn't. With a VPN, it seems like you have your own private network, but it's not really there. It looks like your network and acts like your network, but it's built on the public Internet. A VPN is your private network at the same time that it's a public network.

Part II
Getting Technical with Protocols and Addresses

The 5th Wave   By Rich Tennant

©RICHTENNANT

"Please Dad– do we have to hear the story of Snow White's OSI model and its 7 layers again?"

In this part . . .

*P*art II delves into the ingredients of the TCP/IP suite:
the protocols and services themselves and IP
addressing. You see how the protocols fit into the layers
of the TCP/IP network model and you get a look at the
most important ones. TCP/IP is called a *suite* because it
consists of more protocols than the two it is named for,
plus a set of services and applications. The TCP/IP protocols, services, and applications in the suite work together
just like the rooms in a hotel suite or the pieces in a furni-
ture suite work together. The protocols are also referred
to as a *stack*.

Moving on from the protocols to IP addresses, you get to
see how IP addresses are constructed, including IPv6
addresses for those of you on the cutting edge. You find
out that you don't always need to assign an address the
hard way — that is, manually. You can let a very handy
protocol and service, the Dynamic Host Control Protocol
(DHCP), lease you an address just for the asking. Also, if
you're worried because you read that the Internet is getting low on addresses, Part II eases your worries by cluing
you in on three different ways to make IP addresses go
farther: subnetting, CIDR, and NAT.

After you've gotten the basic theory down, Part II shows
you hands-on how to configure TCP/IP on lots of different
operating systems, including Mac OS X, UNIX, Linux,
Microsoft Windows XP/95/98/Me, and Windows 2000
Server. Last, but not least, you get familiar with the files
that get created when you install and configure TCP/IP.
You find out what those files are for, what they look like
inside, and when you may need to change them.

Chapter 5

Introducing the TCP/IP Model and the Protocols

*I*f you read Chapter 1, you know that a protocol is the set of agreed-upon practices, policies, and procedures used for communication. In this book, we're concerned with TCP/IP as the protocol for communication between two or more computers. Remember that TCP/IP is actually a large suite of pieces that work together. In this chapter, we look first at the layered TCP/IP organization, and then at the protocols themselves.

TCP/IP's interoperability technology is designed to allow all parts of your network to work together, regardless of which suppliers you bought them from. Toward this goal, TCP/IP divides network functions (for example, getting you connected or sending data) into layers and defines how those layers should interact.

How a de facto standard (TCP/IP) beat out the international standard

www.dictionary.com defines the term *de facto* as "In reality or fact; actually." TCP/IP is the de facto internetworking protocol standard but not the official international standard. The international standard for network architecture and protocols is Open System Interconnect (OSI). International Standards Organization (ISO; pronounced eye-ess-oh) specifies worldwide standards for different types of computing. ISO sets standards for networking, database access, and character sets, among other things. OSI is the name for the ISO network and protocol standards. (OSI is pronounced as oh-ess-eye. Often, it's referred to as ISO OSI, pronounced eye-so oh-ess-eye. We know it's not consistent, but don't blame us.)

If OSI is the "official" standard, why are so few OSI protocols in production, as compared to TCP/IP? One reason is that the OSI specification is extremely complicated and took long to implement all the functionality. TCP/IP is already here and in use. The existence of the Internet proves that computers and networks can connect just fine by using the TCP/IP set of protocols. The OSI layered model, however, lives on and influences TCP/IP and other network models.

Taking a Modular Approach to Networking

TCP/IP organizes the protocols in layers. Five layers are stacked up in the TCP/IP model. We love things like desserts and snacks, so we like to call TCP/IP a five-layer cake.

Technically, the five layers in the cake are called a *stack,* and the protocols that sit in these layers are called a *protocol stack.* Each layer of the stack depends on the layers below it; that is, each layer provides services to the layer above it. When two peer computers are communicating, each computer has its own set of layers. When you send a message to another computer on the network, your information starts at the top layer of your computer, travels down all the layers to the bottom of the stack, and jumps across to the other computer. When your information gets to the other computer, it starts at the bottom layer and moves up the stack to the application in the top layer. See Figure 16-1 for a diagram of these layers.

Each layer has a special function. The lower layers are hardware oriented. The highest layer does user stuff, such as e-mail and file transfers. Starting with Layer 1 at the bottom of the cake, we examine each layer.

Layer 1: The physical layer

The physical layer at the bottom of the stack is pure hardware, including the cable, satellite, or other connection medium and the network interface card. This is where electrical signals move around, and we try not to think too hard about how it works.

Layer 2: The data link layer

This is another layer we don't want to strain our brains trying to figure out. Again, hardware is involved. This is the layer that splits your data into packets to be sent across the connection medium. Here's where wiring, such as Ethernet or token ring (see Chapter 2), gets involved. After the information is on the wire, the data link layer handles any interference. If there is heavy sunspot activity, the data link layer works hard to make sure that the interference doesn't garble the electric signals.

Sunspot activity and solar flares tend to disturb all sorts of transmissions, not just network signals. Your cellular telephone and television reception, for example, can degrade during solar episodes. Even cable TV is affected. Wouldn't it be nice if television broadcasts had a data link layer like OSI's and TCP/IP's to fix poor reception?

Layer 3: The internet layer

The bottom two layers are about hardware, while TCP/IP is software. Layer 3 is the first place where a TCP/IP protocol fits into the networking equation. I P is the TCP/IP protocol that works at this layer. This layer gets packets from the data link layer (Layer 2) and sends them to the correct network address. If more than one possible route (or path) is available for your data to travel, the network layer figures out the best route. Without this layer, your data couldn't get to the right place.

Layer 4: The transport layer

Although the network layer routes your information to its destination, it can't guarantee that the packets holding your data will arrive in the correct order or that they won't have picked up any errors during transmission. That's the transport layer's job. TCP is one of the TCP/IP protocols that work at the transport layer; UDP is another one. (We explain what TCP and UDP do in the section "Transport Layer Protocols," later in this chapter.) The transport layer makes sure that your packets have no errors and that all the packets arrive and are reassembled in the correct order. Without this layer, you couldn't trust your network.

Layer 5: The session layer

The other protocols that make up TCP/IP sit on Layer 5 and above. Layer 5 does the following:

- ✔ Establishes and coordinates a *session*. A session is a connection between two computers. A session must be established between two computers before they can transmit data between themselves. A session announces that a transmission is about to occur and at the end of the transmission, determines whether the transmission was successful.

- ✔ Works with operating systems to convert files from one format to another, if the server and client use different formats. Without file format conversion, file transfers could only happen between computers that had the same file format.

- ✔ Sets up the environment so that applications can communicate with each other and with users. Requests for service and data start at the application layer and move down through the remaining four layers before going out across a network. The application layer is also where secure protocols for specific applications such as Web browsing and e-mail reside.

The TCP/IP Protocol Suite

The *TCP/IP suite* is a large collection of protocols, named after the two original pieces, TCP and IP.

Now you may say, "A suite is too big. Can I just have the protocols I need?" Nope. Sorry. The protocols in the TCP/IP suite move the data from one layer to another and interact with one another. You can't really have a functional network with just one of the TCP/IP protocols.

Figure 5-1 shows the TCP/IP five-layer cake with some of the protocols drawn on the individual layers. You don't need every protocol on the stack to run a network application, but you need at least something from each layer in the stack. So even though you may not use every protocol on each layer, you definitely need more than one.

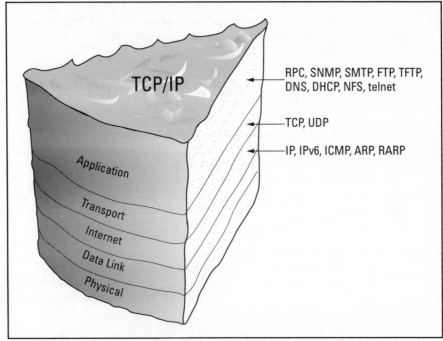

RPC, SNMP, SMTP, FTP, TFTP,
DNS, DHCP, NFS, telnet

TCP, UDP

IP, IPv6, ICMP, ARP, RARP

TCP/IP

Application

Transport

Internet

Data Link

Physical

Figure 5-1:
Here's what
you're in for
in this
chapter.

TCP/IP: More than just protocols

Many pieces of the TCP/IP suite function as protocols, applications, and services. As we talk about all the great things you can do with TCP/IP, we let you know whether you're using a TCP/IP protocol, a network service, or an application — and highlight the places where the same name applies to one or more of these things.

TCP/IP's modular, layered design makes it easy to innovate and add new components. If you envision a new network service, as you go about designing the server and client applications, you can simultaneously design a new protocol to add to the TCP/IP suite. The protocol enables the server application to offer the service and lets the client application consume that service. This simplicity is a key advantage of TCP/IP.

If you create a new protocol/application/service combination for the Internet, be sure to read RFC 2223, "Instructions to RFC Authors."

The CD included with this book includes every RFC in existence at the time of this writing. Because new RFCs appear almost every week, Chapter 23 explains how to get a completely updated listing.

Protocol, application, or service?

In the fabric of a network, you find the protocol/application/service relationship so tightly woven together that it may be very difficult to distinguish the threads in the cloth. We use FTP as an example. FTP stands for *file transfer protocol,* but it's not only a protocol, it's also a service and an application. (Don't worry about FTP itself at this point — it's just an example. If you need to find out how to use FTP, check out Chapter 13.) In this section, we show you how the FTP service, application, and protocol work together to move files around the network.

- ✓ **FTP is a service for copying files.** You connect to a remote computer offering this service, and you can pull or push files from or to that computer. *Pull* is a more techie term for download, which is techie enough. You may have already figured out that *push* is a techie synonym for upload.

- ✓ **FTP is also an application for copying files.** You run a client application on your local computer to contact the FTP server application on the remote computer. Your client application is either FTP, the *file transfer program,* or your Web browser, which uses the FTP protocol behind the scenes for downloads. The server application is often called FTPD, the *file transfer protocol daemon.* (The term *daemon* comes from UNIX. Think of friendly demons haunting the computer to act on your behalf.) You tell the client what you want to do — pull or push files — and it works with the server to copy the files.

- ✓ **Finally, FTP is a protocol for copying files.** The client and server applications both use it for communication to ensure that the new copy of the file is, bit for bit and byte for byte, identical to the original.

FTP is three, three, three things at once — application, service, and protocol. Suppose you need to copy a file from a remote computer. Without the application, your computer doesn't know that you want to copy. Without the service, you don't get a connection to the remote computer that has the files you need. Without the protocol, the client and server can't communicate.

Most of the time, you know from the context whether someone is referring to the service, the application, or the protocol. If you can't quite tell, maybe it doesn't really matter.

And now, on to the protocols!

The Protocols (And You Thought There Were Only Two!)

Hold on tight — here come the pieces in the TCP/IP protocol suite, listed by layer. We start at the bottom with Layer 1 — the physical layer — and move up to the top application layer, which has the most protocols.

In each of the protocol sections, we give you some pointers to RFCs so that you can look up the heavy technical details of the protocols.

The physical and data link layers

Protocols are here in the hardware layers, but they're not part of the TCP/IP stack. The physical layer transforms data into bits that go across the network media. The protocols in the physical layer include protocols for Ethernet, token ring, and FDDI. The data link layer includes MAC (Media Access Control) protocols that understand your network interface card (NIC).

Network layer protocols

While it's the third layer of our cake, the network layer is the first layer where we find TCP/IP protocols. Not only is IP the most important protocol of the network layer, it's the most important protocol of the TCP/IP stack. Without IP, TCP wouldn't know where to send anything. There are a few other network layer protocols. After IP, ARP and RARP are the most known.

IP: Internet Protocol

The Internet Protocol, IP, is responsible for basic network connectivity. IP is like a plate in a basic place setting. When you're eating, you need a plate to hold your food. When you're networking, you need a place to put (send and receive) data — that place is a network address.

The core of IP works with Internet addresses. (You can find the details about these addresses in Chapters 6 through 9.) Every computer on a TCP/IP network must have a numeric address. The IP on your computer understands how and where to send messages to these addresses. In fact, all the other protocols — except for ARP and RARP — depend on IP to get information from one computer to another.

While IP can take care of addressing, it can't do everything to make sure that your information gets to where it's going correctly and in one piece. IP doesn't know or care when a packet gets lost and doesn't arrive. So you need some other protocols to ensure that no packets and data are lost and that the packets are in the right order.

All of this is true for both IP version 4 and the new version 6 (IPv6, originally called *IPng* for next generation). IPv6 is just bigger and better. So if IP is a plate, IPv6 is a serving platter.

Refer to RFCs 791 and 2460 for more information.

ARP: Address Resolution Protocol

When all you know is the TCP/IP address of the remote computer, the Address Resolution Protocol, ARP, finds the computer's NIC hardware address. Every NIC comes with a unique hardware address built into it. You cannot change it. It is not an IP address. ARP is the coordinator between a NIC's hardcoded address and an IP address. With its load of addresses for the devices on the network, ARP is closely allied with IP. (See Chapters 6 through 9 for more on TCP/IP.)

By the way, ARP is a protocol, a service, and an application, although you may never use the application. Refer to RFC 826 for more on ARP.

RARP: Reverse Address Resolution Protocol

When all the computer on your desk knows is the NIC hardware address of a remote computer, the Reverse Address Resolution Protocol (RARP) finds the computer's TCP/IP address.

Check out RFC 903 for more on RARP. Besides being a protocol, RARP is also a service.

Mobile IP

The proposed Mobile IP standard describes how you can connect your mobile device to the Internet from various locations, such as your office, your hotel room, and your car, while keeping the same IP address.

As of this writing, there are 14 RFCs for Mobile IP. We suggest you start with RFC 3220, "IP Mobility Support for IPv4."

IPSec: IP Security Protocol

As the security protocol for VPNs (Virtual Private Networks), IPSec includes some very strong encryption (coding) techniques to protect your data in the public/private world of VPNs. IPSec also makes sure that the computer accessing your private network across the very public Internet is really a part of your network and not a pretender trying to sneak into your VPN. We describe VPNs in Chapter 15, and you can read more about IPSec in Chapter 20.

Transport layer protocols

The protocols in the transport layer include TCP and UDP and some of the routing protocols.

TCP: Transmission Control Protocol

TCP uses IP to deliver packets to those upper-layer applications and provides a reliable stream of data among computers on the network. *Error checking* (to ensure that every packet arrives undamaged) and *sequence numbering* (to put the packets back into the right order) are two of TCP's more important functions. After a packet arrives at the correct IP address, TCP goes to work. On both the sending and receiving computers, it establishes a dialog to communicate about the data that's being transmitted. TCP is said to be *connection oriented* because it tells the network to resend lost data.

Theoretically, you can have TCP without IP. Some other network mechanism besides IP can deliver the data to an address, and TCP can still verify and sequence that data. But in practice, TCP is always used with IP.

Check out RFC 793 by the great Jon Postel (one of the greatest TCP/IP gurus and pioneers) for TCP information.

UDP: User Datagram Protocol

UDP uses IP to deliver packets to upper-layer applications and provides a flow of data among computers. Although it's not as reliable as TCP, UDP nevertheless gets a lot of data across the network. UDP provides neither error checking nor sequence numbering, although these features can be added by the application that has chosen to use UDP. This protocol is said to be *connectionless* because it doesn't provide for resending data in case of error.

Another difference between TCP and UDP is that many TCP implementations are very polite. A polite TCP does not intrude on a congested network. That is, it waits before sending its packets. UDP, on the other hand has no worries about network congestion. It rudely sends packets across even the most congested network. VoIP (Voice over IP), NFS (Network File System), DNS (Domain Name System), RPC (Remote Procedure Call), and API (Application Programming Interfaces) use UDP. For the details about the protocols, applications, and services for DNS, check out Chapter 10; for the same information about NFS, see Bonus Chapter 1 on the CD.

See RFC 768 for more information on UDP.

Connection versus connectionless — TCP versus UDP?

TCP/IP communicates among the layers in different ways. These methods are either *connectionless* or *connection oriented.*

Connection-oriented communication is reliable and pretty easy to understand. When two computers are communicating with each other, they connect: Each understands what the other one is doing. The sending computer lets the receiving computer know that data is on the way. The recipient acknowledges receipt of the data (called *ACKs* for short) or denies receipt of the data (negatively acknowledges, or NACKS). A recipient would NACK if the error checking shows a problem, for example. This ACKing and NACKing is called *handshaking.*

Suppose you send a fax to your friend Ken in Tokyo. If you want to be sure he gets it, you might call and say, "I'm faxing you the baseball results now. Call me when you get it." After the fax comes in and Ken checks it over to make sure it is readable, he calls you and says, "Thanks. I'm thrilled to hear that the Red Sox finally won the World Series." That's connection-oriented communication. This is how TCP behaves.

But suppose you send the fax without first notifying your friend. And, for some reason, it never gets there. Ken doesn't know to expect anything, so he doesn't know that anything is lost. That's connectionless communication. When connectionless data are sent, the computers involved know nothing about each other or the data being sent. If you're on the receiving end, no one tells you that you're about to get anything. If you're sending data, no one bothers to mention whether or not they got it or if it was totally garbled. This is how UDP behaves.

With this in mind, you may wonder why any data communications would be done in connectionless mode. But there's a time and place for everything. First, communication is faster without the ACKs and NACKs. Second, not every network message needs to be as accurate as your e-mail. Finally, some applications do their own error checking and reliability processing, so they don't need the connection-oriented overhead of TCP.

Figure 5-2 shows the relationship between IP, TCP, and UDP, as well as the applications at the upper layers.

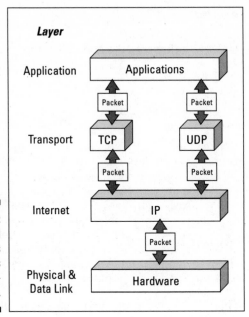

Figure 5-2:
TCP and
UDP pass
IP packets
to the appli-
cations.

OSPF: Open Shortest Path First and other routing protocols

Under your network place settings is a spread of gateways and routers, which have various gateway and router protocols that allow them to exchange network architecture and status information. A router is a physical device that connects networks to allow data to move between them. A *gateway* translates information from one format to another. For example, an SMTP gateway translates e-mail messages from one computer's format to another to interconnect two different e-mail systems when one system uses SMTP and the other uses something else. *Routing* is the process of moving packets between networks.

There are several routing protocols defined in the TCP/IP suite. The Internet today uses mostly OSPF and BGP-4 because of their capability to reroute packets when necessary. When networks change, — perhaps a segment becomes unavailable because a cable fails — OSPF quickly recalculates the route a packet should follow. This ability to recalculate a route is called *dynamic routing*. See RFCs 2328 and 2740 for OSPF details.

Border Gateway Protocol version 4 (BGP-4) — RFCs 1771 and 2545 (for IPv6 networks) is another dynamic routing protocol at Layer 3. The Routing Information Protocol (RIP) — RFCs 1723 and 2080 (for RIP with IPv6) is another commonly used (but older) routing protocol that does not have dynamic routing features.

TLS: Transport Layer Security

The TLS protocol provides privacy for client/server communication. TLS prevents eavesdropping and tampering with the communication between the client and server.

RFC 2246 introduces TLS.

RSVP: Resource Reservation Protocol

To provide the best experience when you're using multimedia applications, such as Internet telephony and videoconferencing, on the network, packets need to be delivered as quickly as possible and always in the correct order. Otherwise, you see strange pauses or blank spots. The Resource Reservation Protocol (RSVP) was created to provide for high quality of service (called *QoS*). Yes, we know that the acronym doesn't match the protocol's name. It's called RSVP because you *reserve* network resources in advance the same way that you reserve a seat at the party by replying to the engraved invitation's request that you RSVP — from the French phrase *repondez s'il vous plait* which essentially translates to "respond, if you please."

You can find a large set of RFCs about RSVP. RFC 2205, "Resource ReSerVation Protocol (RSVP) — Version 1 Functional Specification," is a good place to start. The IETF also has a BCP (Best Common Practice) document about RSVP over ATM — BCP0024 (also labeled RFC 2379), "RSVP over ATM Implementation Guidelines."

ICMP: Internet Control Message Protocol

The Internet Control Message Protocol (ICMP) reports problems and relays other network specific information, such as an error status, from network devices. IP detects the error and passes it to ICMP. A very common use of ICMP is the echo request generated by the ping command.

See RFCs 1256 and 2463 for the scoop on ICMP. Besides being a protocol, ICMP is also a service and an application, although the application is called *ping*. Chapter 17 shows you what ping does.

Application layer protocols

The application layer protocols, applications, and services provide a user interface to the rest of the TCP/IP stack. For example,

DNS: Domain Name Service

DNS is critical to the operation of the Internet (and to any other large network). DNS translates the names that we humans love, such as crwe.org, into the numbers that machines like. Thanks to DNS, you can type www.sorbonne.fr instead of 195.220.107.3. DNS servers are distributed throughout the Internet.

Besides meaning the service that makes the name-to-number translation work, DNS refers to the entire system of DNS servers and databases. In that case, the name changes slightly to Domain Name *System*.

Chapter 10 describes how DNS translates names and addresses. RFCs 1034 and 1035 document the standards for DNS.

FTP: File Transfer Protocol

The File Transfer Protocol (FTP) helps you copy files between two computers. You use FTP either to pull the files from the remote computer or push them to the remote computer. Keep in mind that FTP is also the name of an application and a service, so we'll be looking at it again (and again). (Check out Chapter 13 for lots more on FTP.)

See RFCs 959 and 2640 for more on FTP.

telnet

The telnet protocol lets you connect to a remote computer and work as if you were sitting in front of that computer, no matter how far away that computer may be. With telnet, you can lounge around in Tahiti and work on a remote computer in Antarctica as if you were there surrounded by penguins — without even a shiver. Besides being a protocol, telnet is also a service and an application — three for the price of one. If you've only ever used a graphical operating system, such as a flavor of Microsoft Windows, you may not understand the value of telnet. But your friendly neighborhood Linux, UNIX, and Mac OS X users can use telnet to sign on to remote computers and run programs remotely that may not exist on the computer on their desks (or in their laps). System administrators love telnet because they can take care of computers on the network without having to travel to each one.

Check out Chapter 14 for more on telnet — the protocol, the application, and the service. For more on telnet, see RFCs 854 and 855, also by the great Jon Postel.

TFTP: Trivial File Transfer Protocol

The Trivial File Transfer Protocol (TFTP) is a specialized FTP. One common use of TFTP is to copy and install a computer's operating system from a TFTP server's files. Refer to RFC 1350 for more on TFTP.

SNMP: Simple Network Management Protocol

SNMP is the protocol that's used to monitor and manage networks and the devices connected to them and to collect information about network performance. If you want to write a network management application, you read SNMP messages called *protocol data units* (PDUs) to see when devices connect or disconnect from the network and whether everything is okay on the network.

But wait! Don't waste your time. Why should you write a network management application that uses SNMP when you can buy one from your choice of vendors? IBM SystemView, HP Open View, and other network management products show the state of your entire network with some neat graphics. So watch the pretty pictures and go have a long lunch on your boss.

RFC 2572 has more on SNMP.

SMTP: Simple Mail Transfer Protocol

The Simple Mail Transfer Protocol (SMTP) is the protocol for Internet e-mail. It transfers e-mail messages among computers. The messages may go directly from the sender's computer to the recipient's, or the messages may proceed through intermediary computers in a process known as *store and forward*.

E-mail, of course, is one of the Big Four network applications (along with file transfer, signing on to remote computers, and Web browsing), and many vendors have their own mail protocols. SMTP is the mail transfer protocol for the Internet. UNIX mail understands SMTP, but some other operating systems don't. When users of SMTP-ignorant computers need to get out to the outside world (in other words, get to the Internet), a special SMTP gateway must be established for that communication. In Chapter 11, we tell you more about SMTP gateways and e-mail in general.

RFC 821 also has information on SMTP.

POP3: Post Office Protocol, v3

The latest version of the Post Office Protocol is version 3 (POP3); it provides basic client/server features that help you download your e-mail from a POP3 mail server to your computer. POP3 is designed to allow home users to move their e-mail off their Internet Service Provider's (ISP's) computers and onto their own. You need a POP3 mail client to communicate with a POP3 mail server. See Chapter 11 for more information about POP3 clients and servers.

RFCs 1939 and 2449 have more on POP3.

IMAP4: Internet Message Access Protocol, v4

The latest version of the Internet Message Access Protocol is version 4 (IMAP4); it provides sophisticated client/server capabilities that give you choices about how you handle your e-mail. IMAP4 provides a richer set of features than POP3. You need an IMAP4 client to communicate with an IMAP4 mail server.

POP3 and IMAP4 don't interoperate. You can't use a POP3 client with an IMAP4 server or an IMAP4 client with a POP3 server, but you can find clients and servers that speak both protocols. Read Chapter 11 for more info on IMAP4.

See RFC 2060 for more on IMAP4.

LDAP: Lightweight Directory Access Protocol

LDAP (pronounced as L-dap, which rhymes with cap) is the way to look up information such as usernames and e-mail addresses in an X.500-compatible directory service. Whew! That's a mouthful. Think of the directory service as a big set of telephone books containing all of the information you may need. The problem is, there isn't just one set of phone books. Each organization has several.

LDAP helps applications get what they need from any or all sets of phone books. (LDAP is the main access protocol for Microsoft Windows 2000 Active Directory structure.)

Check out RFC 2251 for more on LDAP.

NTP: Network Time Protocol

The time-of-day clocks that computers maintain are synchronized by the Network Time Protocol (NTP). Time-stamping is important in all sorts of applications, providing everything from document creation dates to network routing date/time information. NTP gets the time data from a time-server computer, which gets it from an official source, such as the United States National Institute of Standards and Technology. In continental Europe, ISO provides a time service used with banking transactions and stock transfers.

RFC 1305 has more on NTP.

HTTP: HyperText Transfer Protocol

HyperText Transfer Protocol (HTTP) is the key protocol for transferring data across the World Wide Web. The HTTP transfers HyperText Markup Language (HTML) and other components from the servers on the Web (or your intranet or extranet) to your browser client. (You can find lots more about the Web in Chapter 12.)

HTTP brings the various Web ingredients to you. It's similar to the wonders of e-mail brought to you by SMTP.

See RFC 2616 for more on HTTP.

S-HTTP: Secure HTTP

S-HTTP is a secure version of HTTP that *encrypts* (codes) sensitive data, such as credit card transactions.

See RFC 2660 for more on Secure HTTP.

BOOTP: Boot Protocol

Not all computers come with the operating system pre-installed — sometimes you have to install the operating system yourself. If the computer has no disks for storage (horrors! — but it happens mostly in large organizations where people share resources), you can download the operating system into your computer's memory from another computer on the network. When you do, your diskless computer uses the Boot Protocol (BOOTP) to load its operating system (or other stand-alone application) via the network. *Booting* means loading the operating system.

RFC 2132 has more information on BOOTP.

If you have disk storage on your new computer, you should install your own local operating system. Some operating system vendors let you perform a remote installation from another computer on the network. The remote installation copies all the operating system files to your computer's disk; from that point on, you can boot the operating system locally.

PPTP: Point-to-Point Tunneling Protocol

The Point-to-Point Tunneling Protocol (PPTP) helps you create a *virtual private network* (VPN) on the public Internet. Using PPTP you can have a secure link to your organization's network — as if you were inside the building and on the LAN — even though you're actually connected to the Internet via an ISP. It's like having a secret tunnel into the office. With PPTP, your communication traffic can even be encrypted to ensure that no miscreants can see your data. You get all of the benefits of a global private network without any of the hassles of launching your own satellites, laying your own undersea cables, or working with any of the pieces we describe in Chapter 2.

See RFC 2637 and RFC 2661, "Layer Two Tunneling Protocol L2TP," for more on PPTP.

DHCP: Dynamic Host Configuration Protocol

DHCP is a client/server solution for sharing numeric TCP/IP addresses. A DHCP server maintains a pool of shared addresses — and those addresses are recyclable. When a DHCP client wants to use a TCP/IP application, that client must first request a TCP/IP address from the DHCP server. The server checks the shared supply; if all the addresses are in use, the server notifies the client that it must wait until another client finishes its work and releases a TCP/IP address. If an address is available, the DHCP server sends a response to the client that contains the address.

This shared-supply approach makes sense in environments in which computers don't use TCP/IP applications all the time or in which there aren't enough addresses available for all the computers that want them. Flip to Chapter 7 for more detailed information about DHCP.

Refer to RFC 2131 for more on DHCP.

SSL: Secure Sockets Layer

SSL (the Secure Sockets Layer) version 2 provides security by allowing applications to encrypt data that go from a client, such as a Web browser, to the matching server. (*Encrypting* your data means converting it to a secret code. We discuss encrypting your e-mail in Chapter 19.) In other words, when you buy that Lamborghini over the Web, no one but the dealer can read your credit card number. SSL version 3 allows the server to authenticate that the client is who it says it is. Check out Chapter 20 to see how secure Web transactions use SSL.

IPP: The Internet Printing Protocol

As of this book's publication, there is no standard for printing. Currently, you may need to use different printing methods depending on how your printer is attached and the maker of your printer. The goal of the application layer IPP is to standardize most Internet printing tasks. In other words, regardless of who makes your printer and how the printer is attached, you only need to know one way to

- Print
- Cancel a print job
- Discover the printer's status
- Find out what a printer can do (print color, print draft quality, and so on)

IPP is on the standards track and is documented by a set of RFCs, including RFCs 2910, 2911, 3196, and 3239. Before IPP can become a standard, however, it needs to include strict authentication and security.

The Kerberos Network Authentication Service

Kerberos is a three-headed dog that guards the entrance to Hell. Or is it a TCP/IP service? If your network security is hellish, Kerberos is both. The TCP/IP service, Kerberos, is designed to allow users, computers, and services to identify themselves to each other without lying. This identity checking is called *authentication*. Without authentication services such as Kerberos, a computer or service could potentially say it is anything or anyone, and TPC/IP would accept the identification without checking. In this age of computer hacking and intrusions, trusting that network services and computers are who they say they are can be dangerous.

Kerberos is a trusted impartial authentication service — or maybe it's just paranoid. It assumes that unauthorized programs will try to read and modify packets that are traveling along a network. It's this very paranoia that makes Kerberos impartial. Kerberos doesn't depend on other programs, the host's operating system, the physical security of the network, or IP addresses to do its work. Instead, it works alone with its own validated tickets. (See Chapter 20 for details on the Kerberos service.) Kerberos is the default authentication mechanism in the Microsoft Windows 2000 operating system.

Kerberos, documented in RFC 1510, is like a bouncer at an exclusive party. It guards the door and kicks out anyone who isn't invited.

Instant Messaging and Presence Protocol (IMPP)

While Instant Messaging (IM) is a handy application for people to send quick messages back and forth across the Internet, the IM vendors use different, proprietary protocols that don't work together. The goal of IMPP is for different IM applications to talk to each other easily across the Internet. RFC 2779 defines the basic requirements for IMPP.

SIP: Session Initiation Protocol

SIP is a protocol for connecting interactive sessions, such as voice, chat, games, and video, between users. RFC 3265 details SIP, a proposed standard.

And many, many more . . .

You can find many more existing pieces of TCP/IP, and new ones are being developed this very minute! The ones that we describe in this chapter are some of the most important and most commonly used. All of the protocols that use an IP address must be updated so that they understand the IPv6 address. Aren't you glad you're not a TCP/IP programmer?

The changes in IPv6 also affect services such as DNS. You can read about IPv6 details in Chapter 9.

Chapter 6

Nice Names and Agonizing Addresses

· ·

In This Chapter

▶ Using a new name for computers: hosts

▶ Understanding why you need both names and numbers

▶ Using TCP/IP network addresses — classy things or classless?

▶ Recognizing the parts and fields of IP addresses

▶ Figuring out how to get an IP address and an address on the Internet

▶ Worrying that the Internet will run out of addresses

▶ Getting a helping hand from DHCP

· ·

If your computer is already on a network, *and* you always call computers by name, *and* you don't give a fig what TCP/IP is doing to your computer's name behind the scenes, you can breathe easy in this chapter. The only thing you really need to know here is another term for a computer — a *host* — and what it means. In other words, you can move on to some other chapter. This whole chapter is techno-geekism for you.

However, if you need to get your computer on the network or the Internet, or you want to know the meaning of all those strings of numbers and dots (not to mention IPv6's letters and colons and CIDR's slashes) that you see when you use an application such as FTP or telnet, stay right here. Most of the information in this chapter is aimed at you — especially if you're a beginning network administrator.

What Did You Say Your Computer's Name Was Again?

If your computer uses TCP/IP, your computer must have a name. You can choose it yourself for your home computer. Most likely, at work, your organization has a naming policy that helps you select a name or limits your choices. In some cases, a system manager or network administrator gets to have all the fun and assign a name to your computer for you.

Playing the numbers game

Your computer has a number, as well. That number is called the computer's *IP address,* and we spend the greater part of this chapter studying it. (Throughout much of this book, we call it a *numeric address* — now you know the correct technical term.) Your computer may have more than one IP address, depending on how many networks it's connected to.

Your computer's name and IP address can change, too. It may never write a book under a pseudonym or take a married name, but it can take on nicknames, change names, and have multiple identities. (If you use it for espionage, maybe your computer has a "cover," too — would you believe Agent 80586?)

You could have a network where all the computers had numeric addresses and no names, but it would make life difficult, almost impossible for most of us.

- ✔ Humans like to name things (dogs, cats, goldfish) and can remember names. Computers like dealing with numbers.

- ✔ You need to be able to connect to a particular computer to use the services it offers. Knowing that computer's name makes it easier to link up. For example, you could connect to **192.168.0.246**, but remembering and typing **pinkflamingo** is a lot easier.

- ✔ You want your e-mail delivered to a specific place. Without computer names and addresses, e-mail would be impossible.

Uniquely yours . . .

What happens if your computer name isn't unique on the network? Let's compare two Lotus companies — one makes cars; the other makes IBM software. If you try to connect via FTP to a computer named just lotus, would you find files about cars or software?

TCP/IP and the Internet require that each and every computer on the network, in the organization, in the world, in the solar system, be uniquely identified by both name and address. To identify a computer named "domino," we need more names — kind of like first, middle, last, and maybe more.

A computer's full name is called a *fully qualified domain name,* FQDN. (Go ahead — just try to say it three times fast.) So for the computer named domino, its FQDN may be

```
domino.lotus.com
```

Computer name = domino; organization name = lotus; and Internet top-level domain = com (short for *commercial organization*). Here's another example:

```
hbs.harvard.edu
```

The computer name = hbs; organization name = harvard; and Internet top-level domain = edu (short for *educational institution*).

Translating Host Names into Numbers

Hosts on a network are identified by their numeric IP address. Yes, you usually type in the host's name, but somewhere along the way, TCP/IP resolves that name into an IP address. Your computer has a hosts file to translate the host name into its IP address. In the case of big networks (and can you get any bigger than the Internet?), where the hosts file would be too big, the Domain Name Service (DNS) does the name/address resolution. You can read the details of the hosts file and DNS in Chapter 8.

What's in an IP Address?

The address where you live is made up of several parts. It may include any of many elements that identify you — your street name, post office box, city, region (province, state, canton, county), country, postal code, and so forth. The same is true of your computer (host). The difference is that you know your address — it's mostly text with a few numbers — but you may or may not know your computer's address, which is all numbers and dots.

Before we start getting technical, you need to know that two versions of IP are currently in use:

- ✓ IPv4
- ✓ IPv6

Although IPv6 is the next generation of IP addressing, most people still use IPv4. In this chapter, we explain IPv4 addressing. Chapter 9 is about IPv6. But don't head to Chapter 9 yet, unless you already understand IPv4 addresses because

- ✔ IPv6 addressing builds on the IPv4 foundation.
- ✔ IPv4 and IPv6 will exist together for a long time to come.
- ✔ If you're not ready for IPv6, you can use a workaround for the IP address shortage.

The IP address (to be specific, the IPv4 address) is a set of numbers separated by dots. (We describe IPv6 addresses later in this chapter.) It identifies *one network interface on a host.* Every device on the TCP/IP network — that is, every network interface on the network because some devices may have more than one — needs a unique IP address. If your host is on a TCP/IP network, that host has an IP address, even if you've always called your computer by name.

You may have noticed this numeric address showing up in messages and wondered what it was. For example, telnet reports the IP address as it tries to connect to the remote host. Here's a brief sample that shows it. You connect to flyingpenguin by name, and telnet announces the flyingpenguin IP address.

```
% telnet flyingpenguin
Trying 192.168.0.241...
Connected to flyingpenguin.
```

An IPv4 address is a 32-bit number. It has two sections: the network number and the host number. (You can't see the division. Wait for the section on subnet masks in Chapter 7.) Addresses are written as four fields, 8 bits each, separated by dots. Each field can be a number ranging from 0 to 255. This style of writing an address is called *dotted decimal notation.*

All hosts on the same network must use the same network number. Each host/network interface on the same network must have a unique host number. The following excerpt is from a hosts file. The last two digits of each address are unique. These are the host numbers. The rest of each address is the network number. Notice that the network number is the same for every host. It's the same because all the hosts are on the same network.

```
# Cardinal Consulting, Inc. LAN
# IP address          Name           Comment
130.103.40.55        flyingpenguin   #Candace-Linux
130.103.40.56        bluebird        #Marshall
130.103.40.61        oldestbird      #VMS server
130.103.40.63        bigbird         #Unix server
130.103.40.64        mazarin         #WNT server
130.103.40.65        macbird         #the Mac
130.103.40.72        uselessbird     #ancient 386
130.103.40.75        pinkflamingo    #Candace-XP
```

Figure 6-1 shows some legal combinations of network and host numbers. The preceding listed hosts are part of a Class C network.

Figure 6-1:
Here are some legal combinations of network and host numbers.

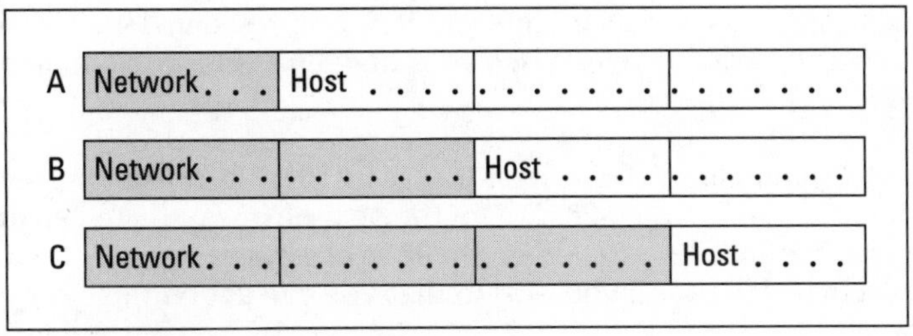

Class A address 1.1.1.1
Class B address 130.103.40.210
Class C address 192.9.200.15

Getting an IP Address

Can you just pick any IP address that's unique on your network? Most of the time, the answer is no, unless you're a network administrator. If your organization uses DHCP (the *Dynamic Host Configuration Protocol*), the DHCP server software automatically assigns an IP address to your host. We show you how to configure DHCP servers in Chapter 7.

Most organizations have network administrators (known affectionately as the network police) who tell you what to use for an address so that yours doesn't conflict with anyone else's. After all, you can't just pick any ol' house on the block and move in — someone else probably already lives there, right? So your network police officer is there to make sure nobody squats at a network address that's already in use. If the police don't do their jobs and you set up your computer to use an existing address, don't come complaining to us that you never receive your e-mail or that you're receiving someone else's junk mail.

Only if your network isn't connected to any other network is it okay for you or your network police to pick a host address out of the blue. If your network is connected, your address must be unique across the combination of linked networks.

On the Internet, where many thousands of networks are interconnected, no one person actually polices to make sure each and every address is unique. The assignment of the network number portion of the IP address keeps the organizations clearly identified and separate.

To connect your network to the Internet, you need an official block of addresses and a registered domain name (to append to your computers' names to create their fully qualified domain names). The official bestower of IP addresses is ICANN, the *Internet Corporation for Assigned Names and Numbers,* but you don't talk to them directly. Your organization actually gets its official addresses from an Internet Service Provider (ISP). Chapter 10 has the information about registering your domain name with an ISP or an accredited registrar.

How do you find an ISP? The best way is by looking at lists on the Internet — but that's kind of a Catch-22. One of the next best ways is to ask neighboring organizations that are already on the Internet whom they use. Some of the big ISPs, such as AOL, send you CDs so that you can get on the Internet quickly and easily.

The Four Sections of the IPv4 Address

An IPv4 address looks like this:

```
field1.field2.field3.field4
```

The meaning of these fields depends on your network class. There are four classes of networks in TCP/IP. While only three classes are widely used today, the fourth is for a special purpose. Whether your organization connects to the Internet or is a private intranet, the first three classes work the same way.

Class A is for a few enormous networks

Theoretically, there can only be 127 class A networks on the Internet, but each one of those 127 can have a huge number of hosts: about 17 million each (16,777,216 to be exact). Only a few very large organizations need class A networks. (By the way, there is no class A network that starts with the number 0 and the entire class A network numbered 127 is reserved. This leaves only 126 class A networks.)

Class B is for lots of big networks

Although they're nowhere near as enormous as class A networks, class B networks are hefty, as well. Each class B network can have about 65,000 hosts — the size needed by some universities and larger companies. The Internet can support up to 16,384 class B networks.

Class C is for the thousands of small networks

Class C networks are much smaller, and the Internet has over 2 million (2,097,152) of these. Most of the networks connected to the Internet are class C. Each one can have only 254 hosts.

Class D is for multicasting

Class D networks are completely different from the other classes — they're used for multicasting, which is a special way of transmitting information from a server to a set of clients all at the same time. Multicasting is the technology that supports such cool applications as audio- and video-conferencing and radio and television stations that exist only on the Internet.

Days or weeks prior to the "broadcast," the sponsoring organization announces (via e-mail or Usenet news) the class D network address that the server is going to use for the transmission. (Radio and television stations are assigned permanent addresses so that they can transmit constantly if they choose to.) Plenty of channels are available because class D addresses go from 224.0.0.0 to 239.255.255.255. At the assigned date and time for the broadcast, you tune — that is, configure — your client software to the proper class D address. The broadcast works just like ordinary radio and television, but it's on the Internet.

Real-time applications require special purpose, multicast-aware *routers* (see Chapter 18 for more on those) so that the packets always arrive in the proper order and none are missing. These routers on the Internet form the MBone, or IP Multicast Backbone.

Take a look at Chapter 9 for more on multicasting, especially about its new uses in IPv6.

For Math Nerds Only: Biting Down on Bits and Bytes

Who decided how many hosts are in class A, B, and C networks? And why can there only be 127 class A networks when there can be a zillion (well, almost) of class C?

It all has to do with the arrangement of the bits inside the addresses. For example, class A addresses use the first field as the network section and the next three fields as the host section. The more fields in a section, the bigger number you get. Because class A only has one field in the network section, it can only have a small number of networks. But the three fields in the hosts part allow each of those 127 networks to have a ton of computers.

Table 6-1 shows how the four fields of the IP address are assigned to the network section and host section.

Table 6-1	The Two Sections of the IP Address	
Network Class	**Network Section of IP Address**	**Host Section of IP Address**
A	field1	field2.field3.field4
B	field1.field2	field3.field4
C	field1.field2.field3	field4

Danger! There's math ahead. If you already understand binary numbers and how to convert from decimal to binary, skip ahead to the next section. If you don't understand binary, this section takes you back to high school. Get ready to look at place values in a whole new way.

Figure 6-2 takes the number 127 apart to show how it's constructed in binary. A computer looks at the number 127 as an arrangement of 0s and 1s. Computers ultimately do everything in *binary,* or base 2. So if you look at the place value columns in Figure 6-2, you don't see the familiar 1s, 10s, 100s, and so on, from the decimal system. Rather, you see the 1s, 2s, 4s, 8s, 16s, 32s, 64s, 128s, and so on. (Remember, in binary, the only possible values in a column are 0 or 1. Also remember that a byte contains 8 bits.) In the decimal system, it takes three columns — the 1s column, the 10s column, and the 100s column — to represent the number 127. To get to 127, then, a binary number has 7 columns: the 1s, 2s, 4s, 8s, 16s, 32s, and 64s.

Classy bits

In a computer, each place-value column in a binary number is represented by a *bit*. In the early days of computers, you could look inside the cabinet and actually see circular magnets called cores; each magnet was a bit. A core magnetized in one direction (say, clockwise) meant the bit was set to 1. The other direction (counterclockwise) meant the bit was set to 0. Today's transistors and semiconductors have replaced the magnets so that seeing what's going on inside is more difficult — but the computer still uses bits of 1 and 0. All numbers inside the computer, from 0 to 1,000,000,000,000 and on up, are made from bits. The computer keeps adding the 1s and 0s until it reaches the total, such as 127.

If each and every bit of the class A network piece were set to 0 or 1, that would result in a higher number than the 127 allowed by the Internet. Figure it out: 128+64+32+16+8+4+2+1. But TCP/IP requires that the high-order bit for a class A network always be 0. According to this rule, when you add up the bits you get 0+64+32+16+8+4+2+1 for the number of class A networks that a 32-bit address allows. To determine how many networks and hosts were allowable for each Internet class, the maximum value was calculated for the field combinations of each section. The rules for class B state that the first two high-order bits must be 1 and 0. For class C, the first two high-order bits must be 1 and 1.

The high-order bits are the bits at the end of the number. Which end depends on whether your computer reads from right to left or left to right. If a computer reads from right to left, as does a PC, the high-order bits are the ones on the far left end.

Figure 6-2:
Binary numbers are as easy as 1, 2, 3. Oops. Make that 0 and 1.

Class A Network

128	64	32	16	8	4	2	1	Place value columns
0	1	1	1	1	1	1	1	Bit values (either 1 or 0)

High order bit ⟵——————————— Low order bit

$127 = 1 + 2 + 4 + 8 + 16 + 32 + 64$

DHCP Gives Network Administrators Time to Rest

Do you hate the idea of doing the math? Let DHCP help you out. DHCP is the TCP/IP protocol that automatically assigns and keeps track of IP addresses and subnet masks while the network administrator takes a stroll on the beach.

Besides giving network administrators a break, DHCP helps a network conserve addresses because addresses aren't wasted on computers that are not connected. To find out how DHCP works and to set up DHCP, see Chapter 7.

Will the Internet Ever Run Out of Addresses?

No, however it is getting low. DHCP servers help the address shortage by assigning addresses only to hosts that need them. IPv6 expands the Internet address space immensely. Read all about IPv6, the next generation of IP, in Chapter 9. If you're not ready for IPv6, read about workarounds such as CIDR (Classless Inter-Domain Routing) and NAT (Network Address Translation) in Chapter 7.

Back to the Comfort Zone

Congratulations. You stuck with it and made it to the end of this arduous odyssey of agonizing addresses. If you're an experienced network administrator, you need to work with numbers to set up IP addresses and possibly subnets (see Chapter 7), so you may be used to this stuff anyway. If you're an end user of TCP/IP and the Internet, you've just acquired a store of valuable mathematical trivia. We doubt that you need to use it, however, unless you become a contestant on the mythical game show "Who Wants to Be a Network Manager?"

In any event, no matter what your role in network fun and games, for the rest of the book, you can relax. Well, you can relax if you don't need to know any technical stuff about IPv6. That's in Chapter 9. Sorry about that. But if you gotta know, you gotta know.

Chapter 7

Not Enough Addresses?
Try Subnets, DHCP, CIDR, NAT

In This Chapter

▶ Finding out how to use IP addresses economically

▶ Understanding subnets and why they wear masks

▶ Letting DHCP do the work and save on IP addresses

▶ Drinking CIDR to relieve Internet address space disorder (for now)

▶ Understanding how NAT can help an IP address shortage

*T*he Internet is running out of addresses. You must have heard that before, maybe in Chapter 6. What that scary statement really means is that the Internet is running out of *32-bit IPv4* addresses. So, what's the problem then? Use IPv6 — 128 bits will hold us for a long time. Actually, IPv6 does much more than provide a massive address space. There's built-in security, for example. But many organizations and people aren't moving to IPv6 yet. So, we need a way to keep surviving on the limited number of IPv4 addresses available. In this chapter, we describe some ways to conserve IPv4 addresses without giving up any Internet connectivity.

Working with Subnets and Subnet Masks

Subnets divide one network into multiple smaller networks. The separate networks are normally interconnected by network devices called *routers*. (See Chapter 16 for more information about routers, hubs, and switches.)

Not every environment requires subnets. For example, if your organization's network has 254 or fewer hosts and the network lives in one building, there's no reason to subnet it. But if your organization's network expands into multiple locations, the network administrator has a couple of options:

✔ Ask for another entire network number for each new facility; this is greedy if your existing network still has enough unassigned host numbers.

✔ Split your existing network into pieces, one piece for each location.

When subnets are necessary and the network administrator (this may mean you!) uses good common sense to subdivide the network, subnets do yield some advantages over one large network:

✔ Smaller networks are easier to manage and troubleshoot, even though there are more pieces.

✔ Network traffic overall is reduced and performance may improve because most traffic is local to its subnet.

✔ Network security can be applied more easily at the interconnections between the subnets. For some mind-numbing details about network security, read Chapters 18, 19, and 20.

Figure 7-1 shows a main network with two subnets. Each network and each host has an address. Look carefully at field3 in each address; can you find some subtle differences?

The address for a subnet uses the address for the main network and borrows some bits from the host part to extend the network section. The borrowed bits enable each subnet to have its own unique network address. Because the subnet addresses come from the main network's address, you don't have to ask a registrar to assign them. These addresses already belong to your organization; you've just decided to deploy them differently.

What is a router?

A *router* is a computer that runs software that figures how a packet should be forwarded on the route to its destination. A router is connected to at least two networks. The routers on the Internet backbones have huge capacity. Cisco Systems Inc., for example, makes most of the Internet backbone routers, including one that can move over 271 million packets per second! Of course, for those of us with small businesses, there are lots of smaller routers to choose from.

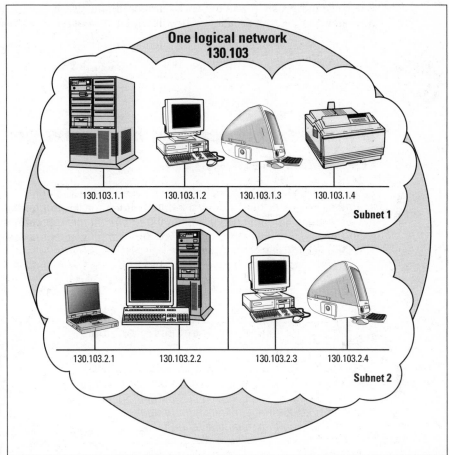

One logical network
130.103

130.103.1.1   130.103.1.2   130.103.1.3   130.103.1.4

Subnet 1

130.103.2.1   130.103.2.2   130.103.2.3   130.103.2.4

Subnet 2

Figure 7-1:
Each
subnetwork
has its own
address.

Defining subnet masks

When the network administrator borrows bits from the main network address's host section, TCP/IP needs to know which bits of the host section are borrowed to be used as the network address. The administrator uses a *subnet mask* to borrow those host bits. A subnet mask is 32 bits that overlay an IP address. (For IPv6, the subnet mask is 128 bits.) The bits for the network address are all set to 1, and the bits for the host address are all set to 0. The mask tells the router, "Look only at the bits that lie under the 1s. Forget about any bits that lie under the 0s." Because the router can skip the masked-out bits (that is, the zeroed-out bits), it can send packets on their way faster than if it had to look at the entire address.

Before defining a subnet mask, the network administrator needs to figure out how many subnets to create and how many hosts will be in each subnet. This determines how many bits should be set to 1.

The more bits used for the subnet mask, the fewer hosts can be on each subnet created.

Why does my network have a mask if it has no subnets?

Your network always has a subnet mask even if it doesn't use subnets. Most TCP/IP implementations supply a default subnet mask, which says, "Hi. I'm a network that's not subnetted." Figure 7-2 shows the default subnet mask for each class of network. Most TCP/IP vendors automatically set the default subnet mask for you.

Figure 7-2:
Each class
has a
default
subnet
mask.

A	255.0.0.0

11111111	00000000	00000000	00000000

B	255.255.0.0

11111111	11111111	00000000	00000000

C	255.255.255.0

11111111	11111111	11111111	00000000

The subnet mask must be the same for each computer on that part of the network; otherwise, the computers don't understand that they're on the same subnet.

The subnet mask is applied to the IP address in every message in order to separate the network number and the host number. For example, when your computer examines the address 192.9.200.15 and applies the default subnet mask of 255.255.255.0, it sees the network number 192.9.200 and the host number 15.

How do you know that this works? Hold on to your techie hats. It's done by converting nice decimal numbers, such as 255, to not-so-nice binary numbers, such as 11111111. And then, after all the numbers are converted to binary, they get ANDed. AND is a binary mathematical operation. If you aren't fed up AND bored by now, read the upcoming sidebar "Boolean arithmetic: AND." Just remember: Although this stuff may seem incomprehensible to you, your computer lives, breathes, and eats binary and thinks this is Really Fun!

P.S. The authors can't be held responsible for any medical or mental complications that result from reading the Boolean arithmetic sidebar.

Subnetting 101

We're going to split one class C network with 256 addresses into two equal subnets of 128 addresses each. We must change the class C default subnet mask of 255.255.255.0.

For an example, we use network number 192.9.202, which means the 256 addresses are numbered 192.9.202.0 through 192.9.202.255. To split the network into two parts, with one part getting addresses 0 to 127 and the other getting addresses 128 to 255, you need the custom subnet mask 255.255.255.128. The 0 becomes 128 because you borrow the high-order bit from `field4`. (In binary, 128 is 10000000. Refer to the "Classy bits" sidebar in Chapter 6 if you need help with the math.)

In the 192.9.202 network, there are 128 addresses that happen to have the high-order bit of `field4` set to 0 and another 128 addresses that happen to have the high-order bit set to 1. If you thought the custom subnet mask would be 255.255.255.1, you were close, but that mask borrows the low-order bit of `field4`. It puts all the even-numbered addresses (0, 2, 4, 6, and so on up to 254) in one subnet and all the odd-numbered addresses (1, 3, 5, 7, and so on up to 255) in the other.

Before subnetting this example network, it was easy to say that all of the hosts were in the 192.9.202 network. After subnetting, they still are.

Probably the most common example of subnetting is splitting a class B network into 256 class C networks. To accomplish this, every host sets its subnet mask to 255.255.255.0.

If you hate this math, read about IPv6 in Chapter 9. The expanded address size removes the need for subnetting.

If you hate the math, and you're a network administrator, try out the IP calculators on the CD-ROM included with this book.

Boolean arithmetic: AND

In the AND operation, regardless of the value in the data bit, a mask bit of 0 yields a result of 0. And a mask bit of 1 preserves the value in the data bit, also regardless of the value in the data bit. Another way to say this is that the result bit is a 1 if and only if both the data bit and the mask bit contain 1. Otherwise, the result bit is 0. Here's a table that demonstrates this:

	0	1	0	1	Data
AND	0	0	1	1	Mask
	0	0	0	1	Result

Suppose you examine how a subnet mask is used to obtain the network number part of an IP address. In your computer, the fields of the dotted decimal IP address 192.9.200.15 are already in binary as

11000000 00001001 11001000 00001111

The fields of the dotted decimal subnet mask 255.255.255.0 are already

11111111 11111111 11111111 00000000

The AND operation yields the network number 192.9.200, as shown here:

11000000 00001001 11001000 00001111 IP address: 192.9.200.15

11111111 11111111 11111111 00000000 Subnet mask: 255.255.255.0

11000000 00001001 11001000 00000000 Result: 192.9.200.0

To get the host number, your computer inverts the bits of the subnet mask — each 1 becomes a 0 and each 0 becomes a 1 — and does another AND. Easy as pi, right?

11000000 00001001 11001000 00001111 IP address: 192.9.200.15

00000000 00000000 00000000 11111111 Subnet mask: 0.0.0.255

00000000 00000000 00000000 00001111 Result: 0.0.0.15

DHCP Gives Network Administrators Time to Rest

DHCP (Dynamic Host Configuration Protocol) is the TCP/IP protocol that automatically assigns and keeps track of IP addresses and subnet masks while the network administrator takes a stroll on the beach.

One administrator's nightmare is another's fantasy

Imagine you're the person in charge of the White Pages of the telephone book. What a hard job it must be! You have to be sure that everyone's name and number are in the book correctly and in alphabetical order. When people move into your area, you have to assign them a number and list it in the directory. If people discontinue service, you have to remove their names and numbers. If you live where people move frequently, you spend all your time keeping that directory up-to-date.

Now imagine that the telephone company gets a new system. Whenever someone needs to be assigned a telephone number, you don't do anything. The telephone system magically assigns a number automatically. If someone no longer needs a number, the telephone system automatically removes it and later recycles the number to someone else. And forget about keeping the telephone book up-to-date. The telephone system magically does that, too. In fact, there's no permanent telephone book. If someone wants to call Emily, she picks up the telephone and says, "Please connect me to Emily's telephone, wherever that is." This system would make your life as a telephone administrator so easy that you could work at the beach with a novel in one hand and a cold drink in the other.

Fantasy? Yes, for telephone administrators, but not necessarily for network administrators. People communicate on an internet or intranet via computer names and IP addresses. The network administrator keeps these up-to-date in a hosts file or a DNS database. Maintaining this information is tedious and time consuming in a volatile environment.

How DHCP works — it's client/server again

When you turn on your computer (a DHCP client), it contacts your network's DHCP server and asks to *lease* an address. The client and server negotiate the lease and — voilà! You have an IP address to use for the duration of the lease.

Here's how it works:

1. **You turn on your computer.**

   TCP/IP starts, but remember, you're leasing. You have no permanent IP address.

2. **Your DHCP client software asks to lease an IP address.**

   This request is called a *DHCP discover message.* The DHCP discover message contains the name of your computer and its hardware address. Your hardware address comes on your NIC (network interface card).

3. **Your computer keeps broadcasting its lease request until a DHCP server responds.**

If there's no DHCP server — maybe an earthquake destroyed it — your computer keeps trying, but never gets its address. That means you can't use any TCP/IP applications or services.

4. **All the available DHCP servers answer your message by offering your proposed IP address, the servers' IP address, a subnet mask, and the duration of the lease in hours.**

    Your computer grabs an IP address so that no one else can take it while you're negotiating.

5. **Your DHCP client takes the first offer and broadcasts its acceptance.**

    The other servers cancel their offers.

6. **Your selected DHCP server makes your IP address permanent and sends you an "acknowledged" message (DHCP*ACK*).**

7. **You have an IP address.**

    You can use TCP/IP applications and services as long as you want — or until your lease expires.

Oh no! My lease expired. Am I evicted?

Usually a DHCP server renews your lease with no problem. In fact, you don't have to do anything. The entire process is automatic and doesn't interfere with what you're doing.

If the DHCP server dies during your lease, you won't be able to renew. When your lease expires, so does your ability to use TCP/IP services and applications.

Because any DHCP server on the network can renew your lease, your network administrator should configure more than one DHCP server.

CIDR (Classless Inter-Domain Routing) Juices Up the Internet

Have you heard about CIDR *(Classless Inter-Domain Routing)?* You pronounce it the same as cider, the drink made from apples. The key word if you're a class expert is "classless"! With the enormous growth of the Internet, everyone needs to accept that IP addresses are an endangered resource that must be managed for the good of the many. CIDR replaces the A, B, C class system with a way to allocate IP addresses that allows the Internet to grow without getting obese.

Scott Bradner, Internet Society VP for Standards and author of the foreword to this book, told us that "no one has been assigned a Class B address since 1992." With CIDR, the remaining enormous Class A networks are split into various sizes, including the traditional Class B size. The Internet backbone's routers understand CIDR and distribute packets to the right destinations.

What's CIDR?

CIDR is an addressing and routing scheme that enables routing decisions to be made more efficiently — CIDR reduces the size of routing tables. Reducing the size of anything in the Internet is a good thing. (Too bad TCP/IP doesn't have a protocol for reducing the size of our waists — excuse the digression.) RFCs 1467, 1517, 1518, 1519, 1520, and 1817 document CIDR. If you're an Internet user who doesn't need to configure TCP/IP on your computer, you now know all you need to know about CIDR. Stop here if you don't want to read too many stressful techie details. If you're a network administrator, read on.

The problem

In late 1990, there were 2,190 routes to be managed by routing tables. In early 1999, that number exceeded 40,000 routes. It takes almost 64MB of computer memory and a powerful CPU to store 60,000 routes. If you use CIDR, you can save lots of router memory and its CPU power, too.

The solution

CIDR offers a solution to the growing demand for IP addresses without making the Internet address space too hefty to manage. One way CIDR does this is to replace a Class B address with a group of contiguous Class C addresses that can be allocated differently. This technique is called *address space aggregation*. It means that fewer Class B addresses are wasted, and it keeps the routing table size nice and slim. CIDR specifies that every IP address include a network prefix that identifies either one gateway or an aggregation of network gateways. The length of the prefix is also part of the IP address.

A CIDR network address looks like this:

```
130.103.40.03/18
```

130.103.40.03 is the IP address and /18 declares that the first 18 bits are the network part of the address. The last 14 bits (because 32 bits minus 18 bits equals 14 bits) represent the host address. A /18 address space aggregation holds 16,384 hosts — that's equivalent to 64 Class C networks and is one-fourth of a Class B network. Table 7-1 lists more details.

Taking CIDR apart

C is for *classless*. Classless means "Let's revolt against the 4-class structure of IP addresses, especially class B networks (65,533 hosts), which often waste lots of IP addresses."

I is for *inter*. Inter-domain means that CIDR is used between domains. The routers on the Internet's backbone network that we describe in Chapter 4 use CIDR as the system for routing between each other. The Internet's regulating authorities now expect every ISP to use CIDR.

D is for *domain*. RFC 1518, "An Architecture for IP Address Allocation with CIDR," defines a domain as the group of "resources under control of a single administration." Internet Service Providers (ISPs) are domains of domains. That is, ISPs let other domains hook into their network. Subscribers are the domains that connect to ISPs. A domain can be both an ISP and a subscriber simultaneously.

R is for *routing*. A router is a computer that runs software that connects two or more networks. Routers determine the path a packet should follow on the network as it moves toward its final destination. A router stores a table of the available routes for packet travel and figures out the most efficient route that a packet should follow.

Table 7-1	CIDR Address Space Aggregations	
Bits in Network Part	*Number of Hosts*	*Number of Class C Networks*
/12	1,048,576	4,096
/13	524,288	2,048
/14	262,144	1,024
/15	131,072	512
/16	65,536	256 = 1 Class B network
/17	32,768	128
/18	16,384	64
/19	8,192	32
/20	4,096	16
/21	2,048	8
/22	1,024	4
/23	512	2

Bits in Network Part	Number of Hosts	Number of Class C Networks
/24	256	1
/25	128	1/2
/26	64	1/4
/27	32	1/8
/28	16	1/16

CIDR works with the OSPF and BGP routing protocols. You can read about them in Chapter 16.

The Internet is a network of networks. Corporate and campus networks attach to transit networks (such as regional networks). Most of these corporate and campus networks consist of subnetworks. These subnetworks are interconnected by routers to form the corporate or campus network.

You say subnet, NEToRAMA says aggregate

Consider the example of a fictional Internet Service Provider (ISP) named NEToRAMA. NEToRAMA is allowed to give out addresses 162.9.*.* (where * represents 0 to 255). When you sign up with NEToRAMA, you get a piece — some subnet — of its address space (numeric IP address range). From NEToRAMA's perspective, it is aggregating your address space into 162.9.*.*. For example, a mythical company called example.com gets 162.9.200.0/24 and your company gets 162.9.201.0/24. With CIDR, it's easier for NEToRAMA to give all of its customers the number of IP addresses they need without wasting very many.

NEToRAMA has 100 customers. Before using CIDR, NEToRAMA's routing table had 100 entries — one for each customer's address. But now it has just one entry on the Internet that benefits all 100 clients. That routing table entry says, "Send me all packets addressed to 162.9.*.*." That makes for a much smaller and, therefore, more efficient routing table. This is what CIDR does. Now, apply this sample routing efficiency across the entire Internet address space. The efficiency savings are impressive! We wanted to say staggering, but maybe we're getting carried away — or maybe we drank too much hard CIDR.

The IP calculators on the CD-ROM included with this book also do CIDR calculations.

NAT (Network Address Translation)

NAT is a way for multiple computers on an intranet to share one officially registered IP address. One computer on the intranet needs an officially registered IP address to get to the Internet. The computer that has the official IP address is a NAT router. Requests from the other computers on the intranet go through the NAT router on their way to and from the Internet.

How NAT works

When a request comes from one of the computers on the intranet, the NAT router replaces that computers' IP address with its own. The NAT router then sends the message out on behalf of the requester. When a response comes back, the NAT router reverses the procedure and removes its own IP address from the message and replaces the originating computer's address.

NAT and DHCP working together

The computer acting as a NAT router can also be the DHCP server that leases IP addresses to the other computers on the intranet. The computer that is the NAT router might also be a DHCP client getting its official IP address from the ISP. Microsoft's Internet Connection Sharing (in Windows 98 Second Edition, Windows 2000, and Windows XP Professional) is a DHCP server and NAT router. The network we use for most of this book's examples uses NAT and DHCP. Instead of requesting a class C network for our small intranet, we have one computer with IP address assigned by our ISP. Figure 7-3 shows a piece of our intranet and how a Web browser request goes from inside the intranet through our NAT router and out to the Internet.

Pinkflamingo, with two NICs inside and running Windows 98 Second Edition with ICS (Internet Connection Sharing), serves three roles:

- ✔ NAT router: Again, this is the computer that has the official IP address.

- ✔ DHCP Client: It gets our official IP address from our ISP. One NIC connects us to our ISP through a cable modem.

- ✔ DHCP server: It leases IP addresses to the other computers on our in-house intranet. The other NIC goes to a hub that connects all the in-house computers.

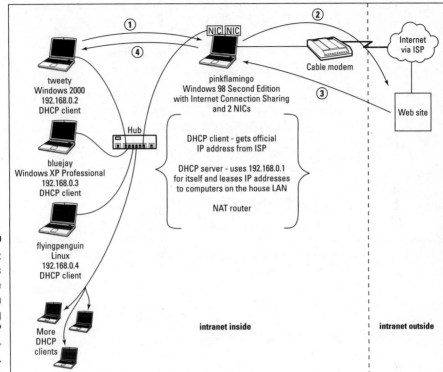

Figure 7-3:
NAT saves
our house
from
needing
seven IP
registra-
tions.

The browser request follows these steps:

1. Marshall, on tweety, types a URL, such as `www.dummies.com`, in his browser. The request's packet includes tweety's address and it goes to pinkflamingo. Pinkflamingo removes tweety's IP address from the packet and inserts its own address.

2. Pinkflamingo sends tweety's browser request to the `www.dummies.com` Web site.

3. The `www.dummies.com` server packages up a response to send to pinkflamingo. Pinkflamingo's IP address is part of the packet. Pinkflamingo receives the response packet. Pinkflamingo removes its own IP address and replaces the address with tweety's IP address.

4. Pinkflamingo forwards the response to tweety.

 CIDR and NAT are workarounds to the IPv4 addressing shortage. They work best in smaller networks. The real solution to the dwindling address shortage is IPv6. Read all about it in Chapter 9.

Chapter 8

Configuring TCP/IP

· ·

In This Chapter

▶ Planning for the TCP/IP installation and configuration

▶ Using commands to find out information about your NIC

▶ Installing and configuring TCP/IP on client operating systems

▶ Installing and configuring TCP/IP on a server operating system

▶ Understanding what network files do

▶ Peeking inside network files

· ·

*I*n this chapter, we describe the steps you need to follow to get TCP/IP up and running and the contents of the basic files that support TCP/IP.

If you're using an operating system or TCP/IP product that's different from the ones that our examples show, your files may vary slightly from the figures in this book. Don't worry. The files may be in a slightly different location, but the general content and the purpose of those files are the same, regardless of what folder or directory they're stored in. *RTFM — Read the Fabulous Manual* that came with your TCP/IP product — always applies.

Setting Up and Configuring TCP/IP: The Basic Steps

No matter what computer, operating system, or vendor of TCP/IP software you use, you follow the same basic steps to set up TCP/IP on both clients and servers:

1. **Decide whether your computer is a client or a server.**

   Setting up a client is much simpler than setting up a server because you don't need to configure server services — you'll be getting those from the server that someone else sets up.

2. **Plan ahead.**

   See the following section ("Planning ahead before you start") for planning advice.

3. **Set up your NIC(s).**

4. **Set up your IP address or say that you're a DHCP client.**

If your computer is a server or a router, you need to continue with optional configurations, depending on what kind of services (such as e-mail, FTP, Web, or DNS) you need to provide. Chapters 10 through 15 and the bonus chapters on the CD help you set up servers.

Planning ahead before you start

Before you start any configuration, have the following information handy:

✔ **Host name:** You set your computer's fully qualified host name, such as flyingpenguin.cardinal.com, when you install the operating system. In Chapter 10, we explain what makes a fully qualified host name. Ask your network administrator for a unique host name.

✔ **NIC type:**

   • Ethernet (cabled or wireless)

   • FDDI (Fiber Distributed Data Interface)

   • Gigabit Ethernet

   • Token ring

✔ **The Administrator username and/or password (except Windows 95/98/Me):** On UNIX and Linux, the Administrator username is "root." Mac OS X prompts you for an Administrator password. Windows XP and NT flavors come with a default Administrator account that you can log on to, or you can set up your own account to have Administrator privileges.

✔ **How your host will get its IP address:**

   Are you going to assign the address manually? If so, will your host only need access to your private intranet, or will you need access to the Internet? If you're going to access the Internet, you need an officially registered IP address that is unique on the Internet. You can get your official IP address from your ISP. If you're an ISP, you can get IP addresses from these Internet Registries:

   • In America, from ARIN (American Registry for Internet Numbers) at www.arin.net/registration/index.html

   • In Europe, from RIPE NCC (Réseaux IP Européen) at www.ripe.net/rs/

> • In Asia and Australia, from APNIC (Asia Pacific Registry) at
>   `www.apnic.net`
>
> *Will DHCP assign your host's IP address automatically?* If so, you don't
> have as much work to do. See Chapter 7 for more information on how
> DHCP works.

✔ **Your subnet mask (if you're subnetting):** In Chapter 7, we also describe
   subnets and subnet masks. Ask your network administrator for the
   value.

✔ **How your host will translate names into addresses — either with a
   hosts file or with DNS (Domain Name Service):** If you're on a small
   private intranet, you might be fine with a hosts file. If you're joining a
   large network, you're probably going to need DNS. In this case, be sure
   to get the IP address of the DNS server from your network administrator.

Deciding whether to be a client, a server, or a router (or all three)

If you're going to be a client, you're not expecting to provide any services
to other computers, so all you have to do is set up your NIC and your IP
address. If you're a DHCP client, you don't even need to set up your IP
address. The DHCP server will lease you an address automatically.

If you're setting up TCP/IP as a server, you need to know what services to
provide. Will your computer be a Web server, FTP server, or DHCP server?

Will your computer function as a router? Chapter 7 defines a *router* as a
computer that runs software that decides how to forward a packet on the
route to its destination. A router is connected to at least two networks. If you
have a router, you need to configure all the NICs and set up some special
routing software.

Yes, you can set up a host to function as all three — client, server, and router.
But don't blame us if it runs slower than molasses. . . .

Setting up your NIC(s)

Your computer connects to a network through a NIC (also called a network
interface or network adapter). A client usually only has one NIC, but a router
has more than one. We use Ethernet for most of the examples in this book
because that's what we have at home and at work. If you have a different
connection media from Ethernet, you still have a NIC to connect to it, and you'll
still follow the same basic steps that we describe in the following sections.

In most cases, your computer recognizes your NIC when you install the
operating system. If you add a NIC after you install the operating system,
you may have to tell your computer about it by installing a device driver.
If your new NIC is Plug and Play, your computer will still be able to recognize
it automatically.

Determining whether you have a NIC

You can find out whether your computer has a NIC inside without even
opening up the cabinet.

Using the ifconfig and ipconfig commands

Most operating systems provide an ifconfig or ipconfig command that lists
your IP configuration, including the name of your NIC. Table 8-1 lists a few of
these IP configuration commands. Figure 8-1 shows using the Windows XP
ipconfig command from the command prompt. Figure 8-2 shows the output
you can expect to see from Mac OS X. Figure 8-3 shows the output from the
Linux/UNIX ifconfig -a command. Adding the -a option to ifconfig shows all
the interfaces.

Table 8-1   Do You Have a NIC and Other Things You Can Learn about Your IP Configuration

Operating System	Folder/Directory	Program	Type
Mac OS X	/sbin	ifconfig	Command
Windows 95/98	c:\windows	winipcfg.exe	Graphical
Windows XP	c:\windows\system32	ipconfig.exe	Command
Linux/UNIX	/sbin	ifconfig	Command
Linux	KDE Control Center	Network Interfaces	Graphical

You can also use the ifconfig command to assign or change an IP address and
configure network settings.

Using graphical tools to see your NIC

Windows 95/98/Me do not include an ifconfig command. Instead, you use the
winipcfg graphical program to see your NIC and other network information.
Figure 8-4 shows the Windows 95/98 graphic equivalent. The Linux graphical
user interfaces (KDE, GNOME) also have graphical tools for finding and configuring your NIC.

```
Command Prompt                                                          _ □ X
Microsoft Windows XP [Version 5.1.2600]
(C) Copyright 1985-2001 Microsoft Corp.

C:\Documents and Settings\Wiley>cd c:\

C:\>windows\system32\ipconfig

Windows IP Configuration

Ethernet adapter Local Area Connection:

        Connection-specific DNS Suffix  . :
        IP Address. . . . . . . . . . . . : 192.168.0.2
        Subnet Mask . . . . . . . . . . . : 255.255.255.0
        Default Gateway . . . . . . . . . : 192.168.0.1

C:\>_
```

Figure 8-1:
Use ipconfig
to find your
NIC on
Windows
XP.

```
● ● ●               Terminal — tcsh (ttyp1)
Last login: Tue Oct  8 13:23:05 on console
Welcome to Darwin!
[Media-Developments-Computer:~] mediadev% ifconfig
lo0: flags=8049<UP,LOOPBACK,RUNNING,MULTICAST> mtu 16384
        inet6 ::1 prefixlen 128
        inet6 fe80::1%lo0 prefixlen 64 scopeid 0x1
        inet 127.0.0.1 netmask 0xff000000
gif0: flags=8010<POINTOPOINT,MULTICAST> mtu 1280
stf0: flags=0<> mtu 1280
en0: flags=8863<UP,BROADCAST,SMART,RUNNING,SIMPLEX,MULTICAST> mtu 1500
        inet6 fe80::203:93ff:fe6b:7442%en0 prefixlen 64 scopeid 0x4
        inet 10.8.1.70 netmask 0xfffff800 broadcast 10.8.7.255
        ether 00:03:93:6b:74:42
        media: autoselect (100baseTX <full-duplex>) status: active
        supported media: none autoselect 10baseT/UTP <half-duplex> 10baseT/UTP <
half-duplex,hw-loopback> 10baseT/UTP <full-duplex> 10baseT/UTP <full-duplex,hw-l
oopback> 100baseTX <half-duplex> 100baseTX <half-duplex,hw-loopback> 100baseTX <
full-duplex> 100baseTX <full-duplex,hw-loopback> 1000baseTX <full-duplex> 1000ba
seTX <full-duplex,hw-loopback> 1000baseTX <full-duplex,flow-control> 1000baseTX
<full-duplex,flow-control,hw-loopback>
[Media-Developments-Computer:~] mediadev% []
```

Figure 8-2:
Use ifconfig
to find your
NIC on
Mac OS X.

```
# ifconfig -a
lo0:
flags=e08084b<UP,BROADCAST,LOOPBACK,RUNNING,SIMPLEX,MULTICAST,GROUPRT,64BIT
>
        inet 127.0.0.1 netmask 0xff000000 broadcast 127.255.255.255
        inet6 ::1/0
en1:
flags=4e080863<UP,BROADCAST,NOTRAILERS,RUNNING,SIMPLEX,MULTICAST,GROUPRT,64
BIT,PSEG>
        inet 192.168.0.6 netmask 0xffffff00 broadcast 192.168.0.255
```

Figure 8-3:
Use ifconfig
to find your
NIC on Linux
and UNIX.

These IP configuration programs give you a lot more information than just
whether you have a NIC. Look carefully at Figure 8-4. Can you see our IP
address, the host name, and when our DHCP lease will expire?

```
IP Configuration                              _ □ ✕
Host Information
                    Host Name    MW600
                  DNS Servers
                    Node Type    Broadcast
            NetBIOS Scope Id
          IP Routing Enabled        WINS Proxy Enabled
  NetBIOS Resolution Uses DNS
Ethernet Adapter Information
                             EL3C589 Ethernet Adapter      ▼
             Adapter Address    00-60-08-8A-AF-D4
  IP Autoconfiguration Address    169.254.118.95
               Subnet Mask    255.255.0.0
            Default Gateway
                DHCP Server    255.255.255.255
         Primary WINS Server
       Secondary WINS Server
            Lease Obtained    09 30 02 10:58:39 PM
             Lease Expires

    OK      Release      Renew     Release All   Renew All
```

Figure 8-4:
Use
winipcfg to
find your
NIC on
Windows
95/98/Me.

Configuring Clients to Use TCP/IP

After you confirm that you have a NIC, you configure the TCP/IP protocols for
it. We show examples using Mac OS X, Linux, and two flavors of Microsoft
Windows — Windows XP Professional and Windows 98. All these operating
systems have tools to help you set up your network. Remember that, while
the menus look different on each one, they perform essentially the same
function: helping you configure TCP/IP and your NIC.

Configuring TCP/IP on a Mac OS X client

Follow these steps to set up and configure TCP/IP on your Mac OS X client:

1. **Log on with the Administrator password.**

2. **Pull down the Apple Menu at the upper-left corner and choose System
   Preferences.**

3. **Click the Network icon.**

4. **Access the Location pop-up menu and choose Automatic.**

5. **Access the Configure pop-up menu and choose your connection
   media, such as Built-in Ethernet.**

6. **If the lock icon (bottom left) is locked, make sure that you click it and enter your password to unlock it.**

   This allows you to save the changes you make in the following steps.

7. **Click the TCP/IP tab, access the Configure pop-up menu, and choose Manually or Using DHCP, depending on how you plan to get the IP address.**

   Figure 8-5 shows the configuration window.

8. **If you're adding the address manually, type the subnet mask (if your network uses one).**

9. **If you're not using DHCP to get an address, type your IP address in the box.**

10. **Click the Save button.**

    You're done. To test your configuration, ping another computer on the network or try using a Web browser to look at your favorite Web page.

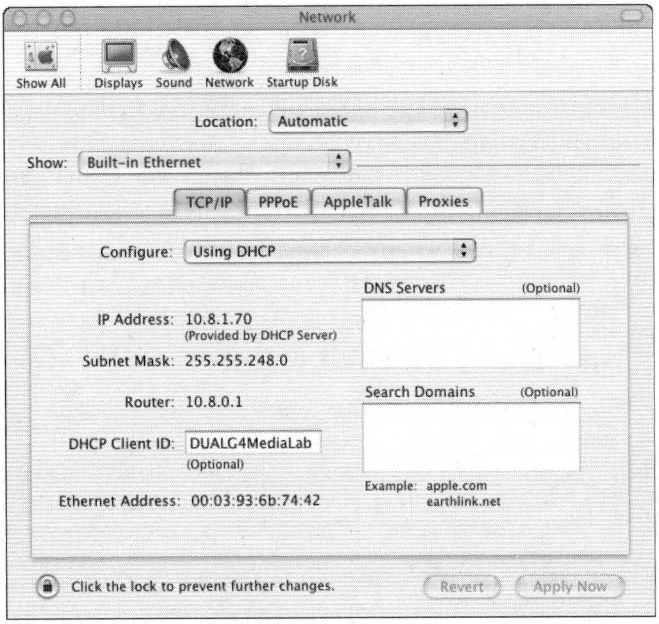

Figure 8-5:
Set your IP
address for
Mac OS X.

Configuring TCP/IP on a Linux client

When you install Linux or UNIX, the installation assumes you are also setting up networking and you must provide the following information:

- ✔ **The network interface that you want to use:** Usually, Linux puts up a list of interfaces that it discovered on your computer. You select from the list. A common Linux name for your Ethernet adapter is eth0. A common Linux name for a token ring adapter is tr0. If you have more than one adapter, the names of the second adapters are eth1 and tr1.

- ✔ **How to assign your IP address:** You must indicate whether you want DHCP to assign your IP address or if you want to set your address and subnet mask manually.

- ✔ **Your IP address and subnet mask:** You're prompted to enter this information only if you don't use DHCP.

- ✔ **The host name:** This is pretty straightforward.

- ✔ **Whether you want to use DNS to translate names into IP addresses:** If you don't choose DNS, you have to put entries in the hosts file (which is coming up later in this chapter).

The installation also sets up networking files. However, if you choose not to set up networking during the installation procedure, you can use the following steps to set up and configure TCP/IP at any time on your Linux client.

How a Microsoft workgroup is different from a domain

To join a *workgroup,* a loose collection of computers sharing file and print services, you type an existing workgroup name. You can also create a new workgroup by typing a new name. Computers in a workgroup can easily share files and printers. For best performance, workgroups should be small; no more than 15 computers is a guideline.

Computers in a *domain,* an organized and managed collection of computers, share one account database managed on the domain controller. The domain administrator sets up resource sharing and assigns your account privileges. You need an account on the domain with administrative privileges to add your computer to a domain. You get this from the network administrator for the entire domain. Domains are more complex to manage than workgroups, but domains can handle large numbers of computers (hundreds, maybe even thousands).

Don't panic if your installation screens look different from ours. Our computer is running the Caldera OpenLinux software with the popular KDE interface. Although every Linux vendor designs its screens differently, the steps to follow for setting up TCP/IP and your network are essentially the same.

1. **Log on with the root password.**

2. **Choose Start➪Control Center and then expand System by clicking the + sign.**

3. **Expand Network and click Interfaces.**

4. **Select your interface and set the IP address.**

   You can allow a DHCP server to assign your IP address automatically, or you can set your IP address and subnet mask by selecting the Manual radio button (see Figure 8-6).

5. **Click Apply.**

6. **When asked if you want to save changes to the interface, click Yes.**

7. **To test your configuration, ping another computer on the network or try using a Web browser to look at your favorite Web page.**

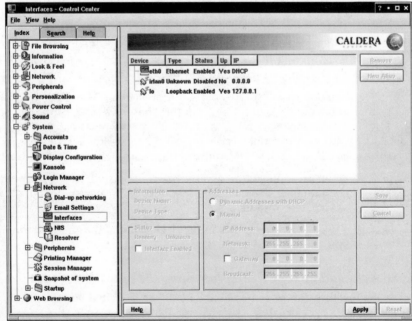

Figure 8-6: You can set your IP address manually or let DHCP assign it.

Configuring TCP/IP on a Windows XP Professional client

Setting up your network connections and configuring TCP/IP as you install Windows XP is easier than doing it later. Unlike Linux and UNIX, Windows clients such as XP do not assume networking setup during installation. You must select Network Services as one of the components to install.

During the Windows XP installation, you must select whether you are joining a *workgroup* or a *domain*. (See the sidebar "How a Microsoft workgroup is different from a domain" for definitions of these terms.) If you don't know, pick workgroup. You can always go back later and join a domain. You can share files, printers and other resources in both a domain and a workgroup.

If you're using Windows XP Home Edition, you won't be able to join a domain. Our examples are from Windows XP Professional.

Configuring TCP/IP during operating system installation

The Setup Wizard helps you install and configure TCP/IP with the following steps:

- ✔ The Windows XP Setup Wizard configures your network adapter cards.
- ✔ If setup can find a DHCP server on the network, it requests an IP address.
- ✔ If setup can't find a DHCP server, it uses Automatic Private IP Addressing (APIPA) to create your IP address.

  You don't want this automatic address. Your computer won't be able to communicate with the computers that have been properly configured. If you're using DHCP, the APIPA address indicates something is wrong with your computer, the network, or the DHCP server. If you aren't using DHCP, get the right IP address from your network administrator.

- ✔ Setup prompts you to choose *typical* or *custom* settings for networking components. Typical installs TCP/IP; if you want to install other services as well, choose Custom.
- ✔ You can also customize network settings after you finish the operating system installation.

Configuring TCP/IP after installing the operating system

Follow these steps to install and configure TCP/IP if you did *not* choose Network Services during the XP installation:

1. **Choose Start⯈Control Panel⯈Network and Internet Connections and then click Network Connections. (See Figures 8-7 and 8-8.)**

2. **Right-click the connection you need to configure, choose Properties, and then click the General tab if you have a local area connection, such as Ethernet.**

   Click the Networking tab for other connections.

   You should now be looking at the Internet Protocol (TCP/IP) Properties window.

3. **Type in your IP address, subnet mask, and default gateway. If you're getting your IP address automatically from a DHCP server, select the Obtain an IP Address Automatically radio button. (See Figure 8-9.)**

4. **In the same TCP/IP window, set your DNS server address.**

   You can get the address automatically, as shown in Figure 8-9, or you can set the DNS server addresses manually.

   Now for the moment of truth.

5. **Click OK to apply the changes, and then close your windows and restart your computer for the changes to take effect.**

6. **When your computer restarts, test your configuration by using the ping command. (See Figure 8-10.)**

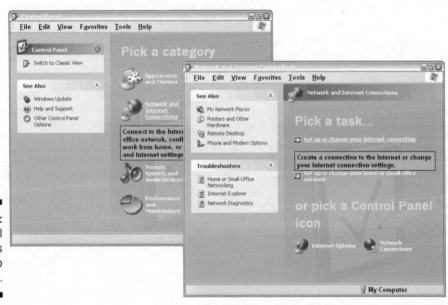

Figure 8-7:
The Control Panel sends you to networking.

Figure 8-8:
The network
connections
window lets
you set
properties
for your
network.

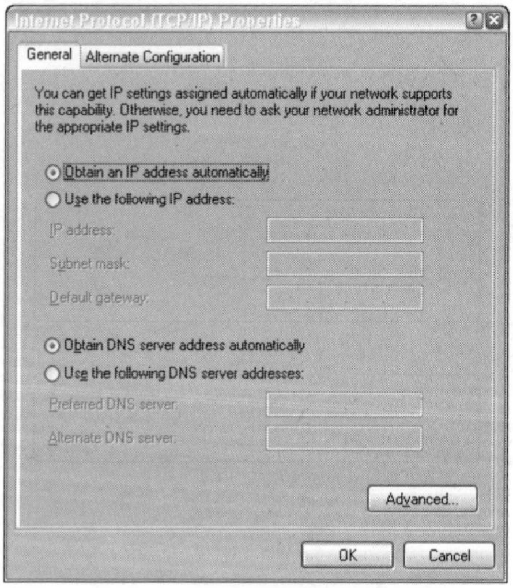

Figure 8-9:
You can
obtain your
IP address
from a
DHCP
server or set
the address
manually.

Figure 8-10:
ping your
computer to
test your
TCP/IP
configur-
ation.

Configuring TCP/IP on a Windows 95/98/Me client

Follow these steps to install and configure TCP/IP:

1. **Open the Control Panel and double-click the Network applet to display the Network dialog box and the Configuration tab.**

   You should see the list of network components installed on the computer, similar to the one shown in Figure 8-11.

Figure 8-11:
There's the
component
we want.

The exact number and type of entries that you see depend on your unique situation. They may include

- *Clients:* Software that lets you use file and print servers.

- *Adapters:* Hardware, such as your NIC or modem.

- *Protocols:* TCP/IP and other software for communicating on the network.

- *Services:* Software that lets your computer be a file or print server.

2. **Scroll down the list until you find a line with an icon of a network cable and TCP/IP, followed by the name of the adapter. Select it and click the Properties button (or just double-click it) to open the TCP/IP Properties Configuration dialog box. It opens to the IP Address tab.**

Your network components may look quite different from ours. Notice that we have two entries on the list of network components for TCP/IP. The second entry is there because we configured our AOL software to run over TCP/IP.

3. **Select the Obtain an IP Address Automatically radio button to request a numeric IP address from a DHCP server.**

See Chapter 7 for the scoop on DHCP. If you're lucky enough to work in a DHCP environment, you may be done with the Network applet.

If you aren't using DHCP, specify your IP address and subnet mask manually, as shown in Figure 8-12.

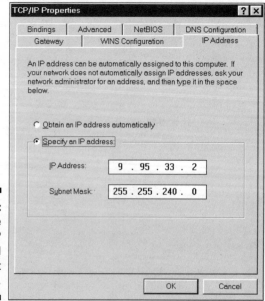

Figure 8-12: Enter the numeric IP address and subnet mask.

4. **Click OK twice to exit.**

   You usually have to restart the operating system after making changes in the Network applet.

You can't just use the numbers from Figure 8-12. They aren't right for your network. You have to get your numbers from your network administrator.

Those are the essential steps for configuring a TCP/IP client for Windows 95 and Windows 98. The next step is to set up DNS if you're in a large network. We describe DNS fully in Chapter 10.

While you can't simply copy the sample data from Figures 8-13 and 8-14, they show examples of supplying information on the DNS Configuration and Gateway tabs. The Internet uses DNS (Domain Name System — see Chapter 10) to find domains, such as `lotus.com`, and translate their names into numerical IP addresses.

Make sure that your network administrator gives you all of the configuration data that you need, such as the following:

✔ DNS domain name and the numeric IP addresses of any DNS servers (for the DNS Configuration tab)

✔ Numeric IP addresses of the routers (for the Gateway tab)

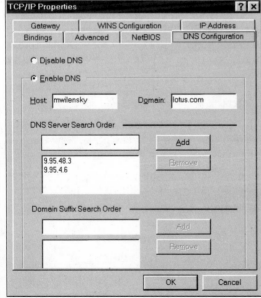

Figure 8-13:
Enter the parts of the computer's fully qualified host name and the addresses of the DNS servers.

```
TCP/IP Properties                               ? X

  Bindings   │   Advanced   │   NetBIOS   │   DNS Configuration
     Gateway    │    WINS Configuration    │    IP Address

   The first gateway in the Installed Gateway list will be the default. The
   address order in the list will be the order in which these machines
   are used.


   New gateway:
   ┌─────────────────────┐        ┌─────────────┐
   │   .   .   .         │        │     Add     │
   └─────────────────────┘        └─────────────┘

   ┌ Installed gateways: ──────────────────────────┐
   │  ┌──────────────────────┐   ┌─────────────┐   │
   │  │ 9.95.32.1            │   │   Remove    │   │
   │  │                      │   └─────────────┘   │
   │  │                      │                     │
   │  │                      │                     │
   │  └──────────────────────┘                     │
   └───────────────────────────────────────────────┘


                         ┌─────────┐      ┌─────────┐
                         │   OK    │      │ Cancel  │
                         └─────────┘      └─────────┘
```

Figure 8-14:
Enter the
default
gateway
address the
network
administra-
tor gives
you.

Configuring a Server to Use TCP/IP

This section gets you started with bare bones TCP/IP on a server. To configure specialized servers, such as DNS, e-mail, and FTP, read Chapters 10 through 15 and the bonus chapters on the CD. Our example uses a computer running Windows 2000, but the basic steps apply to any server-class operating system, such as Linux, UNIX, IBM's mainframe systems — even Compaq's ancient, but still excellent, VMS.

1. **Log on as Administrator.**

   When you open the Control Panel and double-click the Network applet, the first thing you see is a choice between Make New Connection and Local Area Connection, as shown in Figure 8-15.

   Wow, it sure looks different from our other Windows examples! That's partly because they're from clients, while Windows 2000 is a server that can provide network services.

2. Double-click the Local Area Connection icon, and then click the Properties button.

You should see a list of installed components, similar to what you see in Figure 8-16.

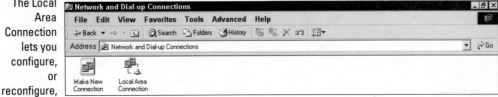

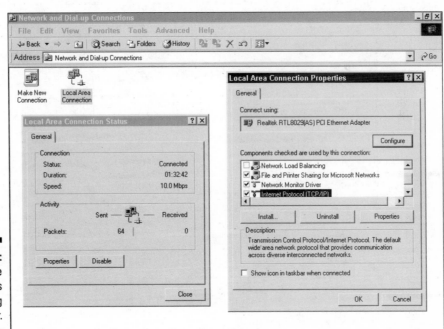

3. **Select Internet Protocol (TCP/IP) and click the Properties button (or just double-click Internet Protocol).**

   The Internet Protocol (TCP/IP) Properties screen appears.

4. **Select Use the Following IP Address.**

   Because this computer is going to provide services to other computers, you can't select the Obtain an IP Address Automatically option.

5. **Enter the numeric IP address, subnet mask, default gateway address, and the IP addresses of the DNS servers, as shown in Figure 8-17.**

   If you click the Advanced button, you can get to even more settings, including the built-in security features on the Options tab, as shown in Figure 8-18. We've gone far enough for this example, though.

   Remember that you can't use the values from our examples for your computer.

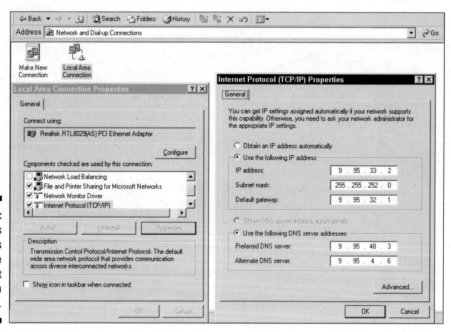

Figure 8-17:
Windows
2000 has
all the
important
fields on
one screen.

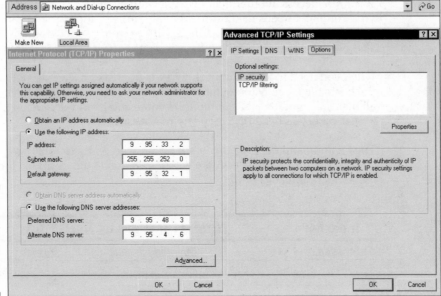

Figure 8-18:
Just how
much
treasure is
buried here,
anyway?

The Network Files

Installing and configuring TCP/IP creates most of the files you need automatically. Just point your mouse, click, and type some text. Your setup program creates and maintains the files for you.

The one exception to this handy tip is when you're working on an older UNIX computer or a very small Linux system that has no network setup program. In this sad case, the network administrator (who is probably you if you're reading this chapter) must create some files and edit others. How you do this is up to you. A text editor works just fine.

The hosts file

We start with the most fundamental file that you need for communicating with other computers on your network — the hosts file. (In Chapter 7, we added the word *host* to your vocabulary — that's host as in a computer on the network. If you think it's host as in "Be our guest," take a look at Chapter 18, about security.)

When you access another host by name on the Internet or any intranet/internet, your computer needs to know the remote host's IP address. You can get remote host addresses from DNS (see Chapter 10) or from your computer's hosts file. This file lists the names and addresses of other hosts known by your computer.

When you need to know about thousands of hosts on the Internet, maintaining the hosts file is really too cumbersome a mechanism. Imagine having to spend all that time updating it as computers come and go or relocate on the Internet! In that case, you need DNS to locate remote hosts.

The location and name of the hosts file depend on the operating system and version of TCP/IP you use. Table 8-2 lists the hosts file locations for a few implementations of TCP/IP.

Table 8-2	Popular Locations for Hosts Files	
Location	*Operating System*	*Vendor*
/etc/hosts	Linux and UNIX	Various
c:\winnt\system32\ drivers\etc\hosts	Windows NT, 2000	Microsoft
c:\windows\hosts	Windows 95, 98	Microsoft
c:\windows\system32\ drivers\etc\hosts	Windows XP	Microsoft
Netinfo database	Apple	Mac OS X
/etc/hosts	zOS	IBM

TIP

Performance: Let DNS and a hosts file share the job

Many versions of TCP/IP allow you to use a combination of DNS and a hosts file to find remote hosts by putting the most frequently accessed hosts into your hosts file. That way, you won't have the performance overhead of accessing a DNS name server on the network to get an address for the hosts that you connect to on a regular basis. Let DNS help you find addresses for hosts that you access only occasionally. This is really the best of both worlds: performance and reliability.

Maintaining the hosts file

Your operating system or TCP/IP product provides a hosts file to get you started. You, the network administrator, the system manager, or whoever is in charge of network configuration, maintains the hosts file. As you add host names and addresses, you need to update the file. If your vendor did not include a network configuration tool, you get to use a plain old text editor, such as Notepad, to type in two columns of information — column 1 for the host's IP addresses and column 2 for its names.

Finding what's in the hosts file

Figure 8-19 shows the contents of a hosts files taken from a computer running UNIX. Looking at Figure 8-19, you may think there are several host names on a line. But the first name is the host name and the following name(s) are nifty host name *aliases*. Look carefully at the entry for the host spiderman. Do you see an alias, peterparker? You can refer to the computer as either spiderman or peterparker. Anything preceded by a # character is a free-form comment about things such as the computer's owner, location, operating system, and whatever else you think is meaningful.

Improving TCP/IP's digestion of the hosts file

Without an up-to-date hosts file, you may not be able to find other computers on the network, so it's important to update the file whenever a computer changes its name or address or joins or leaves the network. Listing the computers in most frequently used order is a good idea. TCP/IP searches the hosts file sequentially from top to bottom until it finds the computer it's looking for, so if you have a large hosts file, ordering the computers appropriately gives you a performance advantage.

Figure 8-19:
This hosts file, created with a text editor, contains the IP addresses and the host names.

```
#
# Sun Host Database
#
#
127.0.0.1       localhost
#
129.103.40.1    spiderman peterparker    # M Wilensky
129.103.40.3    reddwarf                 # Marshall Wilensky
129.103.40.6    giacomo                  # Netware server
129.103.40.7    grapeleaf                # OS/2 Notes server
129.103.40.17   kerwien                  # Erica Kerwien
129.103.40.24   vogon                    # Notes NLM Server
129.103.40.53   zugspitz                 # SparcStation
```

The trusted hosts file

On Linux and UNIX operating systems, the file `/etc/hosts.equiv` lists the other hosts on the network that your computer trusts; this is your *trusted hosts file*. This file is easy to create with any text editor. It has only one column — the host name of each computer you trust. (See Figure 8-20.)

```
vogon
grapeleaf
spiderman
reddwarf
```

Be very careful with the `hosts.equiv` file. Any remote computer listed here is a trusted host, and all of its users can log on to your computer without knowing a password.

Some operating systems implement trust by using other methods besides a trusted hosts file. Microsoft Windows NT and 2000 Server, for example, don't use the `hosts.equiv` file. Instead, you set up trust relationships when you set up security policies for your computer or Active Directory for your domain. Trust relationships are between domains as opposed to individual hosts. See Figure 8-21.

The trusted hosts print file

On Linux and UNIX, you can use the `/etc/hosts.lpd` file to list the remote hosts that can print on the printer attached to your computer. The simplest `hosts.lpd` file possible contains just one asterisk (*) character, which means that any host on the network can share your printer. If you don't have a `hosts.lpd` file, it's the same as having the file with an asterisk in it. So if you aren't prepared to be supergenerous with your printer, you'd better create one of these `hosts.lpd` files. Any text editor will do.

Speaking of generosity, how generous can you afford to be with your printer? If you share your printer with all of the hosts on your network, will the volume of remote print jobs mean that you always have to wait before you can print your own stuff? Will this same print job traffic clog up the network connection media (the cables)? You should ask yourself these questions before editing your `hosts.lpd` file.

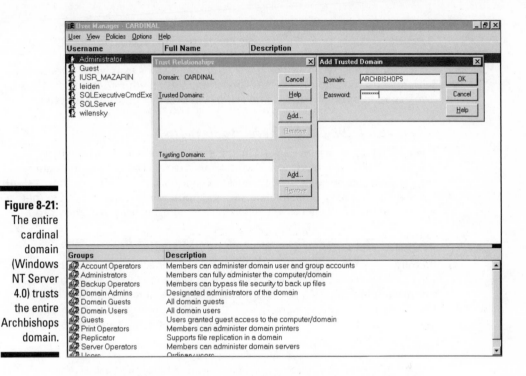

Figure 8-21:
The entire
cardinal
domain
(Windows
NT Server
4.0) trusts
the entire
Archbishops
domain.

Freddie's nightmare: Your personal trust file

You should be aware of a special (and dangerous) file that exists on a "per user" basis. This means that you and all the other users on a computer can create a personal trust file in your home directory. In Linux and UNIX environments, this file is named `.rhosts`, pronounced "dot are hosts." And yes, the dot is part of the filename.

The `.rhosts` file holds two pieces of information: the host name and the account name. Here are the contents of our niece Sarah's `.rhosts` file in her home directory on computer elmst. The file allows her sister, Emily (from computer mainst), to have the run of computer elmst without a password. If you live on Elm Street or elsewhere in cyberspace, don't let personal trust become a nightmare. Please be careful about letting evil players into your computer.

```
#  host   user    comment
mainst   emily  # Let in Emily from mainst
```

Most network administrators, like Freddie, consider .rhosts files to be potential security problems. These files list *trusted remote users* — those who are permitted to log on to your account without entering a password. Logging on without a password allows users to copy any files from your directories with rcp and to remotely execute any command on your computer with rsh. You can read more about rcp and rsh in Chapters 13 and 14, respectively.

This is scary. Why would I ever want .rhosts?

If you do a lot of work on various hosts, it's quite convenient to rlogin as yourself on all the computers on which you have accounts. Your account may be Marshall on one computer, Wilensky on another, and Mwil on a third — with three different passwords. If all of these computers have a .rhosts file that lets you in from anywhere, you can skip remembering all those passwords.

Surprise! The curse of the network administrator lives

If Emily has been wandering all over computer elmst because Sarah lets her, Emily may get a big surprise one day when she tries to log on remotely and permission is denied. Network administrators frequently hunt down and kill these .rhosts files. After Sarah's .rhosts file is gone, Emily needs to know a valid password in order to log on, unless she gets Sarah to re-create the file.

The networks file

Not only do you need a hosts file (or DNS) to list the individual hosts with which you plan to communicate, along with their IP addresses, you also need a *networks file* to hold the network numbers and names with which you plan to communicate. Listing the network names enables you to refer to all of the hosts on the same network (or subnet) as one group. The networks file supplied with the operating system or TCP/IP software rarely needs editing. In Linux and UNIX, the network file is /etc/networks. The file can be at different locations, depending on the operating system. For example, Microsoft Windows 2000 Server stores the file in c:\winnt\system32\drivers\etc\networks.

When you create your networks file, be sure to list only the network section and not the host piece of the numeric IP address. If you're not sure about this, read about IP addresses in Chapter 6. In the file shown in Figure 8-22, some of the network addresses have only one piece, such as arpanet 10. The ending 0s are assumed. You can leave them out for convenience, or you can list them explicitly, as in 10.0.0.

Figure 8-22:
The networks file lists the network name and its addresses.

```
#
# Sun customer networks
# This file is never consulted when the NIS are running
#
loopback        127
sun-ether       192.9.200    sunether ethernet localnet
sun-oldether    125          sunoldether
#
# Internet networks
#
arpanet         10           arpa
ucb-ether       46           ucbether
```

The internet daemon configuration file

What a mouthful! The file named `/etc/inetd.conf` on UNIX systems lists all of the things you want the internet daemon, inetd (see the "Daemons — are we in hell again?" sidebar), to do. The name of this file (`inetd.conf`) is pronounced "eye net dee dot conf." Now try it three times fast.

The `inetd.conf` file shown in Figure 8-23 is nearly identical to the original that came with our UNIX operating system. The TFTP lines were modified slightly, and the bootp line was added to allow down-line loading of X Window terminals.

You don't have this file on Windows 95/98/NT/2000/XP. The registry maintains this information for you.

Daemons — are we in hell again?

Daemons, in general, are programs that provide some sort of services — TCP/IP daemons are the servers for many of the TCP/IP client/server functions. The internet daemon program, inetd, is the heart and soul of TCP/IP services. (By the way, most daemons' names end in *d*.) Inetd supervises the other TCP/IP daemons. The internet daemon configuration file, `inetd.conf`, tells inetd what other servers it is responsible for.

```
# @(#)inetd.conf 1.24 92/04/14 SMI —— This file comes with TCP/IP. Usually you don't
#                                       touch it except for good reasons.
# Configuration file for inetd(8).  See inetd.conf(5).
#
# To re-configure the running inetd process, edit this file, then
# send the inetd process a SIGHUP.
#
#
# Internet services syntax:
# <service_name> <socket_type> <proto> <flags> <user> <server_pathname> <args>
#
# Ftp and telnet are standard Internet services.
#
ftp    stream  tcp  nowait   root   /usr/etc/in.ftpd     in.ftpd
telnet   stream  tcp  nowait   root   /usr/etc/in.telnetd    in.telnetd
#
# Tnamed serves the obolete IEN-116 name server protocol.
#
name   dgram   udp   wait   root   /usr/etc/in.tnamed   in.tnamed
#
# Shell, login, exec, comsat and talk are BSD protocols.
#
shell   stream   tcp   nowait    root    /usr/etc/in.rshd    in.rshd
login   stream   tcp   nowait    root    /usr/etc/in.rlogind    in.rlogind
exec   stream   tcp   nowait    root    /usr/etc/in.rexecd    in.rexecd
comsat  dgram   udp   wait   root   /usr/etc/in.comsat   in.comsat
talk   dgram   udp   wait   root   /usr/etc/in.talkd   in.talkd
#
# Run as user "uucp" if you don't want uucpd's wtmp entries.
#
uucp   stream   tcp   nowait   root   /usr/etc/in.uucpd   in.uucpd
#
# Tftp service is provided primarily for booting.  Most sites run this
# only on machines acting as "boot servers."
#
####
####   Enabled specifically for NCD X-terminals.
####     Marshall Wilensky   Fri Feb  4 17:50:55 EST 1994
#tftp   dgram   udp   wait   root   /usr/etc/in.tftpd   in.tftpd -s /tftpboot
tftp   dgram   udp wait root /usr/etc/in.tftpd   in.tftpd -s /usr1/ncd-install/tftpboot
bootps  dgram   udp   wait   root   /etc/bootpd      bootpd
#
```
There's more to this file, but we've shown you enough.

Network administrator updated this entry. Top of the directory tree for downloading files. ——

Security note: This is the original entry. ⌐

Figure 8-23: The inetd.conf file lists TCP/IP services directed by the internet daemon.

For each service, the `inetd.conf` file contains a line with the following fields:

✔ **Service name:** The service must also have a corresponding entry in the `/etc/services` file.

✔ **Socket type:** An interprocess communication mechanism that's a bit too techie for this book. This field usually specifies `stream` if the service uses TCP and `dgm` or `dgram` for datagram if the service uses the UDP protocol. You may also see `raw` in this column.

✔ **Protocol:** The protocol used by the service, usually either `tcp` or `udp`.

✔ **Flags:** Another technoid. Flags are set to either `wait` or `nowait` to specify whether inetd can accept another connection without waiting for the current server to finish.

✔ **User:** This field holds the account name that's the owner of the service. On UNIX systems, it's usually the username of the privileged user, `root`.

✔ **Server path:** This is the directory and filename for the daemon program.

✔ **Arguments (args):** The name of the daemon or the command that runs a tool and any other command arguments.

The protocols file

The protocols file lists the TCP/IP protocols. It comes with your TCP/IP software. You may need to update this file if you add protocols to your TCP/IP configuration.

Figure 8-24 shows an example of a UNIX protocols file, `/etc/protocols`. Look at Figure 8-25 for a similar example from a Microsoft Windows NT Server protocol file. On Microsoft Windows NT/XP/2000, the file is named `protocol`, with no *s* at the end.

Figure 8-24:
On UNIX, the /etc/ protocols file lists TCP/IP protocols used on the network.

```
# @(#)protocols 1.9 90/01/03 SMI
#
# Internet (IP) protocols
# This file is never consulted when the NIS are running
#
IP       0    IP    # internet protocol, pseudo protocol number
icmp     1    ICMP  # internet control message protocol
igmp     2    IGMP  # internet group multicast protocol
ggp      3    GGP   # gateway-gateway protocol
tcp      6    TCP   # transmission control protocol
pup      12   PUP   # PARC universal packet protocol
udp      17   UDP   # user datagram protocol
```

```
# Copyright (c) Microsoft Corp.
#
# This file contains the Internet protocols as defined by RFC 1060
# (Assigned Numbers).
#
# Format:
#
# <protocol name>  <assigned number>  [aliases...]   [#<comment>]

ip        0     IP        # Internet protocol
icmp      1     ICMP      # Internet control message protocol
ggp       3     GGP       # Gateway-gateway protocol
tcp       6     TCP       # Transmission control protocol
egp       8     EGP       # Exterior gateway protocol
pup       12    PUP       # PARC universal packet protocol
udp       17    UDP       # User datagram protocol
hmp       20    HMP       # Host monitoring protocol
xns-idp   22    XNS-IDP   # Xerox NS IDP
rdp       27    RDP       # "reliable datagram" protocol
rvd       66    RVD       # MIT remote virtual disk
```

Figure 8-25:
On
Microsoft
Windows
servers, the
protocol file
is located in
c:\winnt\
system32\
drivers\etc\
protocol.

The services file

The services file lists the network services being used on your computer. You don't usually have to maintain this file yourself. TCP/IP does it automatically when you enable or disable new services.

Each line in the file has the following columns:

- ✔ Service name
- ✔ Port number
- ✔ Protocol (separated from the port number by a /)
- ✔ Aliases (other, optional names for the service)

Figure 8-26 shows a services file from a UNIX system.

Figure 8-27 shows a services file from a Microsoft Windows NT Server system. Pop quiz: Can you see the difference between Figure 8-26 and 8-27? Answer: It's a trick question. Although the computers in the examples run specific services to support their users (Ingres on the UNIX system, for example), and although the file is located in different directories on the two operating systems, the basic file format is the same.

Any port in a network

With so many services, how does an application know which one it should use? Certainly not by name; that would be too easy, even though many applications, services, and protocols are named the same. Take FTP, for example, which is the name of an application, a service, *and* a protocol.

Applications communicate with services via an object called a *port id number.* ID numbers 1 through 255 are reserved for the most commonly used services, such as telnet and FTP.

Port numbers can also be created, as needed. If you write your own TCP/IP application and service, you simply use a port number greater than 255.

When an application, such as FTP, says to TCP/IP, "Here I am, ready to work," TCP/IP doesn't really care about the application's name. Instead, TCP/IP sees only the numbers: the Internet address of the host that provides the service and the port number through which the application intends to communicate.

```
# @(#)services 1.16 90/01/03 SMI
#
# Network services, Internet style
# This file is never consulted when the NIS are running
#
tcpmux         1/tcp                              # rfc-1078
echo           7/tcp
echo           7/udp
discard        9/tcp          sink null
discard        9/udp          sink null
systat         11/tcp         users
daytime        13/tcp
daytime        13/udp
netstat        15/tcp
chargen        19/tcp         ttytst source
chargen        19/udp         ttytst source
ftp-data       20/tcp
ftp            21/tcp
telnet         23/tcp
smtp           25/tcp         mail
There's more to this file, but we've shown you enough.
```

Figure 8-26: A UNIX services file, /etc/services.

```
# Copyright (c) Microsoft Corp.
#
# This file contains port numbers for well-known services defined by IANA
#
# Format:
#
# <service name>  <port number>/<protocol>  [aliases...]   [#<comment>]
#

# lots of editing to save space

ftp             21/tcp                              #FTP. control
telnet          23/tcp
smtp            25/tcp      mail                    #Simple Mail Transfer
Protocol
time            37/tcp      timserver
nicname         43/tcp      whois
domain          53/tcp                              #Domain Name Server
tftp            69/udp                              #Trivial File Transfer
gopher          70/tcp
finger          79/tcp
http            80/tcp      www www-http            #World Wide Web
kerberos        88/tcp      krb5 kerberos-sec       #Kerberos
rtelnet         107/tcp                             #Remote Telnet Service
pop3            110/tcp                             #Post Office Protocol -
Version 3
ldap            389/tcp                             #Lightweight Directory
Access Protocol
https           443/tcp     MCom
kpasswd         464/udp                             # Kerberos (v5)
biff            512/udp     comsat
login           513/tcp                             #Remote Login
who             513/udp     whod
netnews         532/tcp     readnews
kerberos-adm    749/udp                             #Kerberos administration
nistration
# lots more follows, but we've shown you enough.
```

Figure 8-27: A Microsoft Windows NT Server services file, c:\winnt\ system32\ drivers\etc\ services.

You may notice some interesting security services, including Kerberos, in Figure 8-25. Check out Chapter 20 to see what that security service is all about. Test yourself by trying to recognize some familiar services in these examples.

On Microsoft Windows NT and 2000, you can open the Control Panel and use the Services applet to get information about services, such as whether they're running and whether they start automatically. Figure 8-28 shows the Control Panel running the Services applet on Windows 2000. Interesting — this system is a DHCP client and a DHCP server, as well as a DNS client and a DNS server!

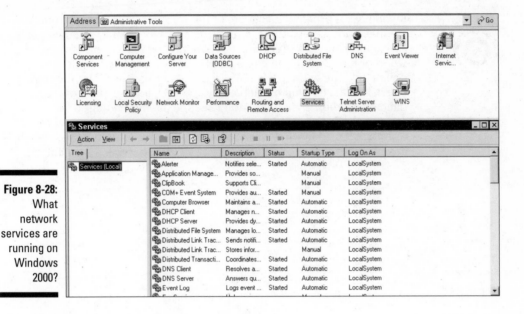

Figure 8-28:
What
network
services are
running on
Windows
2000?

Dealing with the Devil

Earlier in this chapter, we tell you that inetd is the father of all daemons. The following list gives you descriptions of a few other TCP/IP daemons that you should know about:

- **routed (here we go again):** The routed daemon manages routing tables (which we explain in Chapter 16). No, don't say "row-ted" or even "roo-ted." It's either "rowt dee" or "root dee." The routed daemon uses RIP, the Routing Information Protocol (which we also explain in Chapter 16).

- **named:** The named daemon is pronounced "name dee." (Are you getting the hang of it yet?) This handy daemon is the one that runs on your name server to manage DNS and to do the host name/IP address resolution that we cover in Chapter 10.

- **More handy-dandy daemons:** There are lots more daemons. All have names that end with *d* and are pronounced by saying the name of the service followed by "dee." We've listed some of the more famous daemons in Table 8-3, along with the services that they provide. Figure 8-29 shows some popular daemons running on a UNIX system.

TIP

If you have a problem using one of the services in Table 8-2, a quick troubleshooting technique is to check and see whether the daemon is started. On Windows NT and 2000, use the Services applet to see whether it's running. On Linux and UNIX, you can do this with the ps command, one of the tools that we cover in Chapter 17. In the ps output, check the last column of each entry and look for the name of the daemon (ending in *d*). If you don't see the daemon required for the service, that's the problem. To use the service, you need to get the daemon started in whatever way your operating system allows. You may have to simply click an icon, or you may have to type in a command.

Figure 8-29:
The computer has some of our favorite daemons running.

```
$ ps auwx
USER        PID %CPU %MEM   VSZ  RSS TT   STAT STARTED   TIME COMMAND

root         65  0.0  0.0  1160  992 ??   Ss   Thu12PM  1:31.58 named
root         68  0.0  0.0    52  108 ??   Ss   Thu12PM  0:08.83 rwhod
root         70  0.0  0.0    60  108 ??   Is   Thu12PM 5:13.29 nfsiod 4
root         77  0.0  0.0    56   16 ??   I    Thu12PM  1:47.96 nfsiod 4
root         78  0.0  0.0    56   16 ??   I    Thu12PM  0:48.53 nfsiod 4
root         79  0.0  0.0    56   16 ??   I    Thu12PM  0:20.84 nfsiod 4
root         80  0.0  0.0   444  132 ??   Ss   Thu12PM 0:17.39 inetd
root      22947  0.0  0.0    96   72 ??   I    10:28PM  0:00.48 rlogind
root      15491  0.0  0.0   120  172 ??   I     1:00PM  0:00.35 telnetd
root      20008  0.0  0.0   224  556 ??   S     3:03PM  0:00.40 ftpd
root      20033  0.0  0.0    28  232 ??   S     3:03PM  0:00.07 ntalkd
```

Table 8-3	Popular Services and Their Daemons
Service	*Daemon*
finger	fingerd
ftp	ftpd
telnet	telnetd
rlogin	rlogind
rsh	rshd
rexec	rexecd
talk	talkd
NFS client	nfsiod
NFS server	nfsd

Chapter 9

IPv6 — IP on Steroids

*I*f you're interested in the new IPv6 protocols and addresses, this chapter is for you. Take a deep breath, count to ten, and know that IPv6 can make your life a lot easier. But first, here are the reasons why Internet sites can benefit from implementing IPv6:

✔ In the twentieth century, people realized that the Internet was in danger of running out of network numbers. Internet architects came up with some temporary solutions involving NATs (Network Address Translations) and CIDR (Classless Inter-Domain Routing), but those workarounds are not a final solution. The Internet is still running out of addresses.

✔ Large, cumbersome routing tables of addresses slow down the Internet.

✔ The Internet may possibly run out of addresses because it connects hundreds of millions of computers and other devices. Nobody really knows how many. The exact number isn't nearly as important as the fact that the number of computers and devices grows daily by leaps and bounds.

IPv4's 32-bit numbering already provides for 4 billion addresses. How many networks? The Internet probably won't run out before 2010. (That's a wild guess. If we could predict the future, do you think we would be authors?)

If you're a network manager, don't wait until December 31, 2009, to begin planning your migration path to IPv6. Start now! (Remember what happened when you delayed planning for Y2K? The end of 1999 may have been pretty stressful for you.) In the meantime, while you plan, IPv4 and IPv6 can coexist. In fact, you should be considering a coexistence plan right now if you want to be ahead of the conversion tidal wave.

Some analysts believe that everyone in the world should be connected to the Internet. Predictions estimate the world population to exceed 10 billion by 2020. Does that mean 10 billion computers on the Internet? Not really — because people have more than one computer. Not every type of computer is on the Internet. Not yet, anyway. But think of the possibilities, such as your car. You're driving along when your car's computer detects a failing fuel pump. It transmits a message via TCP/IP to your service station to have a replacement ready, uses the Global Positioning System to determine the location of the nearest towing service, and calls for a tow truck. This isn't a fantasy — a concept car like this already exists.

In Chapter 6, we urge you to call your computer a "host," but in this chapter, we change the name of computers again. We're not trying to drive you crazy, we promise! In the IPv6 world, a computer is now called a *node*. Actually, we're not talking just about computers. Any device, such as a router, on an IPv6 network is called a node.

If It Ain't Broke, Don't Fix It — *Well, Maybe It Could Be Improved*

IPv6 retains most of IPv4's characteristics — especially for the stuff that works. For example, fully qualified domain names (FQDNs) stay the same. Thank goodness!

Some things do change, though. Every piece of TCP/IP is affected by a new, longer address format. While the name resolution services (local hosts file, NIS, and DNS) still exist, there should be less need for them in the future thanks to autodiscovery, autoconfiguration, and autoregistration (more about these in the section "IPv6 — and the Using Is Easy" later in this chapter).

Some other things can go away (such as supernet masks and ARP), while still other things could simply stand some improvements (such as switching to a different network number). In this chapter, we highlight the key topics.

If you need a refresher course on IPv4 addressing, see Chapter 6.

Wow! Eight Sections in an IPv6 Address?

A 32-bit IPv4 address provides 4 billion addresses. In order to offer more addresses on the Internet, IPv6 changes the address format. It works like adding an area code to telephone numbers. Does this mean you have to figure out a new way to access the Internet because of IPv6? Not at all. The IPv6 task force mandates that IPv4 and IPv6 addresses must coexist.

IPv6 has its own Web site: www.ipv6.org.

Every IPv6 address is 128 bits long, or four times longer than an IPv4 address. That doesn't mean that there are only four times as many addresses; it means there are an ENORMOUSLY HUGE number of IPv6 addresses because we're talking about exponential growth! The number is so big that we broke three calculators trying to figure it out. It's more than 340,000,000,000,000,000,000, 000,000,000,000,000,000 addresses.

Concerning addressing architecture in detail, you'd better see RFC 2373: "IP version 6 Addressing Architecture."

An IPv6 128-bit address is taken as 8 groups of 16-bit numbers, separated by colons. Each number is written as 4 hexadecimal (hex) digits. This means that IPv6 addresses range from

```
0000:0000:0000:0000:0000:0000:0000:0000
```

to

```
FFFF:FFFF:FFFF:FFFF:FFFF:FFFF:FFFF:FFFF
```

Here's a sample IPv6 address:

```
EFDC:BA62:7654:3201:EFDC:BA72:7654:3210
```

(Hey, these are even more agonizing than v4 addresses.) Aren't you glad that fully qualified domain names are still valid?

If you're curious about all those letters, check out the nearby sidebar "Reading hexadecimal, or since when is *F* a number?"

Don't these long addresses clog network traffic?

The format of the packets is so improved that even though IPv6's long addresses use more of the network's capabilities, the new packet format offsets any performance penalty of the longer address fields. The streamlined packet headers make the store and forward process (which we describe in Chapter 7) go faster.

Why use hexadecimal?

Hexadecimal is very compact inside a computer, saving memory and disk space. It's also easier to write large numbers in hex than it is in decimal.

Reading hexadecimal, or since when is *F* a number?

Everyone knows that digits are 0 through 9. That's true for decimal (or base 10) numbers, but other numbering bases also use letters. In hexadecimal (also called hex and base 16), the allowable digits are 0 through 9 plus A through F. Zero through nine are the same as good old decimal, but then there's

- ✔ A = decimal 10
- ✔ B = decimal 11
- ✔ C = decimal 12
- ✔ And so on

So the decimal value 15 can also be written as hex F.

Fact of life: People love decimal. Computers love hex.

Here's where we get advanced: hex 10 = decimal 16. Yikes! We're talking place value here. Take a look at a decimal example. Remember the 1s, 10s, and 100s columns.

```
100s   10s    1s
 1      3      0      = one 100s
    plus three 10s plus zero 1s
                  = 130
```

In hex, the columns are 1s, 16s, 256s, 4096s, and so on. Try the hex number 101. What number is it in decimal?

```
256s   16s    1s
 1      0      1      = one 256s
    plus zero 16s plus one 1s
                  = 256 plus
 1
                  = 257
```

Here's another hex number to test yourself: AC4.

```
256s   16s    1s
 A      C      4      = A 256s
    plus C 16s plus four 1s
                  = ten 256s
    plus twelve 16s plus four
1s
                  = 2,560
    plus 192 plus 4
                  = 2,756
```

For fun, try FFF. That's

```
256s   16s    1s
 F      F      F      = F 256s
    plus F 16s plus F 1s
                  = fifteen
    256s + fifteen 16s + fif-
teen 1s
                  = ??
```

Now is a good time to get out your calculator and figure it out. Don't call us if it breaks, though.

Most operating systems have a calculator tool that can convert between decimal and hexadecimal.

There's good news and there's bad news

The good news is that if you're what the computer industry calls an end user, you don't really need to worry about this. You still send e-mail to Candace by typing her address, `cleiden@bigfoot.com`.

The bad news is that if you're a system manager or network administrator, you may have to type these awkward addresses into files to set up the network for the lucky end users.

Shorthand for Non-Stenographers

We know it seems like a lot of work to read and write these addresses. Thank goodness IPv6 has some shortcuts to make these addresses easier to handle.

The leading zero (0000) shortcut

When you write an IPv6 address, you can omit any leading zeros — and there may be lots of them — in each group of four hex digits. If all four digits are zero, you need to write just one. For example, you can write

```
1060:0000:0000:0000:0006:0600:200C:326B
```

as

```
1060:0:0:0:6:600:200C:326B
```

The double-colon (::) shortcut

Then there's the double-colon (::) shortcut. In an address, you can replace one sequence of single zeros and colons with a double colon. You can only use the double-colon shortcut once in an address, though. For example, you can write

```
1060:0:0:0:6:600:200C:326B
```

as

```
1060::6:600:200C:326B
```

To re-expand a double-colon address, you have to figure out how many colons are missing and which ones. You may want to draw an address template with asterisks (*) instead of any hex digits and with all seven colons in place, like this:

```
****:****:****:****:****:****:****:****
```

Then look at the address you need to expand and find the : : — everything to the left of it must start at the beginning of the address. Line up any colons you can. Everything to the right of the : : must end at the end of the address. Again, line up any colons you can. Insert spaces or leading zeros to help yourself. Now you can tell which colons are missing and how many!

For example, to re-expand 1060::6:600:200C:326B, the 1060 (before the : :) must start at the beginning of the address, and the 6:600:200C:326B (after the : :) must come at the end, like this:

```
****:****:****:****:****:****:****:****
1060:    :    :    6: 600:200C:326B
```

This means that 0:0:0 is what's missing. Don't worry about the leading zeros before the 6 and 600. They're optional.

Be careful. Sometimes, the double-colon appears at the start or end of the address — as in : :8267:2805 or FEC0:1:A0::.

The IPv4 coexistence shortcut

IPv4 addresses are a subset of the IPv6 address space. You can convert an IPv4 address into an IPv6 address by inserting zeros at the beginning and converting the decimal digits to hexadecimal. All of IPv4 fits in

```
0000:0000:0000:0000:0000:0000:****:****
```

which can also be written as

```
::****:****
```

For example, the IPv4 address 130.103.40.5 is also the IPv6 address

```
0000:0000:0000:0000:0000:0000:8267:2805
```

or

```
::8267:2805
```

There's also a hybrid notation called *IPv4 mapped addresses* in which you can still use dotted decimal notation. It looks like this:

```
0000:0000:0000:0000:0000:0000:0000:130.103.40.5
```

or this:

```
::130.103.40.5
```

Thanks to mapped addresses, you can reduce the risk of typos caused by broken calculators.

What about Subnet and Supernet Masks?

IPv6 addresses maintain the notion of a network part and a host part, but it's much harder to say where the division is. Subnet masks, which we discuss thoroughly in Chapter 7, are mostly gone in IPv6. You don't really need subnet masks because the Ipv6 address space is so large. The systems know what to do and that's what matters. Don't worry about it. Supernet masks are completely obsolete under IPv6. We're absolutely positive that it will be years before anyone will need to link together multiple chunks of IPv6 address space. (At least we hope so.)

In fact, subnets, masks, and supernets have been designed to work around the fact that Class A, B, and C networks are different sizes. This means that these networks are typically either too large or too small.

Special IPv6 Addresses

IPv6 reserves certain addresses for special purposes. These special addresses include the following:

- **The unspecified address:** The *unspecified address* is 0:0:0:0:0:0:0:0 (or just ::). It can be used by a system that needs to send a packet for broadcasting or DHCP client requests but hasn't yet received an address. It can't be used as a destination address.

- **The loopback address:** The *loopback address* is 0:0:0:0:0:0:0:1 (or just ::1). It lets a system send a message to itself for testing.

- **Site-local addresses:** *Site-local addresses* begin with FEC0: — they're designed for use within an organization's intranet and can't be routed on the Internet.

✔ **Link-local addresses:** *Link-local addresses* begin with FE80: — they're designed for use on a single network segment and aren't forwarded by any router. Link-local addresses permit communication with only those neighboring systems directly connected to the same part of the network (link). They allow a system to learn about its neighbors and their services without having a router get involved. (Feeling brave? Read all about routers in Chapter 16.) This kind of address saves time and has a side security benefit. A system can automatically generate an IPv6 address for itself from the link-local address prefix (FE80), the double-colon shortcut (::), and the 48-bit hardware address from its network interface card (NIC). Every NIC comes with a unique hard-coded hardware address called the MAC (Media Access Control) address built in to it. For example, your link-local address may be FE80::0800: 2BBE:1124. You can find out more about NICs in Chapter 2.

✔ **Multicast addresses:** *Multicast addresses* begin with FF**: — while a unicast address identifies one NIC, a multicast address identifies a group of NICs for a group of computers. If a packet is sent to a multicast address, all the members in the group receive that packet.

✔ **Anycast addresses:** *Anycast addresses* also identify a group of NICs. The difference between anycast and multicast is that a packet sent to an anycast address goes only to the nearest member of the group. Anycast addressing is new in IPv6 and is designed to help you find the servers closest to you. For example, you can use anycasting to find the closest DHCP server.

IPv6 — and the Using Is Easy

Suppose you receive a new computer that you need to connect to your organization's IP network or you take your laptop computer to the branch office and want to connect to the intranet. How does your computer get an IP address? In the IPv4 environment, you have to contact your network administrator. He or she configures your laptop with an IP address and updates the appropriate network management files (see Chapter 8). In two or three days (assuming the network administrator is not on holiday and not swamped with requests), your IP address is ready, and you can get on to the network and work. If your site uses DHCP, you may be able to plug your laptop into your intranet and request an address from the DHCP server.

How does your computer get an IPv6 address? The answer is autodiscovery, autoconfiguration, and autoregistration. Together they provide easier management of a dynamic network with no manual intervention. The next sections are pretty technical and more than a little boring, but we spent a lot of time on them, so humor us. Give them a try.

The computer without a country — stateful or stateless

In stateless configuration, your computer builds an IPv6 address by taking the on-link prefix and appending its hardware address. Of course, it must now use Duplicate Address Detection (DAD) to check that the address is okay to use.

In stateful configuration, your computer requests an IPv6 address from a neighboring DHCPv6 server.

In both stateless and stateful configuration, the address has a specified lifetime in order to support automatic renumbering. That means that your assigned IPv6 address isn't permanent.

Checking out the network with autodiscovery

Autodiscovery, also called Neighbor Discovery, uses the link-local addresses and the new *Neighbor Discovery Protocol* (NDP) to find out about the network and the nearby systems. NDP uses ICMPv6 informational messages. The routers on the network segments use Router Advertisement (RA) multicast packets to

- ✔ Advertise the routers' existence.
- ✔ Announce the *on-link prefix* (the "network part" of an IPv6 address).
- ✔ Signal whether systems should perform stateless or stateful configuration.

Hosts hear these advertisements and can generate their own addresses (stateless) or request an address from a DHCPv6 server (stateful), as directed. (See the discussion of autoconfiguration in the next section.)

So how does your computer exchange address information with the other computers on the network? We're so glad you asked — although you may regret it. The following process isn't just for computers but also for routers and every other network-attached device.

Whenever your computer creates an IPv6 address for itself, it transmits a Neighbor Solicitation (NS) query to that address and waits for a response. If your computer doesn't receive a response, the address is available. If another system responds with a Neighbor Advertisement (NA), the address is already in use. Try again. Your system caches the address for that neighbor in case it needs to use it later.

Your computer listens to all of the NA confirmations and all the data communication traffic on the network to learn that the neighbors are still alive and what addresses they're using. Your computer caches this information so that it's available whenever it's needed.

In the absence of NA confirmations and data traffic, your computer periodically transmits an NS query. An NA response is a "Yes, I'm here" confirmation that includes the hardware address. If there's no response, the neighbor is unreachable. Address information can be deleted when it expires this way. We could call this "autoforgetfulness," and it's an important piece because it supports the renumbering of systems.

NS, NA, and this Duplicate Address Detection (DAD) process totally replace the Address Resolution Protocol (ARP). Take a look at Chapter 5 to find out about ARP.

Automatically assigning addresses

Autoconfiguration is a kind of IP address "plug-and-play" process. It automatically assigns an IPv6 address to a NIC. As we describe in the preceding section, the Router Advertisement (RA) packets contain the on-link prefix and indicate whether systems should perform stateless or stateful configuration.

Autoregistration says "Let us serve you"

If your computer is just acting as a client of the services on your organization's network, it should be completely satisfied by autodiscovery and autoconfiguration. But what about the servers — the computers responsible for the services on the network? How do they make sure that the clients can find them? Autoregistration!

Autoregistration refers to the automatic, dynamic adding or updating of a computer's hostname and address information in DNS. You need autoregistration so that the new IPv6 address that a server receives via autoconfiguration is available to the clients as soon as they need it. So maybe there won't be that many typos and broken calculators after all. Even now, we can hear the contented sighs of network managers everywhere. Too bad they have to wait for more IPv6 deployment.

Setting Up IPv6

Setting up IPv6 is not very different from setting up IPv4. In most cases, you follow the same basic steps that we describe in Chapter 8, with a major exception, however: Windows XP Professional.

Configuring IPv6 on Windows XP

Installing and configuring IPv6 on Windows XP is a very different procedure from the IPv4 example that's in Chapter 8. You don't use the Control Panel's Network Connections in the Network Connections folder. You do all your IPv6 work from the command prompt. In fact, the commands look more like UNIX than any flavor of Microsoft Windows.

Microsoft provides a prerelease version of IPv6 for XP so that you can test it in your environment. You should not use IPv6 until Microsoft officially releases and supports it.

To install IPv6 on Windows XP, you must be logged on with local administrator privileges. You need a command prompt to begin the installation.

1. **To get a command prompt, click Start and then choose Programs⇨ Accessories⇨Command Prompt.**

2. **At the command prompt, type** ipv6 install**.**

   When the command prompt returns, not only is IPv6 installed, but the autoconfiguration mechanism has also assigned an IPv6 address for the computer to use on your LAN. You can see the address in Figure 9-1 where the output lists the "link local address".

IPv6 doesn't show up as an installed protocol. If you're not sure whether IPv6 is already installed, type **ipv6 if** at the command prompt. See Figure 9-1.

Figure 9-1:
Checking
your IPv6
installation
and
parameters.

```
C:\Documents and Settings\wiley>ipv6 if
Interface 4: Ethernet: Local Area Connection
    uses Neighbor Discovery
    uses Router Discovery
    link-layer address: 00-60-08-f5-27-09
        preferred link-local fe80: :260:8ff:fef5:2709, life infinite
        multicast interface-local ff01: :1, 1 refs, not reportable
        multicast link-local ff02: :1, 1 refs, not reportable
        multicast link-local ff02: :1:fff5:2709, 1 refs, last reporter
    link MTU 1500 (true link MTU 1500)
    current hop limit 128
    reachable time 27500ms (base 30000ms)
    retransmission interval 1000ms
    DAD transmits 1
```

To remove your IPv6 configuration, type **ipv6 uninstall** at the command prompt.

When you're using Microsoft's IPv6, the familiar network commands add a "6" at the end of the command name. For example, the ping command, which checks to see whether a computer is reachable, becomes ping6 for IPv6. Figure 9-2 shows sample output from the ping6 command. Notice the long IPv6 address.

Figure 9-2:
Remember
to add a "6"
to IPv6
commands
on Windows
XP.

```
C:ping6 fe80: :260:8ff:fef5:2709

Pinging fe80: :260:8ff:fef5:2709
from fe80: :260:8ff:fef5:2709%4 with 32 bytes of data:

Reply from fe80: :260:8ff:fef5:2709%4: bytes=32 time<1ms
Reply from fe80: :260:8ff:fef5:2709%4: bytes=32 time<1ms
Reply from fe80: :260:8ff:fef5:2709%4: bytes=32 time<1ms
Reply from fe80: :260:8ff:fef5:2709%4: bytes=32 time<1ms

Ping statistics for fe80: :260:8ff:fef5:2709:
        Packets: Sent = 4. Received = 4, Lost = 0 (0% loss),
Approximate round trip times in milli-seconds:
        Minimum = 0ms, Maximum = 0ms, Average = 0ms
```

Not all IPv6 implementations add a "6" to the command name. See the example of an IPv6 ping from the Hewlett Packard Tru64 UNIX operating system in Chapter 17.

Welcoming IPv6 to Mac OS X

The ability to set up IPv6 on Mac OS X is a huge change. Before Mac OS X, no released version of Mac OS had support for IPv6. When you upgrade to version 10.2 or higher of Mac OS X, you can configure IPv6 as part of the upgrade procedure.

Tips for getting started with IPv6 on UNIX and Linux

If you need to run IPv6 on a UNIX or Linux computer, you must be sure that the operating system kernel supports IPv6. For Linux, at this writing, the latest stable kernel is version 2.4.18 and has IPv6 support. If your kernel is old, you need to download a new kernel and build it on your computer. Our favorite Linux book, *The Linux Bible* (by Candace Leiden; published by Wiley Publishing, Inc.), has an entire chapter on how to build a new Linux kernel.

To find out the version of your kernel, type the uname -r command as follows:

> # **uname -r**

which yields this:

```
2.4.13
```

On UNIX, you can find out whether your kernel has IPv6 support by using the sysconfig -q ipv6 command as follows:

> # **sysconfig -q ipv6**

The command's output lists the IPv6 subsystems that are in the UNIX kernel.

If your kernel is set up with IPv6, you'll see sysconfig messages that start with inet6, such as the one following, which displays an IPv6 format address:

```
inet6 efdc:ba62:7654:3201:efdc:ba72:7654:3210
```

It makes life a lot easier if your UNIX/Linux operating system provides a setup utility for configuring IPv6. For example, the Compaq Tru64 UNIX has the ipv6_setup utility that you run by typing

> # **/usr/sbin/ip6_setup**

The ip6_setup utility asks you questions and creates and configures the necessary files automatically so that you can run IPv6. It's not quite as easy as it sounds because you need to do plenty of planning and research to answer the questions. The ip6_setup questions include things such as

- ✔ Whether your computer will be a regular IPv6 host or an IPv6 router
- ✔ Your domain name
- ✔ Whether you will be tunneling across to IPv4 networks
- ✔ The names of the network interfaces (NICs) that will handle IPv6 traffic
- ✔ Whether you want to start IPv6 immediately or wait until later

Even if your operating system provides a handy IPv6 setup tool, be sure to read the manual thoroughly.

Other Delicious IPv6 Morsels

IPv6 delivers other features, too. Some are continuations of stuff that works under IPv4 while others are new concepts. While we won't go into detail here, we thought you should hear a little about them.

Security for all

Security services, such as packet authentication, integrity, and confidentiality, are part of the design of IPv6. These capabilities can guarantee that packets are actually from the indicated sender, haven't been altered in transit, and can't be seen by hackers. Because the security services are built into IPv6, they're available to all of the TCP/IP protocols, not just specific ones, such as SSL, PPTP, and S-HTTP. This means that your organization's network can be easily made more secure, but don't assume that you can relax completely. Governmental restrictions against exporting or importing security technology may limit the availability of some capabilities, and hackers can be amazingly crafty.

Here are a couple of IPv4 security problems that IPv6 solves:

- ✔ **IP spoofing:** IP spoofing tricks a computer into believing that a message comes from an authorized IP address. IP spoofing can fool a computer into revealing passwords and data to hackers and crackers. Spoofing is also a common form of denial-of-service attacks, in which crackers flood a site with so many requests that genuine users can't access the site.

  The problem: IPv4 doesn't know how to determine whether the packets it receives are from the end node they claim to be from. Malicious users can impersonate genuine nodes. You need to buy good firewall software to use on state of the art routers to guard against IP spoofing. (See Chapter 18 for an explanation of how firewalls work.)

  The IPv6 solution: The IPv6 packet includes an authentication header that allows you to determine that a packet you receive really comes from the address it claims to come from. The authentication header also assures you that the packets you receive have not been altered. You don't need any add-on software or hardware to prevent the bad guys from masquerading as good guys.

- ✔ **Sniffers:** A *sniffer* is a program that monitors and analyzes network traffic. Network managers use sniffers to find bottlenecks and problems on a network. Sniffers also cause security holes on networks — and we mean all networks, not just TCP/IP networks. Because a sniffer can read the data inside the packet, a cracker can use a sniffer to read data as it moves along the network wires.

  The problem: IPv4 transmits data, including account names and passwords, mostly in regular text. When crackers "sniff" out accounts and passwords, they can really do some damage to your computer and network. Most UNIX and Linux operating systems have tools so that you can search for sniffers on your network, but these tools can be difficult to use and time consuming. For other operating systems, you need to buy sniffer-detection tools. And they still take time to use and analyze the data they return. You can also buy certain specialized hardware and software that prevent sniffer attacks.

The IPv6 solution: An IPv6 packet includes a special extension header that says that the *payload* (that is, the data that follows this special header) is encrypted. This is called *end-to-end encryption* at the network layer.

The IPSec protocol, a component of IPv6, adds an additional level of security and creates a secure, TCP/IP-level, point-to-point connection. In fact, IPv6 offers security to applications that currently lack built-in security and adds security to applications that already have minimal security features. You can find IPSec information in Chapters 5 and 20.

Faster, better multimedia

IPv6 provides new capabilities for high-quality, streaming, multimedia communications, such as real-time audio and video. Huge opportunities for research and experimentation exist in this area of communication, especially as the Internet continues to grow and evolve.

Support for real-time applications

IPv6 improves the performance of real-time applications, such as live radio and television broadcasts and video conferencing.

The IPv6 term *flow* is a noun that means a set of packets that needs special handling along the way between source and destination. Real-time services, for example, need special handling. A flow of packets has a label that's stored in the packet header. By checking this header, a computer on the network can decide how to forward these special packets without taking the time to look at the rest of the headers for each packet in the flow. The result is that IPv6 strips some of the fat from real-time transmissions. In a videoconference, the picture won't seem so jerky, and you won't miss what people are saying.

Improved support for mobile computing

IPv4 has trouble with mobile computers. A mobile computer not only moves around geographically, it also attaches to the Internet at different addresses. When Candace teaches a database class in Tokyo and attaches to her client's intranet, she needs a different address for her laptop. When Marshall delivers a Lotus Domino presentation in Buenos Aires and attaches his notebook to the convention center's intranet, he needs a different address. And at the same time, both Candace and Marshall need to be attached to their companies' networks. IPv4 has a hard time keeping up with these changes in location.

IPv6 has many benefits for mobile users. We won't go into detail here, but check out the Internet draft called "The Case for IPv6" at www.ietf. org/internet-drafts/draft-ietf-iab-case-for-ipv6-05.txt — it discusses the advantages of IPv6 dialup support for road warriors. The improvements involve some of the topics that we discuss in this chapter, such as autoconfiguration, special headers, encapsulation, security, and anycast addresses. As you read this, some satellite work in Europe has already become IPv6 based.

Sharing the Planet — IPv6 and IPv4 Can Coexist

Now that it's here, do you have to use IPv6? No. Most organizations still use IPv4. Also, IPv6 is built to manage both v4 and v6 addresses. If your server has the latest and greatest IPv6, your client computer with IPv4 doesn't have to change. IPv6 server software is backward compatible. That means it understands both IPv4 and IPv6 dialects. Your server knows what to do.

Don't bother upgrading your client computer to IPv6 until your network administrator upgrades your servers and routers.

A key reason to upgrade your routers is to enable the autos (autodiscovery, autoconfiguration, and autoregistration), thereby enabling network administrators to have a well-deserved week at the beach.

Welcome to the 6Bone

Just as there is an Internet backbone (see Chapter 4), there is an IPv6 backbone called the *6bone*. The purpose of the 6bone is to provide an IPv6 test site for interoperability and connectivity: Organizations connect to the 6bone to discover and troubleshoot IPv6 problems and test that their IPv6 applications work as they should. The 6bone is a worldwide test network consisting of over 400 sites spread across 57 countries . . . and still growing. Just as the Internet backbone has regional networks attached, the 6bone has regional 6bones, such as Japan's WIDE6bone.

If you want to join the 6bone to get experience with IPv6, your first step is to get on the 6bone mailing list. Send an e-mail to majordomo@isi.edu with the line *subscribe 6bone* as the contents of the message. Next, get a registered production IPv6 address from an ISP that supports IPv6. If you don't want to go through an ISP, you can get your own address. To see how, go to the 6bone Web page: www.6bone.net/6bone_hookup.html.

Whew . . . You Made It!

Wow, are we ever impressed! You made it all the way here. If you're interested in more details regarding IPv6 and its advanced features and capabilities, you can find many RFCs, articles, and books. Or you can get on the Internet and see what's happening on the 6bone, the real world deployment of IPv6.

As of this writing, there are 70 current RFCs about IPv6. We recommend that you start with the following:

- ✔ RFC 2373, by R. Hinden and S. Deering, "IP Version 6 Addressing Architecture"
- ✔ RFC 1924, by R. Elz, "A Compact Representation of IPv6 Addresses"
- ✔ RFC 2460, by S. Deering and R. Hinden, "Internet Protocol, Version 6 (IPv6) Specification"

Part III
Using and Configuring TCP/IP Services

The 5th Wave   By Rich Tennant

"I know my modem's in the microwave. It seems to increase transmission speed. Can you punch in 'Defrost'? I have a lot of e-mails going out."

In this part . . .

TCP/IP is more than two protocols — it's a whole suite of protocols, services, and applications. With TCP/IP applications and protocols, you can take advantage of everything from reading news to exchanging e-mail and online conversations with your friends to copying good stuff like games, technical articles, and even TCP/IP itself. Is your computer underpowered? In this part, we show you how TCP/IP services let you "borrow" processing power from across the network.

In this part, we also show you popular Internet applications, including e-mail, file sharing, Web browsing, remote access, and dialing up. You find out how these applications and services work with client/server technology, and you get hands-on tips for setting up both the client side and the server side for these popular applications.

Chapter 10

Resolving Names and Addresses with DNS

*H*ere you discover another service: the Domain Name System (DNS, pronounced by saying the letters D N S). But when you fish for information with the DNS rod and reel, you're fishing around not just on your own intranet but also on the Internet.

Getting to Know DNS

A name service *resolves* (or translates) a computer name into a numeric address. The Domain Name System (DNS) is the name service for the Internet, and it translates computer names into TCP/IP numeric addresses.

If your organization's network is connected to the Internet, you must use DNS. If your organization has a private intranet, you may use DNS to provide the name service for your network.

DNS was created specifically to handle the requirement that each computer needs to be uniquely named on the network. By adding some pieces to your computer name to make it unique, DNS solves the problem of duplicate computer names.

Do you drive a Lotus or just work there?

With millions of computers participating on the Internet, finding unique names is difficult. Today, you'd wonder if the computer called lotus belongs to Lotus software or the car manufacturer. And if you send e-mail to user Wilensky on computer lotus, will it go to your friend at the car company (actually www.lotuscars.com) or to someone you never heard of at the software company (which is www.lotus.com)?

DNS = Does Nifty Searches

DNS shares information about computer names and addresses over a TCP/IP network. On a large network (such as the Internet), that's a lot of information.

In techie terms, DNS is the *name-and-address resolution service* used on the Internet. In more straightforward terms, DNS is a kind of directory service. It searches for the numeric Internet address for a computer name and vice versa. (Of course, if we could remember those complicated numeric addresses, we wouldn't need a name-and-address resolution service, but brain cells being what they are, we'd rather think of a computer as bigbird instead of as 192.168.0.1.)

As you may have read in Chapter 6, hosts on a TCP/IP network have both a name and a numeric IP address. When you use a name, either the hosts file (see Chapter 8) or DNS must translate the names into numbers behind the scenes. Let's look at the mythical address abc.university.edu.

Remember that the first piece of this address, abc, is the computer's name; the last piece of the address on the right, edu, represents a domain name — a DNS top-level domain name. The intermediate piece (university) is a secondary domain name, which represents things like organization names.

Revisiting Client/Server — You Can't Get Away from It

A *service* is functionality, such as resolving a name into an address. The *server* is the software that implements the functionality.

DNS is a client/server environment. Clients (applications such as e-mail, telnet, FTP) query a *name server* for a computer name-to-numeric address translation. If the name server can answer the query, it responds with the requested information and all is well. The most common DNS server software is named BIND (Berkeley Internet Name Daemon). BIND started as a graduate student project at the University of California at Berkeley. Microsoft name servers use a proprietary product that interoperates with BIND.

If the name server can't supply the information, two things may occur, based on whether the name server is or is not *responsible for* the information (more on this in the next section).

- ✔ If the name server is responsible, it responds with a message that says the information doesn't exist. (Do you have any fives? Go fish!)

- ✔ If the name server isn't responsible for the information, it forwards the query to, or at least toward, the name server that's responsible. (The name server knows to do this based on how the network administrator sets things up.) When the answer comes back, it travels all the way back down the chain to the client.

- ✔ If the client *times out* — gets tired of waiting for a response — that's the same as receiving a "No Information" answer from the queried name server.

- ✔ If at this point *you* have timed out, too, hang in there. We explain this "responsibility" thing next.

Who's responsible?

What does it mean to be "responsible for" the name and address information? The DNS term for responsibility is *authority.* Several different types of name servers may be deployed in your environment. In the DNS world, there is no single master server. Instead, primary name servers know, via the DNS database, the names and addresses of the computers in your organization. These name servers are responsible for this information, and the answers they give to client queries are said to be authoritative.

Because DNS is *distributed* (that is, decentralized), no one computer has to have all the information about all the addresses. Can you imagine the number and size of the disks you'd need to hold the addresses of all the computers on the Internet? Not practical, even if it were possible. Therefore, multiple name servers work together to translate a name to an address.

There are 13 Root Name Servers across the world that hold the master list of all DNS records. Your ISP's DNS server queries these Root Name Servers to update its own DNS tables.

Name servers and resolvers

The name server program that responds to queries for a resolution of a name to an address is one of the pieces of the DNS puzzle. The name server program may or may not be included in your TCP/IP product. If you need to set up and run your own name server, make sure that you have the program. Most organizations use an ISP to administer DNS.

Another piece of DNS is a library of programs called a *resolver,* which takes the client program's request to get address information and converts it into a query to the name server. (The resolver is part of every TCP/IP product. You need it. You have it. Don't worry.) More specifically, when a programmer writes an application that needs to know a computer's address, the application contains a call to the resolver routines. For example, this request in a program, "Open an FTP connection to computer Jerry," generates a DNS query for the address of computer Jerry. Figure 10-1 shows the resolver communicating with the name server on behalf of a client application.

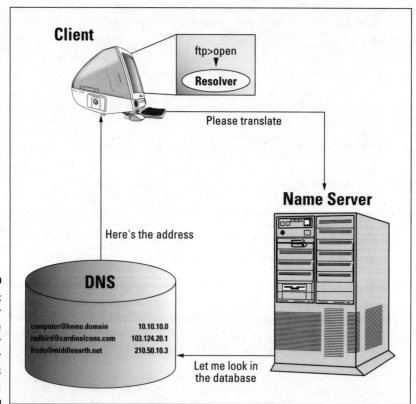

Figure 10-1:
The resolver asks the name server to answer an address query.

Client

ftp>open

Resolver

Please translate

Name Server

Here's the address

DNS

computer@home.domain	10.10.10.0
redbird@cardinalcons.com	103.124.20.1
frodo@middleearth.net	210.50.10.3

Let me look in
the database

Putting the DNS pieces and parts together

Lots of bits and pieces work together for DNS, including hardware, software (programs and some TCP/IP protocols), data files, and people. Here is a summary:

- ✔ **The distributed database** holds information about computers in domains on the Internet or on your internet.

- ✔ **Domains** are logical collections of computers whose requests for network address lookups are all handled by the same server(s).

  DNS domains are different from and unrelated to Windows NT/2000 domains.

- ✔ **Name servers** are programs that implement the name service by accessing information from the database and respond to client queries.

- ✔ **Clients** are programs that request network address information from the name servers.

- ✔ The **resolver** works on behalf of the client applications to get network address information from the name server.

- ✔ **System and network administrators** set up everything and maintain the databases.

In the next few sections, we take a closer look at these pieces.

The Internet's Definition of Domain

Various products and applications use the term *domain* to mean different things. DNS defines *domain* in the context of a large network, such as the Internet.

The Internet is so huge that it organizes its participating computers into groups of administrative units; these units are called *domains.* The domains themselves are organized hierarchically into a tree structure, as shown in Figure 10-2.

The Internet's tree is upside down. The root is at the top. Branches extend from the *top-level domains* (TLDs). Your computer sits in the leaves, at the edge of this hierarchy of domains. There are two types of TLDs:

- ✔ **Generic top-level domains** (gTLDs) (those that do not represent countries). These domains have the generic organization types listed in Table 10-1. You may recognize the suffix in the first column as the last part of many Internet and Web addresses.

✔ **Country code top-level domains** (ccTLDs). A country code domain ends with a two-character country code specified by ISO (International Standards Organization) standard 3166. At our last count, there were 243 country code domains (not all are independent countries: Antarctica, for example, and certain protectorates and territories). Table 10-2 lists a few of these country code top-level domains.

Table 10-1	Generic Top-Level Domain Names
Domain Suffix	*Definition*
.com	Commercial enterprise
.net	Network services
.org	Organization
.edu	Educational institution
.gov	United States government
.mil	Military service
.aero	Air transport industry
.biz	Businesses
.coop	Cooperatives
.info	Unrestricted
.museum	Museums
.name	Individuals
.pro	Accountants, lawyers, physicians, other professions

Table 10-2	Some Country Code Top-Level Domain Names
Country Code	*Country*
ad	Andorra
ca	Canada
in	India
uk	United Kingdom (Actually, the ISO code is gb, but it's hard to make a long story short about whether a country is in Great Britain or the UK.)
us	United States

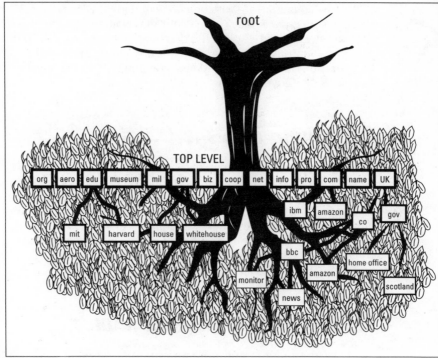

root

TOP LEVEL

| org | aero | edu | museum | mil | gov | biz | coop | net | info | pro | com | name | UK |

mit   harvard   house   whitehouse

ibm   amazon   co   gov

bbc   home office

monitor   amazon   scotland

news

Figure 10-2:
Internet
domains are
hierarchical.

How do you register a domain and what does it cost?

Usually, you register your domain name through your ISP or a Web hosting site. Be sure to register your domain name through an ICANN-accredited registrar or its resellers. You can find ICANN's list of accredited registrars at `www.icann.org/registrars/accredited-list.html`. When you register your domain, either directly or with a registrar, your organization gets a home in one of the top-level domains listed in Table 10-1.

Domain registration used to cost a standard rate. Because so many vendors can now register a domain name for you, it pays to comparison shop. Besides a wide range of prices, many companies run special sales where your domain registration is discounted (or even free) when you buy other services.

Go to `www.registration.fed.gov` to register a site in the `.gov` domain. To register a U.S. military agency, go to the registry at `www.nic.mil`. You must be a legitimate member of the U.S. government or military to register for these domains.

When you communicate with someone outside the United States, be aware that the subdomains may (or may not) have different names. In Australia, they use the same style as in the U.S. (com.au, edu.au, and so on). But in the U.K., some administrative domains are named differently, as in co.uk (corporation) and ac.uk (academic community), and some stay the same, as in gov.uk (government).

Branching into subdomains

The top-level domains branch out into *subdomains,* which are usually named after your organization. A subdomain is any subdivision of a domain. A subdomain of a top-level domain is a second-level domain. If your organization is large, it may further create its own subdomains for administrative purposes; these subdomains are third-level, fourth-level, and so forth. Refer to Figure 10-2 to see a few second-level domains (such as mit.edu and amazon.com), as well as a third-level domain (amazon.co.uk) and a fourth level (news.bbc.co.uk).

Fully qualified domain names

You have already seen some DNS domain names used in this book. The domain name is so important that it actually becomes part of each computer's name. The result is called a *fully qualified domain name,* or FQDN, pronounced by saying the letters F Q D N. For example, the computer named hbs is part of the DNS domain named harvard.edu, yielding the FQDN hbs.harvard.edu. You can see this FQDN in Figure 10-2.

You may wonder why FQDNs are so long. You may be able to use some shortcuts — depending on where you're sending e-mail from. If you send mail to marshall@abc.mythicaluniversity.edu, the mail reaches him no matter where you are when you send it. However, that's a pretty long address to have to type. To make things easier, you don't always have to use an FQDN. If you don't, TCP/IP assumes the domain is the same as yours.

Don't take a domain name for granted

Don't assume anything from the name of the domain. As the popularity of the Internet soared over the last few years, some entrepreneurs got a nasty idea: *cybersquatting.* They register well-known domain names before the companies that really need them do and then try to sell them to the companies for a profit. Hasbro, Inc. had to go to court to prevent an adult nudie site from using candyland.com.

So if you, too, are on computer abc, you can simply send mail to the username marshall and save some typing. If you're on a different machine, say computer xyz, but your computer is also in the `mythicaluniversity.edu` domain, you can leave out the domain name and just send to `marshall@abc`.

Servers, Authority, and Other Techie Stuff

You can have three types of servers in your DNS domain:

- The primary name server
- The secondary name server(s)
- The caching name server(s)

Before we examine their roles in the scheme of things, be sure you know your authority figures. Read on.

Who's in charge here?

In the DNS environment, a name server can be in one of three different states when queried by the client:

- It knows the answer authoritatively. That means it has the answer on the database on its hard drive. This is the same as being responsible for the data. The network administrator maintains a set of the data files that make up a DNS database.

- It knows the answer, but not authoritatively. That means it has stored (cached) the data in memory from some previous query.

- It doesn't know the answer and has to ask another DNS server.

Master of your domain

Primary name servers are the master authority for their domains. A zone is often the same as a domain, but not always. (More on that in a bit.) The primary name server stores the databases for its zone. Also, a primary name server can delegate authority to a secondary name server, to lessen the primary's workload and to give it a backup. (Is this starting to sound like life at the office? To relieve stress, delegate!)

The primary server is the ultimate repository of truth — at least as far as the names and addresses in the domain are concerned. When the primary name server delegates authority, it ships the truth, in the form of the database (or at least part of it), to the secondary name server. That action is called a *zone transfer*. So a zone can be the entire domain, or just a subsection. The more the primary can delegate, the more stress relief it gets. Every domain should have a primary and at least one secondary name server.

The secondary name servers

In school, the little kids in primary school look up to the big kids in secondary school. But on the Internet, it's just the opposite: The big kids are the primary name servers. Secondary name servers download copies of name/address information from a primary or another secondary name server. Secondary name servers relieve primary stress.

The more secondary name servers your organization has, the less chance of clogging up the primary name server and the better protected you are from a failure of the primary. Secondary name servers are the backups for the primaries, and if the primary delegates authority, the secondary can answer address queries from any other name server in its zone.

The big difference between a primary name server and a secondary name server is where each gets its information. The primary gets it from the database files; the secondary gets it from a primary or another secondary name server.

Caching servers

Caching name servers also help relieve stress, but they're not entirely trustworthy because they don't have the real truth in the form of database files on disk. They have what they "believe" to be the truth. Caching servers have no authority in a DNS system. They depend on the kindness of other name servers for information. The caching servers query other servers for name address information and keep (that is, cache) it in memory for users who are geographically close.

All servers do caching, especially of the data for which they're not responsible. Caching servers do only caching because they have no data files and aren't responsible for any information.

If Katherine sends mail to `elaine@mustsee.net`, her local caching server looks up `mustsee.net` in the DNS and holds on to the information. When Katherine sends Elaine another mail message, the `mustsee.net` IP address is now quickly available from the caching server, and her request for the name-to-address translation is spared a long trip across the network.

If `mustsee.net` changes its IP address, Katherine's caching server may still hold the old address information. To avoid this problem, the cached data in a name server expires periodically.

To manage this expiration procedure, the administrator of the authoritative name servers (the ones responsible for knowing the truth) sets a *Time To Live* (TTL) value for the name/address data. Think of the TTL as a timer that limits how long any name server can cache the data. When the timer runs out, the cached data must be discarded. Without the TTL, no updates would ever replace old information. Remember that the resolver issues a query for computer name-to-address translation every time you go out on the network, regardless of the application you're using.

Smaller TTL values mean that the data cached by nonauthoritative name servers (including the caching servers) is updated more often. The trade-off is that those name servers must query more frequently. Larger TTL values reduce network traffic but increase the likelihood that old, possibly incorrect, data are still alive.

Choosing DNS or hosts files . . . or both

Long ago, before the Internet was even a gleam in anyone's eye, keeping track of the names and addresses of a group of computers wasn't a big deal. A text file containing the addresses and names of the computers was the perfect solution. This was the *hosts file,* and each computer kept a local copy. We describe how to use hosts files in Chapter 8. *Host* normally means computer, but it can also refer to any other device connected to the TCP/IP network, including routers, hubs, and terminal servers. If your computer needs to communicate with only a small number of other computers on your intranet, you can easily list them in your own local hosts file.

Every TCP/IP product on every operating system knows how to look in a local hosts file to resolve a computer's name into its numeric address. Every TCP/IP product on every operating system knows how to query DNS servers.

DNS is the best choice for a large private intranet because it eases your maintenance burden and keeps IP addresses reliable. Manually updating and synchronizing local hosts files on all your computers is tedious, time-consuming, and risky. Moreover, those local hosts files can be enormous if your organization has thousands of computers and each one needs its own copy. With DNS, if and when you do attach your organization to the Internet, your domain is ready to go.

You can improve performance and reduce network overhead by using the best of both worlds. Store information about frequently accessed hosts in the hosts file. The default network behavior is for a name resolution request first to look in the hosts file. If the hosts file can't do the name-to-address resolution, DNS takes over. Configure your DNS client to use DNS for everything else.

Configuring a DNS Client

Configuring a DNS client means enabling DNS lookups. You may not even need to do that. If your computer gets its IP address from a DHCP server, you don't need to enable DNS. The DHCP server automatically supplies the DNS settings when it supplies the IP address. Windows XP uses DHCP by default, and you don't need to configure DNS settings.

If you are a power user and know the specific DNS servers that work best for your particular requests, you may decide to enable and configure DNS yourself. For example, if you require an authoritative answer, you can configure your DNS client to avoid caching servers. Follow these steps to configure a DNS client:

1. **Enable DNS.**

2. **List the IP addresses for the DNS servers you want to use.**

Although the preceding steps are the same for any operating system, how you perform the steps varies depending on your user interface.

On Microsoft Windows 95/98/Me clients, you start your DNS configuration in the Control Panel. In the Control Panel, double-click the Network icon. Scroll down to the TCP/IP section and select your TCP/IP Internet connection, such as an Ethernet adapter or dial-out modem. Click the Properties button. Select the DNS configuration tab. Click the Enable DNS radio button. Fill in the host name and domain boxes. Fill in the DNS Search Order box with the IP addresses of the DNS servers in the order you want them searched to resolve a name into an address.

You follow the same steps on Windows XP, but the user interface differs slightly. See Figure 10-3. You still start at the Control Panel. Double-clicking Network Connections takes you to a screen that lists your Internet connections. Double-clicking your Internet connection displays the Local Area Connection Status box. Click Properties. Scroll down the list and select Internet Protocol (TCP/IP). Click Properties. Select the Use the Following DNS Server Addresses radio button. Fill in your preferred DNS server's IP address. Click Advanced to display the Advanced TCP/IP Settings box. Click the DNS tab to set the DNS search order. Fill in the IP address(es) and click the Add button.

If you think you're having trouble with the DNS servers, see Chapter 17 for troubleshooting steps.

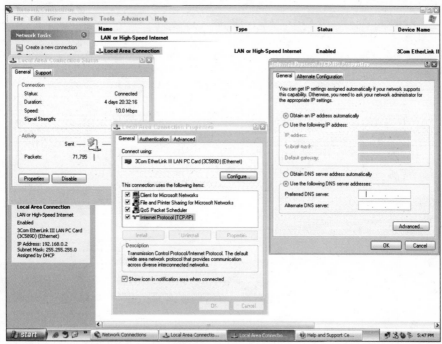

Figure 10-3:
Power
users
configure
DNS clients.

Chapter 11

E-Mail and Other Communication Services

●●

In This Chapter

▶ Understanding how Internet e-mail protocols (SMTP, POP3, IMAP4) work

▶ Understanding how mail clients (MUAs) and servers (MTAs) work

▶ Configuring mail clients and servers

▶ Discovering e-mail services you can get for free

▶ Working with other communication services — news, chat, phone, and instant messaging

●●

*E*lectronic mail is the first network application most people meet. E-mail has been around so long that many of us forget some folks still don't have it yet. The following sections provide an in-depth look at e-mail. And wait 'til you read about MIME, a delicious extra that TCP/IP gives you — at no extra charge.

Talking about TCP/IP without talking about the Internet is almost impossible — it would be like discussing gasoline without talking about cars. In this chapter, you find lots of references to the Internet as we describe the things that TCP/IP lets you do. This chapter also gets you started with other communication services: Usenet news, Instant Messaging, chat, and phone.

Is E-Mail TCP/IP?

The answer is . . . YES! . . . and no. This chapter is about Internet mail, using TCP/IP protocols. There are other proprietary e-mail systems, such as AOL (America Online) mail, that don't use TCP/IP.

When we talk about services and applications in this chapter, remember that, for the most part, we're talking about TCP/IP services and applications. You need to understand what is and what is not a TCP/IP application. It may be different from what you think.

When you start a session to compose and send an e-mail message, the client program you use to create the message is an application, but not a TCP/IP application. In modern e-mail terminology, you use a *Mail User Agent* (MUA) to create your message. Lotus Notes, Netscape Communicator's Messenger, and Eudora are examples of MUAs.

When you send an e-mail message, your MUA hands it to a *Mail Transfer Agent* (MTA). The MTA is a TCP/IP application, and it uses the TCP/IP protocol SMTP (Simple Mail Transfer Protocol). The MTA delivers the message to another MTA. The message moves from MTA to MTA until it gets to the addressee's computer. The addressee then uses the MUA to read the message. Sendmail, with implementations for various operating systems, is the most common MTA. Lotus Domino is another widely used MTA.

The communication between an MUA and an MTA doesn't have to be TCP/IP, but the communication between MTAs does.

E-Mail Addresses: @ Marks the Spot

To send or receive e-mail, you and your correspondent each need to have an e-mail address. These addresses take this form:

```
username@address
```

The first part, `username`, is a username. The @ character is always there. Then comes the `address`: the computer name and some information about the computer's location on the network, separated by periods. Here's a sample e-mail address:

```
emilyd@teenage.example.com
```

In this address, `emilyd` is the username, `teenage` is the computer name, `example` is where the computer is located, and `com` is a domain name that represents educational institutions.

Understanding How Internet Mail Works

E-mail consists of three basic functions:

- ✔ Sending (writing) messages
- ✔ Storing messages in a mailbox
- ✔ Retrieving (reading) messages from the mailbox

A *mailbox* is a file that holds your messages.

Getting the big picture

An e-mail system contains lots of simple pieces that work together in a complex system to perform basic functions. All e-mail systems perform the same basic functions that we list in the preceding section. Some e-mail systems include extra features, such as filtering out SPAM (unwanted junk mail) and adding security. Read about the bells and whistles later in this chapter and also in Chapter 19.

E-mail starts with an MUA (Mail User Agent) — your e-mail client. Some popular MUAs are Lotus Notes, Outlook Express, pine, elm, and mutt. The server side of an e-mail system consists of one or more of the following TCP/IP components:

- ✓ **MTA** (Mail Transfer Agent): A TCP/IP application that helps deliver your mail

- ✓ **SMTP** (Simple Mail Transfer Protocol): A store-and-forward protocol that tells the MTA how to send your message to the right user at the correct address

- ✓ **POP3** (Post Office Protocol3) server: Server software that gets your incoming e-mail messages, also called a *message store*

- ✓ **IMAP4** (Internet Message Access Protocol4) server: Server software that gets your incoming e-mail messages, also called a message store

- ✓ **LDAP** (Lightweight Directory Access Protocol): An optional protocol that defines how to access directory services

Suppose a user, Sarah, wants to send an e-mail message to her sister Emily. Sarah writes the message using her favorite MUA. When she clicks the Send button, Sarah's MUA hands the message to an MTA on her network. Sarah's local MTA must pass the message to an MTA on Emily's network. SMTP defines how messages move from one MTA to the next. Emily's MTA gets the message, and it puts it into Emily's mailbox. The simplest kind of mailbox in an e-mail system is a text file that stores all of a user's messages. After Sarah's e-mail to Emily arrives, it sits in Emily's mailbox until she checks e-mail. Knowing Emily, that's about once a month. Most of us check a lot more often than that! When Emily checks her mail, either POP3 or IMAP4 takes over and gives her Sarah's message from her mailbox. MUAs that work with both POP3 and IMAP4 include Eudora, Outlook Express, pine, mutt, Lotus Notes, and Netscape Communicator. Whether POP3 or IMAP4 takes over depends on how Emily configures her mail client. Figure 11-1 shows the big picture.

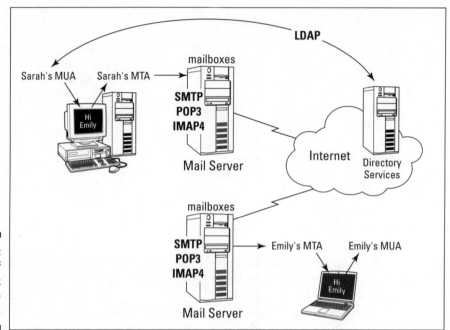

Figure 11-1:
Lots of
pieces work
together to
send mail.

Getting the techie details

The next sections describe how the components of the e-mail system work. If you're just going to be reading and writing mail, you never see these pieces. If you're a system or network administrator, understanding what the pieces do and how they cooperate helps you know where to look if you need to troubleshoot mail problems.

Understanding what the MTA does

The MTA is a program that sends and receives mail messages. The most widely used MTA program is sendmail. MTAs also act as waystations for messages, accepting messages not meant for them and forwarding those messages to their destination or to another intermediary MTA. An MTA determines how to send messages to the appropriate recipient. An MTA sends messages to

- Other MTAs
- Mailboxes
- Other programs for advanced processing, such as filtering SPAM

Understanding how SMTP works with MTAs

SMTP is the part of the TCP/IP protocol suite that MTAs use to communicate with each other. Without SMTP, MTAs wouldn't know how to send e-mail. SMTP defines how messages move from one computer's MTA to another's

MTA, but not what path each message takes. A message may go directly from the sender's computer to the recipient's, or it may proceed through intermediary computers via the store-and-forward process.

In the store-and-forward style, as each message travels through the network on the way to its destination, it may pass through any number of intermediate computers' MTAs, where it is briefly stored before being sent on to the next computer in the path. This is sort of like a weary traveler stopping to rest occasionally before continuing the trip across the network galaxy. Figure 11-2 shows a message for Mr. Spock leaving the source (the laptop where it was created) and being forwarded by three MTAs across two networks before it finally reaches its destination. The computer that connects the two networks is called a *router*.

RFCs 821 and 1869 (also known as STD 10) define SMTP.

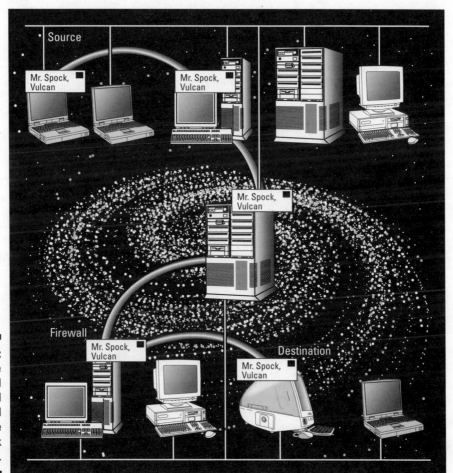

Figure 11-2:
A message is stored and forwarded across the network galaxy.

SMTP is strictly about moving messages from one computer to another. Although SMTP doesn't care about the content of an e-mail message, it does limit the formatting attributes of the message. SMTP can transfer only text; it can't handle fonts, colors, graphics, attachments, or any other of those fancy e-mail features that you may already know and love.

If you like to send deluxe e-mail — sounds, movies, a picture of your dog — you need to read the section about MIME.

Understanding how POP3 and IMAP4 work

POP3 e-mail processing is *offline*. Your MUA connects to the POP3 server, you type a valid username and password, and POP3 downloads the messages in your mailbox to your local MUA so that you can read mail on your local computer.

In contrast to POP3, IMAP4 e-mail processing is *online*. Your MUA accesses the IMAP4 server and your mailbox as if it were on your local computer. An IMAP4 mailbox keeps mail either on the IMAP4 server or on your local computer or both. You set the message storage options when you set up your mail client. You can read e-mail from your computer at home, your workstation at the office, and a PDA on a trip, all without moving messages off the server or transferring them between your various computers. You can scroll through the headers and download only the messages you want to be local.

It's important to match your MUA's protocol to that of the mail server with the MTA you're connecting to. For example, a POP3 MUA cannot communicate with an IMAP4 server.

RFCs 1939, 1957, and 2449 define POP3, while RFC 2060 defines IMAP4.

Spicing up the e-mail mix with MIME and LDAP

Although e-mail works fine without them, MIME (Multipurpose Internet Mail Extensions) and LDAP add user-friendly features that enhance e-mail. It's hard to imagine today's Internet e-mail without the bells and whistles MIME provides. To enhance the body of an e-mail message, some good-deed doers

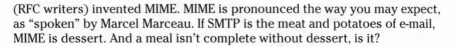

(RFC writers) invented MIME. MIME is pronounced the way you may expect, as "spoken" by Marcel Marceau. If SMTP is the meat and potatoes of e-mail, MIME is dessert. And a meal isn't complete without dessert, is it?

MIME is described in RFCs 2046 through 2049.

MIME allows the body of e-mail messages to have all those cool enhancements, such as colors, sounds, and animation, while still allowing them to be delivered by SMTP (which, as we explain in the earlier section "Understanding how SMTP works with MTAs," couldn't care less about anything but ASCII text).

"How do they do that?" we hear you asking. Well, it requires that you use a *MIME-compliant* mail user agent — that is, your MUA must know how to generate MIME message bodies. When you compose your sophisticated e-mail message, your MIME-compliant MUA encodes the deluxe features into a text-only representation that SMTP can transfer. The message can then pass through the necessary intermediary computers as usual, and none of them needs anything special to process your enhanced message.

When the message arrives at its final destination, your correspondent also needs a MIME-compliant MUA in order to decode the fancy features. Without a MIME-compliant MUA, the recipient may not be able to do much with your message. Most MUAs are MIME-compliant.

S/MIME secures communications between an e-mail sender and the recipient. For example, Candace and her niece Emily need secrecy for sharing important Beanie Baby news. See Chapter 19 for more information about S/MIME.

LDAP is another optional piece of an e-mail system that makes your MUA more user-friendly. If your MUA works with LDAP, you may never need to type another e-mail address. Popular mail clients, including Netscape Messenger, Outlook Express, and mutt, can all use LDAP. When you send a message, LDAP makes it possible for you to enter a name rather than an address. LDAP helps your MUA work with directory services. A directory service is simply some kind of database that stores information — in the case of e-mail, information about people, including their e-mail addresses. Here's how it works. Instead of addressing e-mail to emilyd@emailland.com (a fictitious address), Sarah presses Ctrl+E (or goes through the Edit⇨Find⇨People menu path). Then, as shown in Figure 11-3, she pulls down the Look in: menu and selects a directory service. She fills in Emily's name and clicks the Find Now box. The MUA contacts the directory service following LDAP's rules and looks up Emily. If the directory service finds multiple Emilys, it tells the MUA, and the MUA gives Sarah a list of Emilys to choose from. Sarah selects her Emily and sends the message.

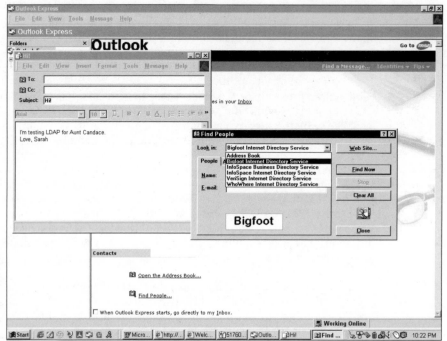

Figure 11-3:
LDAP helps
you find mail
recipients.

Setting Up Your MUA

Every different MUA has a different setup program. Some programs, such as Outlook Express, provide a nifty graphical wizard. Others, such as mutt, expect you to edit a text file. Later, we show you hands-on examples for each client. Regardless of the setup program, you need to provide the following information to your e-mail client:

- ✔ **The protocol you want to use:** Either POP3 or IMAP4; remember that with some clients you have no choice.

- ✔ **The names of your outgoing and incoming mail servers:** The name of the outgoing server is the name of your SMTP server. The name of your incoming server is your POP3 or IMAP4 server. For many ISPs, these names are usually the same computer, for example, `mail.attbi.com`.

- ✔ **The location of your local mailboxes and folders:** Some clients, such as Outlook Express, use a predefined location.

- ✔ **Your account name and password:** Your ISP may assign these to start.

- ✔ **Port numbers:** These are the numbers that SMTP, POP3, and IMAP4 use to communicate.

  Most e-mail clients use the following default port numbers: 25 for SMTP, 110 for POP3, and 143 for IMAP4.

You want Outlook Express, but you run Linux/UNIX

Outlook Express is not just for Windows. There are versions of Outlook Express for Macintosh and Solaris (Sun Microsystems' UNIX). If you need an Outlook-like client for a Linux system, try Ximian evolution (www.ximian.com). It looks just like Outlook Express and supports all the protocols that we discuss in this chapter. You can also import your Outlook mail into Ximian evolution.

Every MUA needs the basic information before you can send and receive e-mail. Most MUAs also accept optional settings: how your e-mail looks, directory services to use with LDAP, and security options, for example.

In large organizations, the system administrator may set up the MUA for you.

Microsoft Outlook Express comes bundled free with Windows Internet Explorer. The following example walks you through setting up the graphical Outlook Express client:

1. **In Outlook Express, choose Tools⇨Accounts⇨Internet Accounts⇨ New Account, click the Mail tab, and then click Add.**

2. **Enter your Display Name.**

   When you write mail, some MUAs automatically fill in the From field with this name. If you're Katherine Duncan, but your username is BigStub, BigStub as a display name looks pretty good on e-mail.

3. **Select a server: either POP3 or IMAP4. (See Figure 11-4.)**

4. **Enter the names of your incoming and outgoing mail servers.**

   You get these names from your ISP.

   Outlook Express creates local mailboxes automatically. See the folder listing in Figure 11-5.

5. **Enter your account name and password.**

   Your ISP may have already assigned these.

6. **If your ISP uses Secure Password Authentication (SPA), you need to select that check box.**

   SPA is a more secure method of checking e-mail. Eudora Pro calls it APOP. Check Chapter 19 for e-mail security details.

7. **Make advanced selections.**

   Depending on your client, advanced setup items may include the port numbers for SMTP, POP3, and IMAP4, whether you will be using the SSL protocol for security, and whether to leave messages on the server. Figure 11-6 shows how to set these options in Outlook Express. Most e-mail clients use the default port numbers 25 for SMTP, 110 for POP3, and 143 for IMAP4.

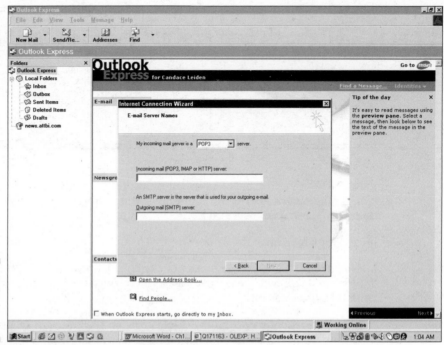

Figure 11-4:
Choose your
server
protocol.

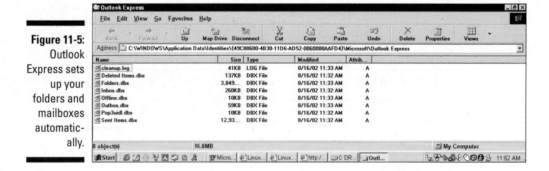

Figure 11-5:
Outlook
Express sets
up your
folders and
mailboxes
automatic-
ally.

8. **Optionally, if you want users to be able to use LDAP to search directory services, you may need to add the directory services.**

   Our copy of Outlook Express came with several directory services preset.

   • To see the preset directory services, choose Main Tools⇨Accounts and then access the Directory services tab.

   • To add a directory service, follow the same menu path, but click the Add button and choose Directory Service from the submenu that appears, as shown in Figure 11-7.

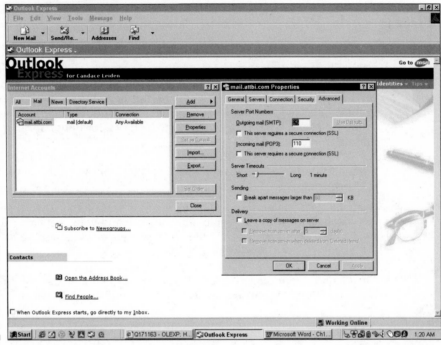

Figure 11-6:
Set up
advanced
options in
Outlook
Express.

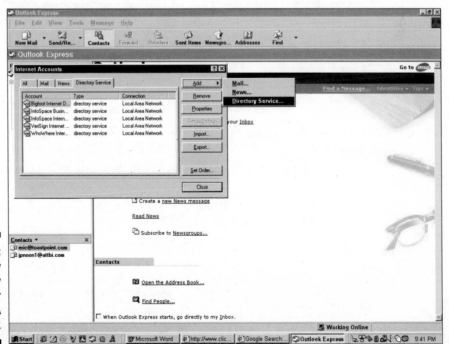

Figure 11-7:
Add a new
directory
service for
the MUA
and LDAP.

Mutt

Mutt is a fast and powerful text-based e-mail client for Mac OS X, Linux, and UNIX. The operating system installation procedure usually installs mutt for you, but it's easy to install manually with the tar command. To set up your mutt e-mail client, you follow the preceding steps but without the pretty graphic interface. Most of what you see in the Outlook Express example is point, click, and type. You set the same kind of information for mutt by editing two files:

- ✔ /etc/Muttrc holds system wide settings for everyone's mutt mail environment.

- ✔ .muttrc, in your home directory, holds your personal mutt settings, such as mailing lists you're a member of and your real name. If you don't have a personal .muttrc file, the first time you run mutt, it asks if you want the file automatically created. Then you edit that file.

The filenames are case sensitive. Don't forget the uppercase "M" in /etc/Muttrc.. The "." is part of the personal filename. Don't forget that either.

Some favorite settings to put into your personal .muttrc file include:

set realname = "your_name_here", a variable that corresponds to the Display Name in our Outlook Express example. Here's BigStub's example, the mutt equivalent to Step 1 in the preceding section:

```
set realname = "Katherine Duncan"
```

set imap_user = "your_username", which sets you up as an IMAP4 user, the mutt equivalent of Step 2.

```
set imap_user=BigStub
```

set hostname and set pop_host to enter the names of your outgoing and incoming mail servers, equivalent to Step 3.

set hostname = the domain name of your POP3 or IMAP4 server, for example:

```
set hostname = "mail.attbi.com"
set pop_host = "mail.attbi.com"
```

You can also set other advanced options. Some typical selections follow.

Setting up mailing lists that you've subscribed to by using the subscribe option, followed by the lists you've subscribed to. Separate the lists by a space, for example:

```
lists mutt-users-digest asian-cats BIG-BAND
```

This is a good option to set in the `/etc/Muttrc` file so that all users get prompted to send CCs (people to send copies of the mail message to):

```
set askcc
```

To tell mutt to use IMAP4, use the following set commands:

To direct the mail queue to the standard IMAP4 mailbox, called inbox:

```
set spoolfile=imap://dodo.cardinalconsulting.com/inbox
```

To use an IMAP4 folder (the folder keyword is the location of the mailbox):

```
set folder=imap://dodo.cardinalconsulting.com/inbox
```

"Alias Smith and Jones"

Mail aliases are nice to have, but definitely not required. Mail aliases provide a handy way to forward e-mail to another address. Suppose you'll be working at a branch office for a month. Instead of connecting to the main office each day to read your e-mail, you can have your e-mail forwarded to a computer at the branch office. The postmaster at the main office creates a mail alias on the main office computer to forward your e-mail to the branch office computer.

The two different kinds of mail aliases are private and public (although they do similar things):

- **Private:** The mail aliases that you create for yourself are private; no one else can use them. To find out how to create your private mail aliases, consult the manual for your MUA. (You define them in the configuration file for your e-mail client, `.muttrc`, for the mutt client.)

- **Public:** The mail aliases that a system administrator (postmaster) creates are public; the system administrator creates these system-wide aliases at the MTA level. Everyone can use them. The operating system and e-mail environment dictate how public aliases are created and maintained. On a UNIX system, the postmaster normally defines them in the file `/usr/lib/aliases`. The sendmail MTA for Windows NT has a graphical interface for creating aliases so that you simply type in the alias name and the real name — no file editing needed.

Mail aliases can also provide assistance to e-mail users in the following ways:

- **Mailing lists:** In e-mail terms, a mailing list is one e-mail address that sends your message to multiple recipients. For example, a mailing list could translate the following alias:
  ```
  tcpip_for_dummies_authors
  ```

into these two addresses:

```
marshall_wilensky@us.ibm.com
cleiden@bigfoot.com
```

Mailing lists are sometimes called *exploders* because one e-mail message "explodes" into many more.

✔ **Friendlier addresses:** It's fairly obvious that this address

```
Marshall_Wilensky@crd.lotus.com
```

takes more effort to type than this alias

```
mw@lotus.com
```

By means of public aliases, a postmaster can create and implement a consistent, more user-friendly naming convention for your organization.

✔ **A way to reach people with difficult-to-spell names:** A lot of people have trouble spelling Marshall's last name, so the postmaster may define this public alias

```
mwilenski@us.ibm.com
```

for this address

```
mwilensky@us.ibm.com
```

(Look closely; the *i* in Wilenski has been changed to a *y*.) Now, Marshall will get the e-mail whether or not you spell his name correctly.

Configuring a Mail Server (MTA)

If you're using a Microsoft operating system, such as Windows NT/2000, as a mail server, the protocols you need are bundled into Microsoft's IIS (Internet Server).

The sendmail program is the Internet's most often used MTA. The UNIX, Linux, and MAC OS X installation procedures usually automatically install sendmail and give you a default configuration file. There are 1,000-page books written about sendmail! If you're a system administrator responsible for a sendmail system, don't despair. The following section gives you enough information to get a basic sendmail MTA up and running.

Before you configure sendmail, make sure that the software is installed and running. Most operating systems have a GUI system administrator interface that shows what software is installed. Linux also has a very simple command, rpm -q, shown here:

```
[root@dodo]# rpm -q
sendmail-8.11.6-8
```

Just because sendmail is installed doesn't mean it's running, although it is
usually configured to start when your computer boots. Figure 11-8 shows two
ways to see whether sendmail is running: by using the ps and telnetting to
localhost on port 25. On Microsoft Windows servers, use Administrative tools
or Computer Management to list the running services.

Figure 11-8:
Checking
whether
sendmail is
running.

```
[root@dodo root]# rpm -q sendmail
sendmail-8.11.6-8
[root@dodo root]# ps -elf | grep sendmail
140 S root    17689    1 0 68  0    - 1126 do_sel 03:34 ?        00:00:00 sendmail: accepting connections
000 S root     9339 9249 0 73  0    -  414 pipe_w 05:36 pts/1    00:00:00 grep sendmail
[root@dodo root]# telnet localhost 25
Trying 127.0.0.1...
Connected to localhost.
Escape character is '^]'.
220 dodo.cardinalconsulting.com ESMTP Sendmail 8.11.6/8.11.6; Thu, 15 Aug 2002 05:39:02 -0400
```

On Mac OS X, sendmail is disabled by default. You enable it by opening the
Terminal and editing the file /etc/hostconfig. Find the line "MAILSERVER=-
NO-". Change "NO" to "YES". Exit and save the file. When you restart your
computer, sendmail will start.

The default sendmail configuration file, sendmail.cf, is set up to accept mail
deliveries and to send outgoing mail. Usually you do not need to change the
configuration file.

You can use telnet to localhost to verify that other services, such as POP3
and IMAP4, are running by typing port number **110** for POP3 and **143** for
IMAP4.

```
# telnet localhost 143
Trying 127.0.0.1. . .
telnet: Connected to localhost.
Esc character is '^'.
* OK localhost IMAP4 rev1 v11.240 server ready
```

Interconnecting Internet Mail with Proprietary Mail

Because of the long-standing relationship between UNIX and TCP/IP, Internet
mail servers use SMTP. The same can't be said, however, about some other
e-mail products. Those other e-mail systems need an SMTP gateway. For
example, AOL (America Online) Mail travels across the Internet, but it is not
Internet mail because it is proprietary.

An *SMTP gateway* is software that translates e-mail messages between RFC822/MIME format and the format of another e-mail system. For example, suppose your organization doesn't use an SMTP e-mail system. In order to exchange e-mail with people who do use one, your organization needs an SMTP gateway. The gateway converts outbound mail messages into RFC822/MIME format and inbound mail messages into the correct format for your system.

Every SMTP gateway has to deal with the fact that no two e-mail systems are exactly alike, no matter how similar their features. Some things just won't match up when the gateway translates the message formats. The simple elegance of SMTP means that its mail system usually appears less sophisticated than other systems, although MIME does help narrow the gap.

Free E-Mail with All the Trimmings

You can find lots of free e-mail services on the Web — they're free because they support themselves with advertising fees. Even if you already have an e-mail account on your work or home computer, a Web-based e-mail account can be handy for keeping in touch when you're out of the office or away from home. If you don't have a computer, you may be able to access your free e-mail at a library, senior-citizens center, youth center, or a cybercafe. Free e-mail services range from basic read/write e-mail to sophisticated solutions for pagers and PDAs (Personal Digital Assistants).

`www.thefreesite.com/Email_Freebies/Free_E_mail_software/index.html` links to dozens and dozens of free e-mail services with a wide range of features and languages.

Going Beyond E-Mail with Usenet News

News via TCP/IP is known by various names, including Usenet news, netnews, and Network News. We call it Usenet news in this book.

Usenet news is a TCP/IP service consisting of a worldwide collection of online newsgroups. Each newsgroup is an electronic conversation group about a particular topic. Topics range from Disney and Star Trek, to home repair and gay and lesbian rights. Anyone on the Internet can post an article stating an opinion and/or asking for information. You've heard the stories of people meeting online through newsgroups and falling in love, sight unseen — it really happens!

Newsgroups to help newcomers

If you're new to Usenet news, you can check out a few newsgroups to help you find out how to read and write articles. Here are some of the most useful ones:

✔ `news.announce.newusers`: The articles in this newsgroup are about Usenet news features.

✔ `news.newusers.questions`: You can post articles here asking questions about how Usenet news works.

As of this writing, our NNTP (news) server lists over 50,000 newsgroups and new ones are being created every day. Newsgroups are categorized by interest areas, and the pieces of a newsgroup name are the hierarchy for those interest areas, separated by dots (periods). The first part of the name is the most general topic, and each subsequent part of the name gets a little more specific. Newsgroup names look somewhat like the part of an e-mail address on the right-hand side of the @ sign, but it's just a coincidence.

The news server that stores the articles is running NNTP, the Network News Transfer Protocol. (NNTP is pronounced by saying the letters N N T P.) NNTP, another invisible part of TCP/IP, moves articles from server to server and from server to newsreader (client). Note that the terms *news server* and *NNTP server* mean the same thing. RFCs 977 and 2980 describe NNTP.

Table 11-1 lists the major newsgroup hierarchies that you often see in newsgroup names. There are other hierarchies besides these.

Table 11-1	Some Major Newsgroup Hierarchies
Hierarchy	*Subject*
`alt.`	Alternative; weird and serious stuff, as well as all sorts of miscellany; our "weirdness" is someone else's "normality"
`biz.`	Business
`comp.`	Computers and related topics
`humanities`	Fine arts, literature, music
`misc.`	Miscellaneous
`news.`	Usenet news subjects; not the evening news or the newspaper

(continued)

Hierarchy	Subject
Table 11-1 *(continued)*	
rec.	Recreation and the arts
sci.	Science
soc.	Social and cultural issues; sometimes relevant, sometimes wildly theoretical
talk.	Discussion; often controversial

Reading news with a free newsreader

The end-user application for accessing Usenet news is called a *newsreader*. It's similar to the MUA for e-mail: The newsreader passes your requests on to the TCP/IP service. The newsreader communicates directly with TCP/IP components for you. News is usually stored on a server, and you use a newsreader client to read articles, post follow-ups or new articles, mail a response directly to the article's author, forward an article via e-mail to another person, and so on. Newsreaders come in all shapes, sizes, and flavors. You may have several to choose from on your computer.

Many are free (called *public domain*) — Figure 11-9 shows the setup for a free newsreader, NewsXpress, which is a Usenet newsreader for Windows 95/98/NT/2000. (You can download it from `ftp.malch.com`.) It has an easy setup and interface and still provides lots of features. To run NewsXpress, you need to give out some information about your NNTP (news) server and your SMTP server. You can get this information from your ISP (Internet Service Provider).

Figure 11-9:
NewsXpress
is easy to
set up.

Setup		☒
Hosts and Ports Information		
NNTP Server :	netnews.attbi.com	119
SMTP Server :	mail.attbi.com	25
Personal Information		
Fullname :	Candace leiden	
E-Mail :	cleiden@bigfoot.com	
Organization :	Cardinal	
Signature File :		...
Authorization Information		
Username :		
Password :		
File and Path		
Home Directory :	c:\newsexpress	
News RC File :	newsrc	
Time Zone : GMT		OK

Every newsreader needs to keep track of which articles you've already read. A good newsreader helps you by organizing the articles by discussion thread. Sometimes, this means that the newsreader looks at the article's subject or summary line to see whether it's similar to other articles. Without this kind of feature, you're stuck reading articles in the chronological order in which they arrived on your computer or the server.

Watch out! Reading news articles in chronological order can give you mental indigestion. For example, suppose a news user in Honolulu posts an article. As the article flows via the Internet around the world and toward you, another news user in San Francisco reads it and posts a response. The response, too, flows via the Internet around the world and toward you. It's entirely possible that the response arrives before the original article. If the original article was a question and the response is an answer, you may see the answer before the question!

Figure 11-10 shows three NewsXpress windows that avoid this situation:

- ✔ An alphabetical listing of all available newsgroups on our server

- ✔ A threaded listing of all articles in the selected newsgroup called `comp.protocols.tcp-ip`

- ✔ The article from the TCP/IP newsgroup that we want to read

Check out the newsreaders on the CD that comes with this book.

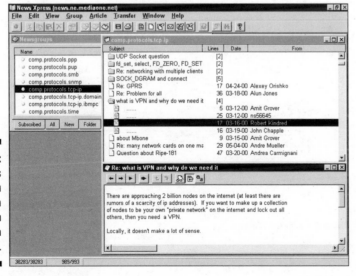

Figure 11-10: NewsXpress helps you follow a discussion thread in a newsgroup.

Reading news with a Web browser or mail client

Web browsers also provide the functions of most TCP/IP client applications. If you have a browser, you no longer need a separate FTP client, newsreader client, or mail client.

Some clients, such as Outlook Express, Lotus Notes, and Netscape Communicator, are newsreaders as well as e-mail clients. Figure 11-11 shows how to set up Outlook Express for newsreading. You start your setup just as you did for e-mail — by choosing Tools⇨Account. Click the News tab, and then choose Add⇨News. You need to get the name of the news server from your ISP. Did you notice back in Figure 11-4 that you can name the port for the newsreader at the same time as for SMTP?

Just because you don't *need* separate clients doesn't mean that you don't *want* them. The Web is like dessert. As fun and delicious as it may be, it adds a lot of fat to your Internet diet. And it doesn't always taste as good as it looks. An old-fashioned newsreader gets the news to you faster than a glitzy browser.

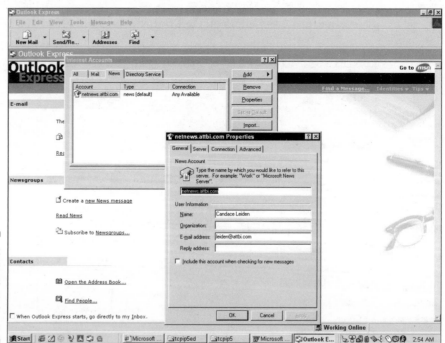

Figure 11-11:
Set up the Outlook Express newsreader client.

Are E-Mail and News Too Slow for You?

E-mail and Usenet news carry messages among users that are separated by both space and time. Other Internet services carry online messages among users that are separated only by physical space — both of you must be online at the same time. Some of the most popular are Instant Messaging (IM), talk, and Internet Relay Chat (IRC).

Messaging in an instant

Instant messaging (IM — it's both a noun and a verb) refers to short notes that you exchange with a buddy over the Internet. Most IM products limit the shortness of the message to 32 or 64Kb. The notes fly back and forth almost instantaneously. When we say "buddy," we're not necessarily talking about your friend. Buddy has become a technical term. A buddy can be a friend, boss, a co-worker you don't even like. A *buddy* is simply someone you add to your *buddy list* so that you can see when that person is online. After all, there's not much point in sending a note if no one's home.

When you type in a message, it pops up immediately on your buddy's screen. AIM (AOL Instant Messenger) is currently the IM leader: People use AOL's Instant Messenger programs to send over 1 billion instant messages a day. You don't need to use AOL as your service provider to use its IM software. You can go to www.aol.com and download it for free. Marshall (on IBM's Global Network ISP) and Candace (who uses a cable modem and a TCP/IP connection) communicate frequently with AOL's IM software. Neither of them starts AOL when they IM each other. It's a whole lot cheaper than a mobile phone call when all you want is for your buddy to bring home a loaf of bread! By the way, you can IM from your mobile phone. To get a free screenname so that you can AIM, go to www.aim.com.

You can find several competing instant messaging systems. Because no IM standard exists yet, not all IM systems interoperate. In other words, if you and your buddies want to IM, you must use compatible messaging systems. To be able to reach all of your various buddies, you may need to have several different IM clients and manage separate buddy lists.

RFCs 2778 and 2779 lay the groundwork for a future IM standard. You can follow the work of the IETF's Instant Messaging and Presence Protocol (IMPP) Working Group at www.ietf.org/html.charters/impp-charter.html.

Talking the talk

Talking, in this case, doesn't mean speaking out loud, unless you like to talk to yourself. *Talk* lets you have live, interactive keyboard conversations. (If you want to speak out loud and hear voices answer over the Internet, you need Internet phone — coming up in the "ET Should Have Used Internet Phone" section, later in this chapter.) Talk, developed in the early days of UNIX, is the oldest of the interactive messaging programs.

Talk provides a private, one-to-one connection. There are no party lines or conference calls. (See the following section on IRC for multiparty conversations.) There's also no server involved. When you talk to someone, your screen gets split into two sections; your words appear in one half, and the other person's words show up in the other half. Every character you type is sent across the network immediately! That means the other person sees exactly what you type, including mistakes and "mistalks," so think before you type!

Internet Relay Chat (IRC): TCP/IP's version of CB radio

Internet Relay Chat (IRC) is the citizen's band (CB) radio of TCP/IP. (You pronounce IRC by saying the letters I R C.) Chatting was created to overcome the primary limitation of talk — namely, that only two people at a time can communicate. IRC provides a party-line environment.

Chatting is done on channels, which are named rather than numbered. Each channel is supposed to be for a specific topic, but you'll have to judge the situation for yourself when you're connected. Chatting is a pretty "loose" environment, although discussions can be scheduled in advance for a specific time, topic, and channel. Each channel has at least one operator, who can't moderate the discussion but can disconnect individual chatters. Because the chatters can simply sign in again, however, disconnecting them may not help keep the discussion focused and free of unruly behavior.

As you may expect, in order to chat, you use an IRC client that communicates with IRC servers via a TCP/IP protocol. The client helps you communicate with the IRC server, connect to the channel of your choice, and chat with the other users. The servers keep track of the chatters and the channels, and they exchange the messages so that all the chatters see all of the chatting.

A typical IRC client is Microsoft Chat for Windows 95/98/NT/2000/XP. If you need a free IRC client, check out www.thefreesite.com. This site lists plain-vanilla chat clients, fancy chat clients that let you have a graphical 3D persona to represent you, and chat clients that are voice enabled.

RFC 1459 defines the IRC protocol.

How do you choose?

IM, talk, and IRC let you communicate live with people anywhere in the world. You don't have to bathe or put on clean clothes. No one will ever know that you're in your pajamas. So how do you decide which one to use? Here are some tips:

- ✔ Use IM if you have a quick question and your buddy has a fast answer.
- ✔ Use talk if the question is more complicated, and you need to have a conversation.
- ✔ Use chat if you want to discuss the question with a larger group of people.
- ✔ If these simple communication solutions don't have enough features for you, look for audio- and video-conferencing products. Most of the big vendors have products, such as IBM Lotus Sametime, which uses VOIP (Voice Over IP) technology. There are lots of products from smaller vendors as well. Our Google (`www.google.com`) search on "conferencing solutions" returned 78 pages of vendors and information.

You won't find any answering machines for any of the services, so if you want to leave a message at the tone, send e-mail instead.

ET Should Have Used Internet Phone

Can you imagine the telephone charge when that cute little alien, ET, phoned home? *Internet phone,* also known as *Internet telephony,* is a toll-free option.

Okay — you don't incur any charges from the telephone company, but you do need the following:

- ✔ Internet phone software
- ✔ A sound card and speakers for your computer
- ✔ A headset or a microphone
- ✔ An Internet connection

After you have the equipment and software, you pay the same to talk to the Philippines for one hour as you do to talk to Podunk for one minute.

Before you become too excited about phoning your friends around the world, you should realize that you can only call people who are connected to the Internet and have Internet phone software, usually the same kind as yours.

In order to make a call with Internet phone, follow these steps:

1. **Connect to the Internet.**

2. **Start your phone software.**

3. **Type in your mom's IP address, or select it from an electronic phone book that comes with your phone software.**

4. **After your mom answers, ask her for money.**

You can attach cameras to your computer and your mom's to send your picture, as well as your voice. See Chapter 15 for wireless and mobile options.

Chapter 12

Getting Started with Web Clients and Servers

*T*here is an absolute glut of information and files available on the Internet — so much that you may feel overwhelmed. Even when you know what you want, it can be really hard to find. The information services that we describe in this chapter help you navigate the Net, including the World Wide Web. The World Wide Web (also called "the Web," "WWW," or "W3") is the worldwide hypermedia information service on the Internet. A common misconception among newcomers is that the Web and the Internet are two different things. The Web is the graphical interface to the Internet, compliments of HTTP.

On the client side, this chapter focuses on Web browsing and services. We also include some oldies but goodies — tools that may help you get to information faster than a Web browser. On the server side, this chapter describes how a Web server works and what steps you need to follow to set up a Web server.

TCP/IP applications give you more than one way of doing things. The applications that we describe in this chapter give you options. There is no "best" way of doing things — only the way that you prefer. We don't recommend one way of finding information over another. It all depends on what suits your personal preference.

Surfers' paradise

Cruising around the Internet to see what's out there is often called *surfing the Net.* Vinton Cerf is known as the Father of the Internet. So shouldn't it be Cerfing the Net?

In this chapter, we show you several ways to download files and information from the Internet. All the reputable download sites on the Internet check files for viruses before they make them available to the public. However, new viruses appear all the time, and you should be responsible for protecting your own computer. Be sure to run your own antivirus software and always check downloads regardless of where you get them. And try really hard to avoid downloading files from unfamiliar sites.

Like most of the applications and services we talk about in this book, Internet information services are client/server environments. You use a client application, such as a browser, to connect to a server.

Most clients running on Microsoft Windows, Macintosh, or X Windows/Motif have a *GUI* (graphical user interface). Other tools have only a plain-character interface that you can run from a DOS PC or even a dumb terminal connected to a minicomputer or mainframe. But whatever the user interface, there's a TCP/IP protocol, service, or application in there somewhere.

What Are Hypertext and Hypermedia?

You may have heard the terms *hypertext* and *hypermedia* used in conjunction with the latest and greatest Internet tools. However, both hypertext and hypermedia have been around for a long time, but TCP/IP, the Internet, and the Web have given them new life.

✔ *Hypertext* is text that contains in-line pointers to other text in the same file or another file. A common example of hypertext is the Microsoft Windows help system, in which you click a highlighted word or icon or button, and you receive more information about what you clicked. The linked, multipage information you click around in is hypertext.

✔ *Hypermedia* extends the hypertext concept beyond just text and into multimedia. In hypermedia applications, a pointer can take you to a sound byte, or a graphic image, or even a video clip. These days, there's much more to life on the Internet than just text! You can check out movie trailers, take courses, listen to foreign-language radio stations, and even climb Mt. Kilimanjaro — all thanks to hypermedia.

You may already be familiar with the most common use of hypermedia on the Internet — the World Wide Web.

Understanding How Web Browsers Work

Microsoft Internet Explorer, Lotus Notes, and Netscape Navigator are popular graphical Web clients. There are many more. Lynx is another Web client that's completely text based. Web clients, also called *browsers,* communicate with the servers via HTTP, the HyperText Transfer Protocol.

A Web browser is an HTTP client that sends requests to Web server software. When you type a *Uniform Resource Locator* (URL) or click a hypertext link, your browser creates an HTTP request and sends it to the IP address that's represented by the URL (or Web address). Figure 12-1 shows a URL, `www.homepage.mac.com/vandeusen/PhotoAlbum2.html`, and a link inside a Mozilla browser window.

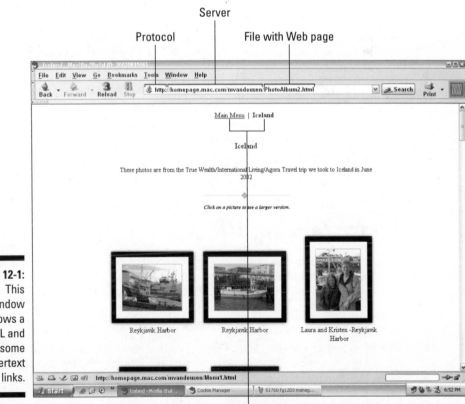

Figure 12-1:
This window shows a URL and some hypertext links.

We use the Mozilla browser for some of the screen shots in this book. Mozilla is a free browser that runs on most operating systems. It may look a little like Netscape. That's because Netscape Version 6 uses the Mozilla core engine (code-named Gecko) and the Mozilla code base. If you're interested in Mozilla, browse to `www.mozilla.org`.

The browser follows these steps to send you the Web page that you request:

1. The browser separates the URL into

   • http — the protocol

   • www.homepage.mac.com — the name of the Web server storing the page you asked for

   • vandeusen/PhotoAlbum2 — the directory and filename for the Web page

2. The browser asks a DNS server to translate the name "www.homepage. mac.com" into an IP address.

   If you're on a small intranet and your Web server is local, the browser may find the name-address translation in your hosts file. We explain DNS and host files in Chapter 10.

3. Using HTTP, the browser connects to the Web server's IP address through port 80 and sends a request to GET a file that holds the Web page.

4. The browser checks your hard drive for cookie files containing information about you. If it finds any cookies, the browser sends them to the server.

5. The server sends the Web page's source code, written in a special language (HTML) to the browser.

6. The browser reads the HTML instructions (called tags) and text and displays the page.

Understanding URLs

A *Uniform Resource Locator* (URL) is the string of characters, usually starting with `http`, that your browser uses to find and display Web content. (You pronounce the acronym by saying the letters U R L.) Here's an example URL:

```
http://www.ibm.com
```

The `http` is the protocol, HyperText Transfer Protocol, that you use to access the resource. Everything following the colon is the location of the Web resource. The location starts with `//`, followed by the site name. If anything follows the final `/`, it is a filename on that host. (Throughout this book, we drop the "http://" part of the URL because many browsers no longer make you type that part to access sites.)

A browser that eats cookies

With all the free browsers available, one of the reasons we like Mozilla is because it has some advanced cookie handling that we can't live without. Not only does Mozilla block pop-ups, it also allows you to view and manage cookies easily. To prevent uninvited pop-ups, choose Edit⇨Preferences and expand Advanced. Uncheck Open Unrequested Windows, and you won't have to look at advertising you didn't ask to see. To manage cookies on your hard drive, choose Edit⇨Preferences and expand Privacy and Security. Here you can disable cookies altogether, have the browser ask you if you want a cookie, and limit the life of a cookie on your hard disk. Clicking the Manage Stored Cookies button displays the Cookie Manager, where you can see who's sending cookies, examine the contents of your cookies, and remove all or selected cookies. If you remove a cookie that you never want again, check the box Don't Allow Removed Cookies to Be Reaccepted Later. The accompanying figure shows how to manage cookies with Mozilla.

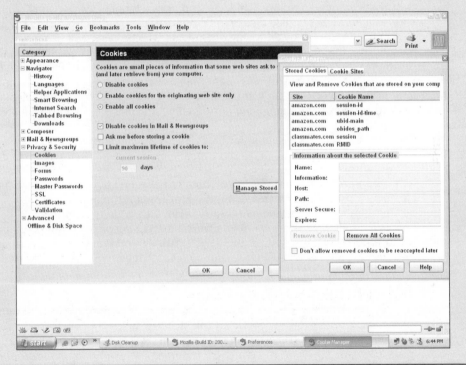

While you're busy browsing, the Web can actually take you to a non-HTTP resource. Here are examples of URLs that point to an Anonymous FTP site and an LDAP server:

```
ftp://ftp.microsoft.com
ldap://ldap.bigfoot.com
```

Although we always start the URLs in this book with www (such as www.homepage.mac.com), the www is not always necessary. If you simply type the domain (homepage.mac.com) in your browser's address window, it works. It's not magic; it happens because a very nice network or system administrator set up the browser to assume the www.

Understanding how cookies work

Web sites keep track of visitors with files called *cookies*. A Web server may store one or more cookies on your local hard disk. For example, a Web page might ask for your postal code. The server stores the postal code and a unique ID number within a cookie file on your own computer. The next time you visit the Web site, the server knows where you live and the browser displays your local weather automatically. Web shopping carts need cookies to keep track of the product you plan to buy. Candace, who does a lot of browsing and Web shopping, has 1,271 cookie files in the directory C:\Windows\Cookies. Some of those cookies are left by annoying pop-up ads. The browser you use may store cookies in a different directory. The cookies directories vary depending on the browser you use, the operating system, even the user interface. The cookie files in Figure 12-2 that start with anyuser come from uninvited pop-ups. See the later section "Reducing the Web's Wait" to see where to get the popup blocker, POW to get rid of those annoying pop-ups if your browser doesn't do it for you.

RFC 2616 is the proposed standard for HTTP. RFC 2660 describes Secure HTTP.

HTTP (HyperText Transfer Protocol) and its baby, HTML (HyperText Markup Language), provide the standard method for transmitting information between Web servers and clients (browsers). The interconnections and links between hypermedia documents delivered by HTTP form the Web piece of the Internet. HTTP is a fast protocol. HTTP tries to minimize the processing load on the Web server's CPU and memory resources — at least compared with other protocols.

A browser that speaks

IBM's talking browser, Home Page Reader for Windows, was developed for blind and visually impaired Web surfers. Home Page Reader browser reads aloud the information on a Web site. Home Page Reader is available in French, English, German, Italian, Japanese, and Spanish. The browser uses IBM's ViaVoice speech technology to speak Web pages.

If disk space and memory are a concern, a small, efficient browser is Arachne, from Arachne Labs in Prague, Czech Republic. Arachne is a graphical browser that runs on DOS and Linux operating systems. To find out more about Arachne and download a copy, browse the site `www.arachne.cz`.

Name	Size	Type	Modified	Al
anyuser@216.34.146[1].txt	1KB	Text Document	7/26/01 10:48 PM	
anyuser@64[1].txt	1KB	Text Document	7/26/01 10:48 PM	
anyuser@ads.link4ads[2].txt	1KB	Text Document	7/26/01 10:56 PM	
anyuser@aol[1].txt	1KB	Text Document	7/27/01 9:19 AM	
anyuser@coldwatercreek[1].txt	1KB	Text Document	7/27/01 9:26 AM	
anyuser@doubleclick[1].txt	1KB	Text Document	7/26/01 10:53 PM	
anyuser@ebay[1].txt	1KB	Text Document	7/27/01 9:18 AM	
anyuser@ehg.hitbox[2].txt	2KB	Text Document	7/26/01 10:57 PM	
anyuser@google[2].txt	1KB	Text Document	7/26/01 10:41 PM	
anyuser@mediaplex[2].txt	1KB	Text Document	7/26/01 10:53 PM	
anyuser@microsoft[1].txt	1KB	Text Document	7/26/01 10:42 PM	
anyuser@netscape[1].txt	1KB	Text Document	7/26/01 10:59 PM	
anyuser@S005-01-4-13-12062-68611[2].txt	1KB	Text Document	7/26/01 10:52 PM	
anyuser@S009-00-11-8-190682-35131[2].txt	1KB	Text Document	7/27/01 9:24 AM	
anyuser@support.microsoft[2].txt	1KB	Text Document	7/26/01 10:55 PM	
anyuser@tamu[2].txt	1KB	Text Document	7/26/01 10:54 PM	
anyuser@thecreek.coldwatercreek[2].txt	1KB	Text Document	7/27/01 9:26 AM	
anyuser@valueclick[1].txt	1KB	Text Document	7/26/01 10:52 PM	

1,271 object(s)   583KB   Internet

Figure 12-2:
Too many cookies lead to an upset stomach.

If you're concerned about security on the Web, S-HTTP (Secure HTTP) is undergoing the Internet's Request for Comments process and should become an international standard. S-HTTP is basically HTTP with extensions for secure client/server communications. Chapter 20 has more information on S-HTTP.

Help! I'm the only person in the universe who doesn't have a browser!

Don't despair. If you don't have a browser, you can connect via telnet to a public host that has a non-graphical browser. In Chapter 14, we show you how to use telnet. Figure 12-3 shows telneting to Maryland's Public Information Network.

If you don't have a browser and you prefer not to telnet to someone else's browser, you can use a non-graphical browser. Use Google or your favorite search engine to find sites from which you can download the Lynx text-based browser. Figure 12-4 shows a home page with all the graphics removed for the Lynx browser.

```
        SAILOR, Maryland's Public Information Network (p1 of 3)

 You are here: Home | [1]Cruise the Internet [2]About Sailor
| [3]Contact Us | [4] Help
SAILOR:  Maryland's Public Information Network
[5]Maryland weather
[6]e-Mail Links
[7]Maryland Association of Counties conference
Maryland:
[8] Around The State This Week
[9]Arts & Entertainment
[10]Business/Employment
[11]Education
[12]Government and Law
[13]Health
[14]History
[15]Kids
[16]Libraries
[17]Places and People
[18]Science and Technology
[19]Families
URL to open: www.homepage.mac.com
Arrow keys: Up and down to move. Right to follow a link; Left to go back.
H)elp O)ptions P)rint G)o M)ain screen Q)uit/=search[delete]=history list
```

Figure 12-3:
Type the
URL for the
site you
want to
browse
non-
graphically.

```
                                                       Apple (p1 of 2)

#[1]home     [2] index

[3] Apple [4]The Apple Store [5] Switch [6] .Mac [7] QuickTime [8] Apple
Support [9] Mac OS X
[10]Hot News [11]Hardware [12]Software [13] Made4Mac [14]Education
[15]Creative [16]Small Biz [17]Developer [18]where to Buy


                          [19]Power Mac G4
                  [20]Introducing the new Power Mac G4.
        [21]Dual G4 Processors [22]All with dual processors, starting at
                                  $1699.
          [23]Dual 1.25GHz, dual 1GHz or dual 876MHz processors Xserve
        technology with up to 2GB DDR SDRAM 1 or 2MB of DDR L3 Cache per
          processor New 167MHz or 133MHz system bus ATI Radeon 9000 Pro or
        NVIDIA GeForce 4 graphics Dual digital display support from one AGP 4x
        card 4 internal hard disk drives for up to 480GB Preloaded with Mac OS
                                X v10.2 Jaguar

                  [24]Hot News Headlines Hot News Ticker
--press space for next page--
Arrow keys: Up and Down to move. Right to follow a link; Left to go back.
H)elp O)ptions P)rint G)o M)ain screen Q)uit/=search[delete]=history list
```

Figure 12-4:
This URL is
automatic-
ally
converted to
text for
Lynx.

If you use a non-graphical browser, you need to know the commands listed in Table 12-1 to help you navigate.

Table 12-1	Non-graphical Browser Commands
Browser Command	**Function**
home	Go to the home page.
recall	Review documents you've already viewed.
top	Go to the first page of the document.
bottom	Go to the last page of the document.
next	Follow the next link in the chain of information.
previous	Retrace the prior link.

Mousing across the Web

Graphical browsers bring the Web to life. To get started, just double-click the icon for your browser and you get a *home page* — the Web term for a "welcome" screen. Typically, the home page explains what the Web site is all about and points you in the right direction for the information that you're looking for. At many sites, the home page is a *portal* — a combination of search engine, categorized content, news, sports, weather, and shopping.

How Does Information Get on the Web?

Web authors use Web-authoring technologies to write the text, place the pictures, and interact with you on the Web. Because a Web language isn't a protocol, service, or application, it's not part of TCP/IP. However, the Web wouldn't be the Web without all the creative, exciting pages created by the following languages and tools.

The following sections discuss these Web-authoring technologies and tools:

  ✔ **HTML (HyperText Markup Language) and dynamic HTML:** HTML tells a Web browser how to display a Web page's text and graphics. You can use *dynamic HTML* (sometimes called *HTML 4.0*) to create snazzier Web pages than with HTML — with more animations and more response to user interaction than with HTML. For example, when you move your mouse over a graphic, the graphic speaks and changes color.

✔ **XML (eXtensible Markup Language):** The latest language to hit the Web is XML, and more and more companies are creating new Web languages and products based on XML. XML is more powerful than HTML because it *describes* the Web data as well as how the data should look. This description makes Web searching more efficient. Because XML is more descriptive than HTML, Web searches are able to filter out the irrelevant topics that you often see in today's HTML-based world.

✔ **XSL (eXtensible Style Language):** XSL is a W3C recommendation (see the "Who's in Charge of the Web?" section, later in this chapter, for more on the W3C) that specifies how to separate the style from content when building an HTML or XML page. Web-page authors and designers can apply style sheets to multiple pages. XSL also allows developers to decide how Web pages should be formatted for printing.

✔ **Java and JavaScript:** Java is a programming language specially created by Sun Microsystems for use on the Internet. A Java *applet* is a small program that's part of a Web page. A Java application can run on any operating system platform without having to be built specifically for it.

JavaScript is Netscape's scripting language. A *scripting language* is a mini-programming language. If you're creating Web pages, you can include JavaScript in HTML pages. The Web browser knows how to interpret the JavaScript code, which makes the browser act more like a Web application client. You can also run JavaScript on the server side with the Microsoft Active Server Pages (ASPs).

✔ **ASP (Active Server Page):** ASPs are HTML pages that include *scripts* (small programs) written by Web developers. The scripts are processed on a Microsoft Web server, which sends the HTML page to any Web browser. These pages are called *active* because you can use scripts to customize the pages for different users.

✔ **ActiveX:** ActiveX, a set of object-oriented technologies, is Microsoft's answer to Java. An ActiveX *control* is a program that runs in the ActiveX environment and is conceptually similar to a Java applet. ActiveX controls run on Windows 95, 98, NT, and 2000. Microsoft also plans to support ActiveX controls for UNIX.

Using Your Search Engine

One of the toughest things to do is find what you need on the Web. If you know what you want to see on the Web but not where it is, you need a search engine.

XML, HTML — what's the difference?

HTML came first. Most of the information for the Web page is *hard coded,* which means that most things on the page are preset in HTML. Your browser displays the page to the best of its ability. If the browser isn't exactly clear on what the Web page creator meant, it tries to guess what was intended. If it guesses wrong, it displays an error.

With XML, browsers work harder at processing Web pages. The Web-page programmer gets to take it easier. Here are some advantages (and tradeoffs) of using XML to create Web pages:

✔ The browser can generate stuff on the page on the fly — ad lib — which, to some extent, adds flexibility.

✔ The browser does its on-the-fly work at the client computer (helped by scripting languages such as Java and JavaScript). This reduces the workload on the server computer but increases it on your client. Some client computers have a hard time processing some of the fancier pages, and not all clients are enabled to handle scripting languages.

✔ The same content can look completely different, based on use. For example, an entertaining but complex display can have a simpler format for printing.

HTML is a simpler, less flexible way to publish data quickly on the Web. It's especially useful for simple data such as meeting agendas or advertising brochures. If the data needs more structure and flash and will be on the Web a long time, XML is a better choice for Web-page creation. By the way, "a long time" in Web time is probably a month or more.

Sifting through the information on the Web

A *search engine* is a site with specialized software that maintains a database of Internet sites. You tell the search engine what you want to look for, and it hunts through its database to give you links to the sites that match the word or words that you asked for. We had a lot of fun searching for our names. There were only a few matches, so it wasn't bad, but when we searched for the name "Bill Gates," we got more than 600,000 matches. Two of our favorite search engines are AltaVista (www.altavista.com) and Google (www.google.com).

A search engine includes a program that compares your search request to the entries in the index and then returns results to you. A search engine also includes a component — called *spider, crawler,* or *bot* — that searches every searchable page on the Web and reads it to see whether it contains the information that you requested.

Check out the Easy Searcher site (www.easysearcher.com/index.html) to find the locations of hundreds of specialized search engines, including an index of other search engines.

Using a slimmed-down search engine

Much as we love those great big multifunction search engines, we find that the advertising and the animations, while sometimes adding fun and usefulness, just get in the way. For a slimmed-down engine, take a look at the Google home page at `www.google.com`. It's so simple to use, it's practically empty. Google finds things quickly and easily, based on the keyword(s) you type. If you want to find only pictures and images, click Images. You can also browse Usenet news through Google. When you click Groups, Google displays the Usenet hierarchy, and you point and click your way to the information you want.

Structured directories of topics are often miscategorized as search engines. Yahoo! (`www.yahoo.com`) is an example of a popular directory on the Web. Several Web portals, including Yahoo!, combine both the search engine and directory approach to finding information.

Enjoying multimedia

Most people, even Internet newbies, have probably heard about multimedia on the Web — listening to audio, watching animations and videos, playing 3-D games, even attending conventions and training. Life online is more enjoyable when you can access more than words and pictures.

The Internet, compliments of TCP/IP protocols, lets you listen to CD-quality music with a click of your mouse. *MP3* is a file format that shrinks digital audio files (which are usually quite large) while preserving audio quality. You can download MP3 music fairly quickly. One minute of music is about 1 megabyte, so an average song is about 4 megabytes. With a 56K modem, you can download that song in just a few minutes. With our cable modem, it only takes seconds to download MP3 files. To play the song, you need an MP3 player, such as the free WinAmp high-fidelity player (`www.winamp.com`).

Sound and videos, however, use a lot of space on your computer. You need hardware power. Some of the recommendations we've seen on the Web are ridiculously low. You don't want your Internet music refusing to play or hiccupping all the time, do you? That's what happens if you're underpowered. To play music, we suggest at least a Pentium 266 computer with a sound card, 64MB of memory (128MB if you're going to be doing other things on your computer while you listen) and a fast network connection (at least a 56K modem). For video, try to use a faster network connection than a dialup modem — a cable modem or DSL connection, for example. See Chapter 16 for more information about fast network connections, such as cable modems and DSL. You also need software called *plug-ins* that your browser uses to turn your computer into a radio receiver, television set, or meeting place.

If you browse a Web page that uses a plug-in you don't have, you usually get a message asking if you want to download the plug-in right then. If you use a lot of plug-ins, create a folder to store them in the same place. If a plug-in becomes obsolete, the browser helps you update to a newer version.

Microsoft Internet Explorer browser doesn't support plug-ins; it uses ActiveX controls that do pretty much the same things as plug-ins. Just in case there's no plug-in equivalent to an ActiveX control, Netscape Navigator has a plug-in that helps it run some — but not all — ActiveX controls.

Table 12-2 lists some of the most popular free plug-ins.

Table 12-2	Plugging In with Plug-Ins	
Plug-In	*Use(s)*	*Web Site for Free Downloads*
Shockwave	Enjoy interactive Web content, such as games, presentations, and entertainment	www.macromedia.com
Flash Player	Watch vector graphics and animation, including cartoons, interactive seminars, and comedy routines	www.macromedia.com
Adobe Acrobat Player	View and print Adobe Portable Document Format (PDF) files	
RealOne Player	Listen to radio or watch TV from around the world	
QuickTime	Enjoy virtual reality scenes, film clips, sound, animation, graphics, text, music, and more	www.apple.com/quicktime

Streaming video and audio allowed Candace to attend Lotusphere, one of the biggest technical conferences in the world, without leaving home. Lotus provided the keynote address and more than 100 technical sessions on the Web. Many readers of our previous editions have recognized Marshall from his appearance on IBM/Lotus Web presentations.

Streaming video of live events such as Lotusphere is called a *Webcast*. Webcasts aren't just for technical conferences. Watching Webcasts lets you catch events like Sting's concert in New York and lots of movie premieres. Webcasts let you attend auctions without leaving your desk.

TCP Unicast streams over the Internet using the TCP protocol over port 1755. This protocol provides the highest performance. HTTP Unicast streams using the HTTP protocol over port 80. This protocol works fine but is slightly less efficient than TCP because of the HTTP overhead. Multimedia is called *streaming* because your browser receives the data in a continuous stream from the server so that you don't have to wait to download large multimedia files. A broadband connection helps streaming video stream. With a dialup modem, the video sort of bumps along.

Web Services

E-mail may be the most popular of the Big Four network tasks (along with file transfer, using remote computers, and Web surfing), but people keep focusing on the Web, looking for more and better ways to do e-business. Their latest and greatest plans involve Web Services.

Web Services are self-contained, connectable business components that are built on open, Internet standards. That's a nice digestible definition, but a hypothetical example is more valuable. Our friends at Odd Octopus Pies and Sushi (OOPS; see Bonus Chapter 2 on the CD) built an e-commerce Web site and are happy that you use it to place your orders. They would really like to make it more valuable by

- Accepting your credit card for payment (rather than sending you a bill by snail mail)

- Offering you special prices and purchase discounts — online — based on your bill-paying history and the value of your previous orders (without having to review those records by hand)

- Reordering from the suppliers automatically when inventory gets low (instead of placing orders by telephone)

Instead of hiring Web developers to custom build these new features, the management at OOPS is planning to

- Link to the credit card processing Web Service that their bank provides

- Link to the Customer Relationship Management (CRM) Web Service from the vendor they've chosen

- Link to the online ordering Web Services on their suppliers' e-commerce Web sites

That's a lot less code to write!

The standards for Web Services include

✔ SOAP (Simple Object Access Protocol), which defines the communication between Web Services clients and servers

✔ WSDL (Web Service Definition Language), which defines how a Web Service describes itself to potential users and their applications

✔ UDDI (Universal Description, Discovery and Integration), which defines how potential users and their applications find the Web Services

✔ XML (eXtensible Markup Language), which defines how Web Services clients and servers exchange potentially complex data

This book isn't about programming, so that's as far as we're going on this subject. For more information on Web Services, use a search engine and consult these Web sites:

✔ www.w3c.org/2002/ws

✔ www.soapware.org

✔ xml.coverpages.org/wsdl.html

✔ www.uddi.org

✔ www.xml.com

Reducing the Web's Wait

Even though HTTP is an efficient Internet protocol, some people think that WWW really means World Wide Wait. Web speed ranges from tortoise speed to warp speed. All of those fancy graphics that you see on Web pages are high fat and take a long time to get to you.

If you would like things to go faster, here are a few tips:

✔ **Use faster hardware:** For dialup access, a 56 Kbps modem should help — see Chapter 16 for the details. Using a broadband connection, either cable modem or DSL is even better especially for multimedia.

✔ **Clear out your cache:** Your browser *cache* is an area of temporary storage on your hard disk. Cleaning it out is particularly helpful when you're low on disk space and if you browse a lot of different sites during your session. A side effect is to protect your privacy by erasing evidence of sites you've visited from your computer. When you browse a Web page, your browser caches the data on your hard disk. If you go back to that same page, your browser retrieves it from the cache, and the page loads quickly. Using cache instead of requesting the file from the Web server speeds up Web browsing. To purge your cache in Internet Explorer 6, choose Tools➪Internet Options and click the General tab. In the Temporary Internet Files section, click the Delete Files button. Click Apply, click OK, and your cache is clear.

If you read Web pages that change frequently, such as those containing news, sports scores, or stock market listings, your cache doesn't show you the most current information. Be sure to click the Reload button on your browser to download fresh data from the server.

✔ **Try a Web accelerator:** An *accelerator* is a program that pre-fetches Web pages and caches them on your local computer. So while you're looking at that first recipe for cheesecake, the Web accelerator program brings the page with the next recipe to your local computer. You see the next recipe more quickly when you click to see it because it has already been moved from the Web site to your computer. You can buy a Web accelerator program for about $30 (U.S.). You can also do a Google search on "web accelerator" to find free downloadable accelerators. These free accelerators typically don't optimize Web browsing as much and don't include as many features as the products that cost you.

✔ **Automatically download files:** You don't have to sit in front of your computer to download Web pages and files. You can exercise and work off the junk food that this book makes you crave by using *download scheduling software.* You can use the software to download Web pages and files automatically on schedule. These scheduler programs disconnect from the Internet when your download successfully finishes. You can find free download schedulers by doing a Google search for "download scheduler". Apple provides a free download scheduler for Macintosh at www.macscheduler.com.

✔ **Use Lynx:** Little-known Lynx saves lots of time. When surfing for text, use the Lynx browser for speed. Lynx outperforms Netscape Navigator and Microsoft Internet Explorer when reading pages of text and FAQ files. You can get a free copy of Lynx for Windows 95 or Windows NT at www.fdisk.com/doslynx/lynxport.htm.

✔ **Create a shortcut on your desktop that links directly to an Internet site:** A shortcut can save you the time and effort of opening your browser and typing in a URL. That doesn't sound like much of a savings, does it? If you need to go to the same few places over and over, though, you may be pleasantly surprised at the convenience. To create a shortcut in Internet Explorer, choose File➪Send➪Shortcut to Desktop. From this point on, double-click the shortcut to launch Internet Explorer and go to the site.

✔ **Multitask:** Let your Internet connection do two things at the same time. Contrary to popular belief, you can surf while you download or perform a couple of downloads at the same time and still get good performance.

✔ **Avoid Web rush-hour congestion:** Check MAE West's traffic report before you start browsing (`www.mfst.com/MAE/west.ds3.overlay.html`). MAE helps you pick the best times to surf and download files.

✔ **Use a popup blocker:** Analogx offers its popup blocker, POW, free. Popup blockers automatically block annoying popup ads from displaying. We like POW because you can configure it to retain any popups you want to see and block the ones you don't want. Not only are popups annoying, they also use system resources and slow down your browsing.

You can download POW from several free download sites, or you can go to the source at `www.analogx.com/contents/download/network.htm`.

✔ **Upgrade from Windows 95:** Starting with Windows 98, Windows clients automatically optimize TCP/IP transmissions if you set the IP Packet Size to Automatic; just follow these steps:

1. **Choose Start➪Settings➪Control Panel.**

2. **In the Control Panel dialog box, click the Network icon, click Dial-Up Adapter, and then click the Properties button.**

3. **Click the Advanced tab and look at the list of properties.**

   The IP Packet Size entry should say Automatic. If not, click to list the IP Packet Sizes and click Automatic. Setting the IP Packet Size to Automatic allows the MTU size to match the connection speeds. By the way, Windows NT and 2000 also have an automatic MTU adjustment feature.

MTU (Maximum Transmission Unit) defines how many bytes are in each packet that flows across a network. The ideal packet size depends on the kind of network and network hardware that's handling your packet. If a packet is too large for your kind of hardware, TCP/IP automatically breaks up the packet into smaller quantities. This slows down your network performance. The automatic setting in Windows 98 adjusts the packet size before it goes out from your PC onto the network.

Who's in Charge of the Web?

The Web is part of the Internet. (See "Who's in Charge of TCP/IP and the Internet, Anyway?" in Chapter 4.) The *World Wide Web Consortium* (W3C), develops protocols for the Web. The W3C is international; consists of industry members from all over the world; and is hosted by the Massachusetts Institute of Technology in the United States, the Institut National de Recherche en Informatique et en Automatique (INRIA) in Europe, and the Keio University Shonan Fujisawa Campus in Japan.

Making the Web accessible for everyone

The W3C sponsors the Web Accessibility Initiative (WAI), which works with many organizations to produce guidelines for creating accessible Web sites and for creating accessible authoring tools for Web content. For example, the WAI recommends using auditory descriptions to help make Web sites accessible for people who are sight impaired. An *auditory description* is a voice (either human or synthesized) that describes the scene, actions, body language, and graphics in a Web video. A side effect of auditory descriptions is that they make Web information available to users whose computers aren't powerful enough to show video.

Accessible Web sites bear a WAI logo — sort of a *Good Housekeeping* Seal of Approval — representing its conformance level, as defined by WAI. The three levels, in order of increasing accessibility features, are as follows:

- Level A

- Level Double-A

- Level Triple-A

The W3C provides several practical services, including

- Sample applications that demonstrate upcoming Web technology.

- A library of information about the Web and its specifications. The library is useful for both application developers and users.

Many members of the W3C also belong to IETF working groups. W3C research and proposals can be put on the IETF track to become standards. The W3C and the IETF work together on the HTTP protocol, and W3C specifications undergo a review and finalization process similar to RFCs. W3C members approve specifications in a process that goes through stages: working draft, proposed recommendation, and recommendation. The W3C has approved almost 50 recommendations so far. To see a list of W3C recommendations, go to www.w3.org/TR.

Chapter 13

Sharing Files with FTP and rcp

*I*n this chapter, we look at ways that TCP/IP enables you to share files on remote computers over a network. Before TCP/IP, *sneakernet* was how people shared files. You copy a file onto a portable storage medium, such as a diskette. After you copy the file, you can take it to any computer anywhere in the universe that can read the storage medium. Sneakernet isn't efficient, and it doesn't always work between different operating systems, with large files, or with lots of files. One thing we miss about *Sneakernet*: Carrying those disks from one computer to another was a way to get some exercise.

Be sure to perform a virus scan on every file you transfer. You never know what's contagious.

The FTP Blue Plate Special

FTP is a protocol, a service, and an application. Use FTP to copy files to and from a remote computer. (Keep in mind that the computer where you're sitting is the *local computer*. The *remote computer* is the other one farther away from you.) Recall that you use the FTP client application to connect to a remote computer that's providing the FTP service. The FTP protocol comes into play when you ask the application to transfer the files.

Suppose it's dinnertime and you're hungry for egg rolls, Hungarian goulash, and crepes suzette, with an Alka Seltzer chaser. You have some choices:

✔ Travel around the world to China, Hungary, and France to assemble your meal.

✔ Order in. Get on the phone or fax to China, Hungary, and France and talk to the best restaurant in each country. Have everything shipped to you at the same time by the fanciest messenger service you can find.

It works the same way with computers and files. If you want files from three different computers, you can travel to each one and get what you need. Or you can stay put and use FTP. It's the next best thing to being there.

The client process of copying files from a remote computer to your local computer is called *downloading*. The server process of copying files from your local computer to a remote computer is called *uploading*. Either way, it's FTP.

With FTP, it doesn't matter what operating system is on the computers because they all have TCP/IP. This ability to transfer files to and from computers running different operating systems is one of the best benefits of FTP. For example, suppose your local computer runs Microsoft Windows 2000, but you need files that are on a Linux system. No problem. Start up an FTP client application on your PC, connect to that Linux system, and transfer those files.

Using Anonymous FTP to Get Good Stuff

The Internet has a large number of public FTP servers. These are known as *Anonymous FTP sites* or *Anonymous FTP archives*. When you connect to them, type **anonymous** as the username. Use your e-mail address as the password.

All anonymous FTP sites contain files that you can retrieve for free. Some have shareware; others hold graphics, music, and movies; and still others contain weird and wonderful things. Companies, universities, and numerous other do-gooders provide the sites. Many of these organizations have interconnected their Web sites and Anonymous FTP sites, which simplifies how they store things and how you get the stuff you want.

Although all Anonymous FTP sites are publicly readable, only a very small percentage are publicly writeable. You can connect to any of them and download all the files you want, but only rarely can you upload files. (If you're providing an Anonymous FTP site, be sure to protect your site so that some scoundrel doesn't fill it up by uploading objectionable or even illegal content.) In addition, some organizations have private FTP sites that don't accept the username "anonymous." If you've been given a username and password to allow you to use the archive, be sure to keep them secret.

Choosing Your FTP Client Application

These days, you have many choices in FTP client applications — these choices fit into three categories:

- **Web browsers:** You can use your Web browser. All of them can download files but if you need to upload files, you must choose one of the other two types of FTP client application (see the next two bullets). Using a browser is easy: Just surf to the appropriate site, point the mouse at what you want, and click.

- **Text-mode program:** You can use the old, reliable text-mode client application, which is simply called *ftp*. It's free and built-in to almost every operating system. You have to type some commands, but this is the fastest way to download or upload a large group of files.

- **Graphical program:** You can use an FTP client application that has a graphical user interface (GUI). There are dozens to pick from — some are freeware, but most are shareware. Most, including CuteFTP and FlashFXP, provide two windows so that you can see the files on your local computer and the remote computer at the same time. Then you can just highlight the files to transfer in one window and pull them into the other (called *drag and drop*).

Using FTP to Transfer Files

We show you step by step how to download five files with all three types of FTP client application: browser, text-mode, and graphical. For this example, we want RFCs 2771 through 2775 from the IETF archive.

You must follow six basic steps to transfer files by using FTP:

1. **Start your FTP client application.**

   - **Browser:** Launch your favorite browser.

   - **Text-mode:** At an operating system command prompt, type **ftp**.

   - **Graphical:** Launch your favorite graphical FTP client application.

2. **Connect to the remote computer that has the files you want.**

   Like many organizations, the IETF has linked its Web site and its Anonymous FTP archive, which means that we can get to the same files through two different addresses.

- **Browser:** Surf to `ftp://ftp.ietf.org`.

- **Text-mode:** Use the open command. At the `ftp>` prompt, type **open ftp.ietf.org**.

- **Graphical:** Connect to `ftp.ietf.org`.

3. **Tell the remote computer your username and password.**

- **Browser:** The browser automatically sends anonymous as your username and your e-mail address as the password.

- **Text-mode:** At the User prompt, type **anonymous** and press Enter. At the Password prompt, type your e-mail address. When you type the password, nothing appears. That's for security.

  If you have your own account on the remote computer, type that username and password.

- **Graphical:** The graphical FTP client automatically sends anonymous as the username and your e-mail address as the password.

4. **Locate the files you want.**

- **Browser:** Click the rfc folder.

- **Text-mode:** Use the cd command. At the `ftp>` prompt, type **cd rfc**.

- **Graphical:** In the window for the remote computer, double-click the `rfc` subdirectory.

On most Anonymous FTP sites, the good stuff is in or below the subdirectory named `pub`, which is short for public.

5. **Transfer the files.**

- **Browser:** Scroll down the list until you find a file called `rfc2771.txt`. Don't click it! If you do, the browser displays it rather than downloading it. If you use Microsoft Internet Explorer, right-click `rfc2771.txt` and choose Save Target As (or Copy to Folder for Internet Explorer 6) from the context-sensitive menu that appears. If you use Netscape Navigator or Communicator, right-click `rfc2771.txt` and choose Save Link As from the context-sensitive menu that appears. Figure 13-1 shows the pop-up menu that appears. Choose a destination directory and click Save.

  Repeat this step for each of the other four RFCs: `rfc2772.txt`, `rfc2773.txt`, `rfc2774.txt`, and `rfc2775.txt`. Right-click each one in turn and choose the Save option.

Even though we are browsing the Web, this address is an FTP archive.

Address	ftp://ftp.isi.edu/in-notes/

```
02/08/2000 02:57PM      95,255  rfc2769.txt
02/18/2000 10:43AM       8,988  rfc2770.txt
02/17/2000 10:11AM       8,988  rfc2770.txt~
02/04/2000 11:02AM      20,954  rfc2771.t
02/04/2000 11:05AM      28,565  rfc2772.t
02/09/2000 08:59AM      20,008  rfc2773.t
02/09/2000 12:34PM      39,719  rfc2774.t
02/10/2000 03:23PM      42,956  rfc2775.t
02/16/2000 11:01AM      61,628  rfc2776.t
02/17/2000 10:22AM      30,064  rfc2777.t
02/23/2000 03:13PM      35,150  rfc2778.t
02/22/2000 11:02AM      47,420  rfc2779.t
03/05/1997 12:00AM       7,526  rfc278.tx
03/03/2000 08:46AM      18,954  rfc2780.t
02/23/2000 11:34AM      29,870  rfc2781.t
02/23/2000 11:32AM      24,013  rfc2782.t
03/02/2000 05:10PM      61,421  rfc2783.t
03/14/2000 12:21PM      16,627  rfc2784.t
```

Open
Open in New Window
Save Target As...
Print Target
Cut
Copy
Copy Shortcut
Paste
Add to Favorites...
Properties

Figure 13-1:
A right-click
is the right
thing to do.

- **Text-mode:** You can use the get command one time for each file, like this:

```
ftp> get rfc2771.txt
ftp> get rfc2772.txt
ftp> get rfc2773.txt
ftp> get rfc2774.txt
ftp> get rfc2775.txt
```

TIP

Under DOS and Windows, rfc2771.txt, RFC2771.TXT, and rFC2771.tXt are all the same file. But under Linux and UNIX, these are three different files! Be sure to type the filenames exactly as you see them.

You have to wait for each download to finish before you start the next. But there's a better way. First use the prompt command to eliminate the need to authorize each file download; then use the mget command to get the files:

```
ftp> prompt
Interactive mode Off.
ftp> mget rfc2771.txt rfc2772.txt rfc2773.txt rfc2774.txt
        rfc2775.txt
```

Figure 13-2 shows the text-mode session.

- **Graphical:** In the window for the remote computer, scroll down the list until you find rfc2771.txt. Click to highlight it. Hold down the Shift key and click rfc2775.txt to highlight the five files you want. Drag them to the window for the local computer to start the downloads. Figure 13-3 shows the convenience of drag and drop.

```
C:\TEMP>ftp
ftp> open ftp.ietf.org
Connected to www2.ietf.org.
220 www2 NcFTPd Server (licensed copy) ready.
User (www2.ietf.org:(none)): anonymous
331 Guest login ok, send your complete e-mail address as password.
Password:
230-You are user #4 of 50 simultaneous users allowed.
230-
230 Logged in anonymously.
ftp> cd rfc
250 "/rfc" is new cwd.
ftp> prompt
Interactive mode Off .
ftp> mget rfc2771.txt rfc2772.txt rfc2773.txt rfc2774.txt rfc2775.txt
200 Type okay.
200 PORT command successful.
150 Opening ASCII mode data connection for rfc2771.txt (21573 bytes).
226 Transfer completed.
ftp: 22192 bytes received in 0.39Seconds 56.90Kbytes/sec.
200 PORT command successful.
150 Opening ASCII mode data connection for rfc2772.txt (29352 bytes).
226 Transfer completed.
ftp: 30139 bytes received in 0.60Seconds 50.23Kbytes/sec.
200 PORT command successful.
150 Opening ASCII mode data connection for rfc2773.txt (20515 bytes).
226 Transfer completed.
ftp: 21022 bytes received in 0.44Seconds 47.78Kbytes/sec.
200 PORT command successful.
150 Opening ASCII mode data connection for rfc2774.txt (40842 bytes).
226 Transfer completed.
ftp: 41965 bytes received in 0.99Seconds 42.39Kbytes/sec.
200 PORT command successful.
150 Opening ASCII mode data connection for rfc2775.txt (43967 bytes).
226 Transfer completed.
ftp: 44978 bytes received in 0.99Seconds 45.43Kbytes/sec.
ftp> bye
221 Goodbye.

C:\TEMP>
```

Figure 13-2:
The text-
mode FTP
client
application
is the most
efficient
way to
download.

6. **Exit from FTP when you're done.**

   • **Browser:** Close the browser (or surf somewhere else).

   • **Text-mode:** Use the bye command or the quit command. (Some text-mode FTP client applications also provide an exit command that's identical to bye and quit.) They do exactly the same thing:

   ```
   ftp> bye
   ```

or

   ```
   ftp> quit
   ```

   • **Graphical:** Close the graphical application.

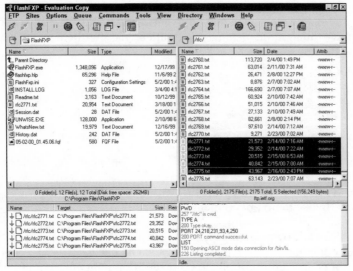

Figure 13-3:
The best of
both
worlds?

Beyond the Basics (Just a Little)

The text-mode FTP application offers many other features.

If you're not sure which text-mode FTP command to use in any situation, type **help** or **?** at the `ftp>` prompt to get a list of FTP commands, as shown in Figure 13-4.

Figure 13-4:
There are
lots of
text-mode
commands.

```
% ftp
ftp> ?
Commands may be abbreviated.  Commands are:
!            debug        mdir         sendport     site
$            dir          mget         put          size
account      disconnect   mkdir        pwd          status
append       exit         mls          quit         struct
ascii        form         mode         quote        system
bell         get          modtime      recv         sunique
binary       glob         mput         reget        tenex
bye          hash         newer        rstatus      tick
case         help         nmap         rhelp        trace
cd           idle         nlist        rename       type
cdup         image        ntrans       reset        user
chmod        lcd          open         restart      umask
close        ls           prompt       rmdir        verbose
cr           macdef       passive      runique      ?
delete       mdelete      proxy        send
ftp>
```

To upload a file, use the put command:

```
ftp> put file1.txt
```

You can rename a file as part of the download or upload; in fact, you may *have* to rename files when you copy between two different operating systems that have different file-naming capabilities. Just put the new file name at the end of the command:

```
ftp> get file1.txt newfile1.txt
ftp> put file2.txt newfile2.txt
ftp> get unusual-Linux.file.name dosfile.txt
```

To upload multiple files at once, use the mput command:

```
ftp> mput file1.txt file2.txt file3.txt
```

You can't rename the files you copy with mget and mput, so you may have to use multiple get and put commands.

If you want to download or upload a group of files so large that all of their names don't fit on the command line, you can use *wildcards* to condense the string of names. For example, to copy files that contain account records for multiple customers whose names start with "smit," you use the asterisk wildcard (*), attached to a partial filename, like this:

```
ftp> mget smit*
```

This tells FTP to get all of the files with names that start with the characters preceding the *. The asterisk wildcard (*) means "any number of characters, including no characters."

If you want to copy every file in the directory, it's even easier: Just use a single * with the mget or mput command, as shown here:

```
ftp> mput *
```

The question mark wildcard (?), on the other hand, means "any single character." So instead of:

```
ftp> mput file1.txt file2.txt file3.txt
```

you can use:

```
ftp> mput file?.txt
```

Just looking at a file

Want to check out the contents of a file without actually transferring it? Just specify an output filename of hyphen (-):

```
ftp> get README -
```

This command transfers the README file to your screen. It doesn't matter which operating system you're using; the hyphen always means "the screen." The file isn't saved in any way. If you want your own copy, get it again without the hyphen.

FTPing non-text files

So far, we've only shown you how to transfer text files. If you want that neat new computer game, it's going to be stored as a *binary file*. Binary files are made up of 0s and 1s instead of letters so that they can be executed by your computer, but to us, they look like transmissions from outer space.

A filename extension gives you a clue as to whether the file contains text or binary code. Text files usually have names that end with the extension .txt. Files in binary have names that end with various extensions, such as .exe, .zip, and .tif.

Unless you tell it otherwise, FTP assumes that you're moving plain old text files. But if you want to transfer something a bit more exotic, like that new game or maybe a zipped file with a special format, FTP has the binary option to take care of that. (*Zipping* is one form of file compression; see the next section, "Smart FTP Tricks.")

To switch to binary mode, type **binary** at the ftp> prompt any time before you type **get** or **put**. Then, after transferring your binary file, you can easily switch back to text transfer mode by typing **ascii**. ASCII stands for the American Standard Code for Information Interchange, where each text character has a standard code. A space, for example, is code 20 in ASCII representation.

If you transfer a file in the "wrong" mode, you may not be able to use it, especially if you copy a binary application in text (ASCII) mode. You'll have to redo the copying operation in the correct mode. The FTP client application doesn't warn you.

If your Windows XP/2000 computer has an infrared port, there is an additional FTP command: irftp (infrared ftp). When you run irftp, the Wireless Link dialog opens, and you select the files that you want to send. The irftp command transfers these files via the infrared port instead of your NIC. At the command prompt, typing

irftp -h

and the filenames to transfer lets you skip the Wireless Link dialog box.

Smart FTP Tricks

FTP, transferring files, get and put — sounds pretty basic, doesn't it? But what if you copy a compressed file — can you use it? You can use these smart FTP tricks to make life on the Internet easier.

Disk space is nearly always a problem for almost everyone. The unwritten rule is: The more you have, the more you fill it up — and you never have enough. To save space and make even more files available to you, many FTP sites compress their files. After you find the file you want, you need to decompress it so that you can use it. Here's where you have to get smart.

Unfortunately, there's no neat little utility called FTP Unzip to get you by. So your first task is to determine what compression method was used on the file. You have literally dozens of (and maybe more) ways to compress files. Look for a file named README, which should tell you how the files were compressed and where to get the decompression utility.

Sometimes you can tell what compression software was used by looking at the file type, also called the *file extension*. Table 13-1 lists some of the most widely used file types and the compression method used.

Table 13-1	Popular File Compression/Decompression Methods	
File Type	*Operating System*	*Compression Utility*
.zip	Windows	PKZIP/PKUNZIP
.z or .Z	Linux, UNIX	compress/uncompress
.tar	Linux, UNIX, and many others	Actually, this is a personal backup utility that groups one or more files into an archive. Tar stands for *tape archive*, but you frequently find tar archives on disk (that's UNIX for you . . .).
.gz	Linux, Unix	GNU zip
.sit	Macintosh	StuffIt

Installing and Configuring an FTP Server

As a general rule, most server-type operating systems (Linux/UNIX, Windows 2000 servers, MAC OS X) come with FTP server software built in. Most client-type operating systems (Microsoft Windows 95/98, PDA operating systems) do not come with FTP server software built in. If you need FTP server features, that is, if you want to upload files as well as download them, and you don't have FTP server software on your computer, don't despair. You can easily get free FTP software from the Internet.

Do you have FTP server software?

There are lots of different ways to find out whether FTP server software is on your computer. For Linux, we like the KPackage program to search for software. Besides telling you whether the package is on your computer, KPackage also tells you whether the package is installed.

In Figure 13-5, KPackage finds a popular FTP daemon, wu-ftpd, and gives you lots of information about the software. If you look at the package list on the left panel, you can see that the Installed tab is open. This means that the wu-ftpd server is already installed. If you see the FTP package under the All tab, but it isn't installed, click the Mark column and then the Install Marked button to install the FTP server software.

Figure 13-5:
Lots of files
make up
one FTP
package.

Click the File List tab to see every file that's part of the software package. Forty-six different files make up our copy of the wu-ftpd server software. Luckily, installing the package takes care of the separate files automatically.

Another Linux program for finding software is RPM, the Red Hat Package Manager. If you don't have graphical interface to UNIX/Linux, you can always use the file command. To find FTP files on Microsoft Windows operating systems, we usually search for files named *ftp*. Use the Finder window in Mac OS X.

Installing and configuring an FTP server

In the following example, we install the RhinoSoft Serv-U FTP server software on a Windows 98 laptop. Serv-U is available for the following operating systems:

- ✔ Windows 95/98/98SE/Me
- ✔ Windows NT Server/Workstation 4.0
- ✔ Windows 2000 (Advanced) Server
- ✔ Windows 2000 Professional
- ✔ Windows XP Home/Professional

You can download a free personal edition of Serv-U from www.rhinosoft.com.

To install and configure the Serv-U FTP server, follow these steps:

1. **Double click the Serv-U file to start the Install Wizard.**

   The Wizard does all the usual things:

   - Asks you which folder to install the software in
   - Copies files to the folder you select
   - Starts the Serv-U administrator program
   - Puts an icon on your desktop

2. **Restart your computer to complete the installation.**

   When your computer restarts, Serv-U automatically starts and connects you to it so that you can configure FTP. Figure 13-6 shows the configuration window.

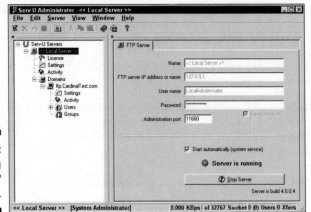

Figure 13-6:
Configuring
the FTP
server.

3. **Provide answers to Serv-U's requests for configuration information:**

   • The IP address of the server. Leave this blank if your computer gets its IP address from DHCP.

   • Whether you want the server to start automatically each time the computer boots — install as system service.

The Serv-U installation asks the second question only for Windows 9*x*/Me. If you answer No, you have to start the server yourself when you log on to Windows. On Windows NT and Windows 2000, Serv-U automatically becomes a system service.

   • Whether you want to allow Anonymous access.

   • Whether you want a named account so that users must log on with a username and password.

   • The username, password, and home directory.

   • Whether you want to lock FTP users into the FTP home directory so that they cannot look around at other directories and folders.

   • Whether you want the FTP user to have Administrator privileges.

Now our laptop is an FTP server as well as a client.

Monitoring FTP activity

After you install and configure the Serv-U FTP server, you can keep track of what people are doing. Figure 13-7 shows the Domain Log tab where you can examine the IP addresses to see where on the network people log on. The local address is the address of the FTP server. The Connected To address is the computer that opens the FTP connection. You can also use the domain log to troubleshoot FTP problems. For example, the third line in the log file in the figure shows that the user, CARDINALFTP, doesn't have a valid home directory. This explains why CARDINALFTP complains that she can't log on.

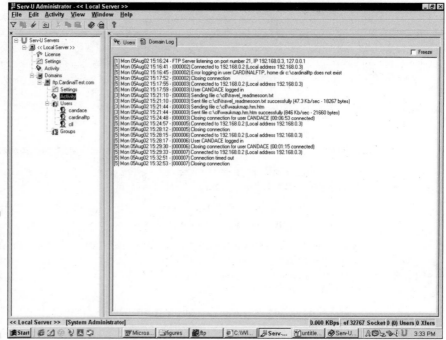

Figure 13-7:
Use the
Activity:
Domain Log
to trouble-
shoot FTP
problems.

The original FTP protocol, service, and application presents a security risk because usernames and passwords went across a network in clear text. The original RFC (959 — written almost 20 years ago) didn't include security provisions. In those early days of networking, trust was a big factor. As the Internet has grown, some nasty folks have become cyber-delinquents, even cyber-criminals, so many people avoided standard FTP. RFC 2228, "FTP Security Extensions," relieves security worries by providing for authentication, integrity, and confidentiality for both passwords and data.

In addition to the provisions in RFC 2228, we recommend that your FTP server also include some other security features:

  ✔ A remote administration feature so that you can connect to the FTP Server by using SSL

  ✔ The ability to deny access to the server based on incoming IP addresses

Using rcp (Not Just Another Copy Program)

An alternative to FTP is rcp (pronounced by saying the letters R C P), another of the Berkeley UNIX r utilities for remote access. (rcp is available on many, but not all, computers that use TCP/IP.)

The rcp utility is a little more lightweight than FTP and, therefore, faster. For one thing, you don't explicitly log on with a username and password. For another, there's no Anonymous rcp variation.

Following are the three ways to use rcp, with the syntax and a sample command for each:

✔ To copy a file from your computer to a remote computer across the network:

```
rcp local_file remote_computer:remote_file
rcp profits1 candace1:profits1
```

✔ To copy a file from a remote computer on the network to your local computer:

```
rcp remote_computer:remote_file local_file
rcp candace1:profits2 profits2
```

✔ To copy a file from one remote computer to another:

```
rcp remotecomputer_a:remotefile remotecomputer_b:remote-
          file
rcp marshallcomp:profits3 candace1:profits3
```

Trust is essential for rcp. When you rcp to the remote computer, you may or may not be prompted for a username and password, depending on trust. You aren't prompted for your username and password if the remote computer *trusts* you or the computer from which you're logging on. The notion of trust in this discussion comes from UNIX and the TCP/IP environment that grew up with it. When two UNIX computers are set up so that they trust each other, all the users on one computer are allowed to use the other computer. The concept of trust has spread to other operating systems, such as Microsoft Windows NT Server.

Trust isn't automatically reciprocal. Just because computer A trusts computer B (and all of computer B's users) doesn't mean that computer B trusts computer A and all of its users. Nevertheless, trust is commonly defined in both directions.

Chapter 14

Sharing Compute Power across a Network

. . . .

In This Chapter

▶ Using someone else's computer power from a distance — a l-o-o-n-n-g-g distance

▶ Understanding telnet versus rlogin — the same but different

▶ Working with other remote access commands: rsh and rexec

▶ Checking your running telnet server

▶ Figuring out how to be trustworthy in a network environment

▶ Installing, configuring, and using secure telnet, rlogin, and rsh

. . . .

*I*s your computer working too hard? Is it hungry for power? Is it low on disk space? (Whose computer isn't at some time or other?) Well, worry no more. Thanks to TCP/IP applications, such as telnet and rlogin (remote login), you can connect to another computer and use its power and disks. In this chapter, we show you how to use remote access clients and servers, such as telnet, rlogin, rsh, and rexec, to read and edit files across the network and do much more. Look Ma, no copying! The computer you use — maybe you're sitting in front of it right now — is the local computer. The remote computer is another one, on someone else's desk or in someone else's computer room in another country on another continent.

Both telnet and rlogin send all data, including username and password, across the network in clear text. This means that anyone sniffing network traffic can steal your data. Evildoers like to collect usernames and passwords to break into other people's computers and networks.

If you're concerned about security holes with telnet and rlogin, you should use secure telnet and rlogin clients. We do. These secure telnet and rlogin clients are based on the SSH (Secure Shell) protocol that encrypts usernames and passwords before sending them across the network. Some of the figures in this chapter use secure products. You can't really tell by looking. In a screen shot, secure telnet and rlogin look the same as their bare-bones ancestors. It's the inner workings that make them secure. More on secure clients later after you get through with the basics.

Sharing Other People's Computers

In a network environment, the computers within your organization are often shared resources. In Chapter 3, we introduce the client/server concept of a compute server, a computer willing to share its CPU power. In this section, we look at some of the TCP/IP clients that you can use to access a compute server.

Cycle stealing — TCP/IP style

Sharing a computer's CPU resources is called *cycle stealing.* No, we're not talking about going out to a biker bar and committing a felony. In this case, we're talking about stealing computer-processing cycles. The computer component that does the processing is called the *central processing unit* (CPU). A CPU cycle occurs each time a computer's internal clock ticks. (Those clocks tick a lot faster than your alarm clock, by the way.) So when you cycle steal, you use the CPU power of another computer.

To distribute power in an organized way, many businesses set up compute servers for you to steal from or share with. A compute server is a powerful computer that's configured especially for sharing among many users. When you "steal" CPU cycles from a compute server, you don't have to feel guilty.

In this chapter, you discover how you can cycle steal with TCP/IP, but computer etiquette requires that you always do it with permission. After all, if you cycle steal from a computer that has an underpowered CPU, you're stealing from someone who can't afford to share, and, as a result, work for both of you goes slower. Besides, if your victim is a techie, she knows how to detect your theft, and you may wind up in worse shape than if you had tried to steal Jay Leno's Harley. (It's a cycle joke!)

If you try to steal CPU cycles without permission from a well-secured computer and network without permission, you won't be able to. (In Chapters 18 and 20, we explain some of the techniques network administrators use to protect computer resources from thieves.) The security on protected networks not only prevents your theft, it also writes your IP address and other information to log files. A good network administrator can track you down and report you to worldwide agencies, including the U.S. Federal Bureau of Investigation (FBI).

Don't steal a moped

Not every computer can be a compute server. Some operating systems can't provide this service — others are set up so they don't. Unless you install extra software, personal computers running DOS or Microsoft Windows 95/98/Me/XP don't provide compute services for network users. They're designed to be used by only one person at a time. (Why do you think they're called "personal computers"?)

A multiuser operating system, regardless of the computer running it, is designed to be used by more than one person at a time. Most multiuser systems, such as Linux, UNIX, Mac OS X, Windows NT/2000 Server, and IBM's OS390, are capable of providing compute services, such as telnet servers. The system administrator can protect telnet servers and may decide not to start a telnet server at all.

But let's deal with the positive. You know that you have a computer somewhere on your network that you can use to steal more power. Luckily, for you to borrow some compute cycles from another computer, that computer doesn't need to have the same operating system you have. In fact, this is one of the big benefits of telnet and rlogin, two TCP/IP applications for cycle stealing. You can see them in action a bit later in this chapter.

How can you use stolen cycles?

You can put your stolen cycles to various uses. Suppose you have an older Macintosh without much CPU power and you need to do some major calculations about weather systems. You don't want to tie up your Mac by making it grind out the calculations. Instead, you can telnet to the big supercomputer at the central office and use the remote CPU to do your math in seconds rather than minutes or hours.

Oldies but goodies

Most telnet applications emulate an ancient Digital Equipment Corporation (DEC) VT100 terminal and its successors (VT220, VT320). The VT100 is so ancient that Digital, in fact, no longer exists. In its time, starting in the early 1980s, a VT100 was *the* terminal to have.

VT100s may not be the leading edge of technology anymore, but they refuse to die. VT100s are very reliable. We have one that still works.

Another standard in its day was the IBM 3270 terminal. A special version of telnet, called tn3270, emulates an IBM 3270. (The tn is short for telnet.)

Does your organization maintain a large database? Or several? Say you have access to a database that tracks restaurants. To use it, you don't need to install database software on your PC. When you're hungry, you telnet over to a remote computer to read through the restaurant database. While you're on a business trip, you can use telnet or rlogin to connect to your home office and read your mail remotely.

Many people also use telnet to do research. Public telnet sites give you access to libraries around the world.

On the Internet, you can find public telnet sites (that is, remote sites accessible via telnet) that publish their usernames and passwords. And some really public sites don't even require usernames and passwords. Use a search engine (such as Google) to search for "public telnet sites". You'll find lists of them.

telnet: A Protocol, Application, and Service

telnet is both a TCP/IP protocol for connecting to a remote computer and a TCP/IP application for running a telnet program (to use that remote computer interactively as if you were sitting right in front of it). telnet is also a TCP/IP service that runs on the remote computer. The telnet client application connects to the telnet server, also called a daemon. Communication runs from the client application (on the local computer) to the protocol (also on the local computer), across the network to the telnet protocol (on the remote computer), to the telnet service (on the remote computer).

The telnet application acts as a terminal emulator, making your expensive, high-powered computer act just like an old-style computer terminal. Whatever commands you type on your local keyboard are sent across the network for execution by the remote computer.

If you're telneting to a Windows computer, with its graphical interface, you can type only commands, so brush up on your DOS commands.

What you need to know before starting telnet

Before using telnet to grab those cycles, you need the name of the computer to which you want to connect and its domain, or its IP address. If you only use e-mail addresses, the computer name is the part right after the @ sign. For example, in `emily@teenage.example.com`, the computer name is `teenage` and the domain name is `example.com`. See Chapter 6 for the full discussion of IPv4 TCP/IP names and addresses. See Chapter 9 if you're using IPv6.

Next, because you're connecting to a multiuser operating system, you need to know a username and password for the remote computer. A system administrator can restrict access to a compute server or prevent a computer from acting as a compute server in the first place by turning off the telnet service.

After you have the computer name (or IP address) and a valid username and password, or you're connecting to a public site, you're ready to start stealing cycles. Keep in mind that whenever you're asked for a computer's name, you can supply that computer's IP address instead. From now on in this book, we just say "computer name," but you can give either the name or the numeric address. (For more about computer name-to-address translation, see Chapter 10.)

Using a telnet client to steal cycles

Master telnet by following these steps:

1. **Run the telnet client application program on your local computer.**

   This usually means typing the command **telnet**, followed by the computer name that you're accessing. The remote computer needs to be running a telnet service. On Microsoft Windows operating systems, choose Start↩ Run and type **telnet** in the Open box. You should see the Connect dialog box, as shown in Figure 14-1. Fill in the host name and click Connect. In Figure 14-1, a Windows 98 telnet client connects to a telnet server running on the Linux operating system.

   You can be a telnet client *from* just about any computer. However, you can't usually telnet *to* a Windows 95/98 or Mac computer (pre-Mac OS X). These computers come with just telnet *client* software. If you want a Windows 95/98 or an older Mac to function as a telnet server running the telnet service, you must install a special telnet software package. You can read about a couple of telnet packages in the "Serving telnet where you least expect it" section later in this chapter.

   If the telnet connection messages tell you about the Escape character, remember it. You may need to use this character later, to interrupt your remote computer session temporarily and issue some additional commands to telnet itself. You'll find more on this in the next section ("The great escape").

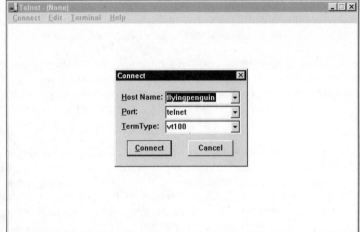

Figure 14-1:
Opus,
running
Windows 98,
telnets
to flying
penguin,
running
Linux.

2. **Log on to the remote computer using a valid username and password, as shown in Figure 14-2.**

3. **Start typing the commands that you want to use in your remote work session.**

   You need to know the commands that work with the operating system on the remote computer. For example, if you know only Linux commands, telneting to a Windows 2000 system won't be useful unless you know how to use the Windows 2000 command line.

   In Figure 14-2, the user, miss_scarlett, telnets to a Linux system from her Windows 98 client. Remember that now, even though miss_scarlett's computer runs Windows 98, everything she types in her telnet window must be Linux. miss_scarlett is now using Linux commands, such as cat and ls, to display a file and get a directory listing. Notice that the error messages are Linux error messages.

4. **When you're finished stealing cycles from the remote computer, exit or quit from your telnet session.**

In our sample telnet session (refer to Figure 14-1), the computer takes care of the terminal emulation mode automatically by setting it to be a VT100.

The great escape

By pressing the key(s) that represent the Escape character in your telnet application, you can switch from issuing operating system commands to issuing telnet commands. We know it seems odd, but on some computers the Escape key doesn't send the escape signal to telnet. It has to do with terminal emulation quirks. Table 14-1 contains some useful telnet commands.

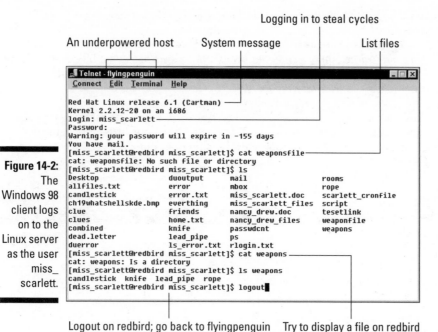

An underpowered host   System message   Logging in to steal cycles   List files

```
Telnet - flyingpenguin
Connect  Edit  Terminal  Help

Red Hat Linux release 6.1 (Cartman)
Kernel 2.2.12-20 on an i686
login: miss_scarlett
Password:
Warning: your password will expire in -155 days
You have mail.
[miss_scarlett@redbird miss_scarlett]$ cat weaponsfile
cat: weaponsfile: No such file or directory
[miss_scarlett@redbird miss_scarlett]$ ls
Desktop              duoutput      mail                  rooms
allfiles.txt         error         mbox                  rope
candlestick          error.txt     miss_scarlett.doc     scarlett_cronfile
ch19whatshellskde.bmp everthing     miss_scarlett_files   script
clue                 friends       nancy_drew.doc        tesetlink
clues                home.txt      nancy_drew_files      weaponfile
combined             knife         passwdcnt             weapons
dead.letter          lead_pipe     ps
duerror              ls_error.txt  rlogin.txt
[miss_scarlett@redbird miss_scarlett]$ cat weapons
cat: weapons: Is a directory
[miss_scarlett@redbird miss_scarlett]$ ls weapons
candlestick  knife  lead_pipe  rope
[miss_scarlett@redbird miss_scarlett]$ logout
```

Figure 14-2: The Windows 98 client logs on to the Linux server as the user miss_scarlett.

Logout on redbird; go back to flyingpenguin   Try to display a file on redbird

Table 14-1	Some Useful telnet Commands
telnet Command	*Function*
open	Initiates a connection to a remote computer.
close	Terminates your connection to a remote computer. If you started telnet with a computer address, close also quits telnet. If you used the open command to start your remote connection, the close command closes the connection, but telnet remains active so that you can open a connection to another computer.
quit	Terminates your connection and quits telnet.
set echo	If the characters you're typing aren't appearing on-screen, set echo may fix the problem.

Serving telnet where you least expect it

TCP/IP for Macintosh (pre-OS X) or Windows 95/98/Me/XP usually includes only a telnet client — no server. That's because those platforms aren't usually used as compute servers. However, given the powerful CPUs you now get in even the least expensive personal computers, you may have plenty of CPU cycles to share with others. What you don't have is the telnet server software to make the sharing possible. No problem! Many telnet server packages for what have traditionally been client-only computers are available as shareware (which usually means that you try it for free and pay a small amount to run it permanently) or freeware on the Web.

Figure 14-3 shows a *telnet reversal*. The powerful computer running Red Hat Linux acts as a telnet client and connects to Opus, our little IBM ThinkPad laptop. Opus is running a shareware version of a telnet server for Windows 95/98/Me/XP from GoodTech Systems.

```
TELNETPS                                                    _ 回 ×
 Auto     ▾  ▢▢▨  ▨ ▨▨ A
2. Modify user
3. User list
ctrl-z to exit
1
Enter username, or ctrl-z to exit: wilensky
Enter password, or ctrl-z to exit: ********
Confirm password, or ctrl-z to exit: ********
Options availale for password utility, Please select one option

1. Create new user
2. Modify user
3. User list
ctrl-z to exit
3
User list:
leiden
wilensky

Options availale for password utility, Please select one option

1. Create new user
2. Modify user
3. User list
ctrl-z to exit
```

Figure 14-3: Opus reverses roles and becomes a telnet server for the big flying-penguin.

The CD that comes with this book includes a copy of Telnet Server, a telnet daemon (server) from GoodTech Systems that you can install on Windows 95, 98, NT, XP, and 2000.

telneting in the palm of your hand

Mobile, handheld computers are more than just organizers — these little devices are really handheld computers with built-in TCP/IP. To telnet from a Palm Pilot handheld device across the Internet to a computer running the telnet service, for example, all you need is one piece of hardware (a modem, and possibly a cable depending on the type of modem), your ISP's phone number, and one piece of software (a telnet client for your Palm Pilot). We tell you more about the hardware in Chapter 16. For software, if you simply need a basic terminal emulator, you can download freeware or shareware from several sites; if you want a fancy terminal emulator with more sophisticated functions, you can purchase the software pretty cheaply. Table 14-2 lists some Web sites that you can browse to find terminal emulator software for your Palm. Most modern PDAs (personal digital assistants) and handheld computers have a Web site where you can find links to telnet client software.

Table 14-2	Holding telnet in the Palm of Your Hand	
Product	*Web Site*	*Special Features*
Online VT-100	www.markspace.com/online.html	N/A
TermPilot	www.shop.store.yahoo.com/pilotgearsw/termpilot.html	Japanese and English support; direct dialing to a BBS or online service.
SSH Telnet	www.airstreamws.com/ourproducts/sshtelnet.html	Splits your screen into halves: You use one half for regular commands and operations, while the other half functions as a numeric keyboard. Secure telnet with encryption for the RIM 957 Blackberry.

R you Ready foR MoRe Remote log-ins?

An alternative to telnet is rlogin, which comes with most UNIX and Linux systems. The rlogin application is one of the *r utilities,* a group of network utilities developed at the University of California at Berkeley for accessing remote computers. The utilities in the group all start with the letter *r*. Although they provide the same kind of functionality, telnet and rlogin were implemented by separate groups of people, and each works differently behind the scenes to accomplish the same thing.

If your computer runs a Windows or Mac client, you probably need to get an rlogin client separately. If you get what we call a *combo-client,* such as SecureCRT or OpenSSH (a free Open Source client; www.openssh.com), rlogin is bundled with telnet and other remote access tools. If you search for "secure rlogin client" on your favorite Internet search engine, you'll see lots of clients with telnet and rlogin bundled together.

When you rlogin to the remote computer, you may or may not be prompted for a username and password, depending on trust. If the remote computer *trusts* you or the computer from which you're logging on, it doesn't prompt for your username and password. The notion of trust in this discussion comes from UNIX and the TCP/IP environment that grew up with it. When two UNIX computers are set up so that they trust each other, all the users on one computer are allowed to use the other computer. The concept of trust has spread to other operating systems, such as Microsoft Windows NT Server.

Trust isn't automatically reciprocated. If computer A trusts computer B (and all of computer B's users), it doesn't mean that computer B trusts computer A and all its users. Nevertheless, it is quite common for trust to be defined in both directions. Figure 14-4 shows an rlogin session on an untrusted computer: The user has to type a password. After the password is entered, the user can list the files in the remote computer's directory and send e-mail.

You don't trust trust? Many security conscious administrators don't. Read the "What? They Don't Trust You? No Problem: rexec to the Rescue!" section, later in this chapter, to find out how to provide secure encrypted communications between two untrusted hosts.

Figure 14-4:
miss
scarlett
needs to
type her
password
because
tweetie
doesn't trust
flying-
penguin.

```
tweeties$ whoami
root
tweeties$ rlogin flyingpenguin
login: miss_scarlett
Password:
Warning: your password will expire in -85 days
Last login: Mon Feb 21 09:09:21 from opus
You have mail.
miss_scarlet> mail
Mail version 8.1 6/6/93. Type ? for help.
"/var/spool/mail/miss_scarlett": 11 messages 10 new 11 unread
 U  1 root@flyingpenguin.c Mon Nov 29 15:59 18/661   "Cron <miss
_scarlett@flyingpenguin> date"
>N  2 root@flyingpenguin.c Mon Nov 29 16:00 17/676   "Cron <miss
_scarlett@flyingpenguin> echo "Clue is a"
 N  3 root@flyingpenguin.c Mon Nov 29 15:59 17/651   "Cron <miss
_scarlett@flyingpenguin> date"
 U  1 root@flyingpenguin.c Mon Nov 29 16:01 17/651   "Cron <miss
_scarlett@flyingpenguin> date"
 & Held 4 messages in /var/spool/mail/miss_scarlett
miss scarlet> who
root      pts/0    Feb 17 14:03
root      pts/1    Feb 17 14:03
miss_scarlet pts/2    Feb 21 18:01      tweetie@cardinalsg.com
```

In Chapter 5, we ever so briefly describe IPSec, RFC 2401. IPSec (Internet Protocol Security) is a proposed standard for IP security that verifies who's sending data across the network and also encrypts the data. See Chapter 20 for more about IPSec. SSH1 and SSH2 are protocols in the Internet draft stage for secure network services, including remote logons, over an insecure network. As of this writing, there are more than ten Internet drafts about SSH1 and SSH2 that describe how products can provide secure encrypted communications between untrusted hosts. Find them on the Web at www.ietf.org/ids.by.wg/secsh.html.

Stealing Cycles with rsh

Sometimes you need to connect to a remote computer and work interactively to perform a variety of tasks, as with rlogin or telnet. At other times, you simply have just one thing to accomplish. The University of California at Berkeley's r utilities include rsh, short for *remote shell*. With rsh, you can tell a remote computer to execute one command.

When you use rsh, the command you enter must include the following three elements, separated by spaces:

- ✔ The rsh command itself
- ✔ The name of the remote computer you want to use
- ✔ The command to perform on the remote computer

Here is the syntax:

```
rsh remote_computer command_to_execute_over_there
```

So a sample command to list files residing on the Linux computer flyingpenguin looks like this:

```
rsh flyingpenguin ls
```

For rsh to work smoothly, the remote system must trust you. (See the description of trust in the previous section.)

rsh is another feature of many combo-clients.

What? They Don't Trust You? No Problem: rexec to the Rescue!

Another r application, rexec, is like rsh — it allows you to connect to a remote computer to issue one command at a time. rexec is different from rsh because you must know a valid username and password for the remote computer.

Before it attempts to execute your command, rexec always prompts you for a username and password. Your password is encrypted before it is sent "across the wire" to the server. (See Chapter 20 for more information about encryption and other security issues.) rexec uses the TCP/IP service rexecd.

Although rsh is quicker because it doesn't involve thorough logon processing, rexec is more secure because it does. Take your pick.

Sniffing Out Security Holes with SSH

SecureCRT, from VanDyke Technologies (www.vandyke.com), is one of many Windows 95/98/NT/XP/2000 terminal emulators that provide both telnet and rlogin clients and supports the Secure Shell (SSH1 and SSH2) protocol. To find out more, read the next section and check out the discussion on encryption and authentication in Chapter 20.

The CD that comes with this book includes SecureCRT, a secure telnet client for Windows 95, 98, XP, and NT from VanDyke Software, Inc.

You can use SSH-based software to replace rlogin and rsh.

Working with Secure Clients and Servers

For basic telnet clients and servers, you may not need to do any installing or configuring. Most vendors' TCP/IP stack comes with a telnet client already set up, waiting for you to use it — no installation or configuration required. Now that's helpful! Just run the telnet command (refer to Figure 14-1), connect to a server, and go. If you want more than the plain vanilla telnet — security features, for example — install a different telnet client. Many telnet clients are available as freeware or shareware on the Web.

Check out the GoodTech and VanDyke clients included on the CD.

Most server-type operating systems come with telnet server software built in. Installing the operating system automatically sets up telnet services to start whenever the computer boots up. Linux and UNIX do this. With Microsoft NT and 2000 Server, you need to click the Network Services button to have the installation procedure set up networking. Otherwise, you can configure telnet and other network services later.

Installing and configuring a secure client . . . telnet and more

Actually, these secure clients provide more than telnet. Most vendors' secure clients combine telnet, rsh, rlogin, and ftp functionality.

Most telnet clients come with an Installation Wizard that makes them easy to install. For example, with our Windows XP SecureCRT client from VanDyke Software, Inc., the wizard takes you through the following steps (after displaying preliminary screens, such as the license agreement):

1. Selecting a directory to hold the SecureCRT files.

2. Choosing a profile — either for all users or a personal profile.

3. Choosing the protocols you want.

   Because we don't dial out, we skipped TAPI (the Telephony API that manages access to your phone lines). We also skipped the Serial protocol, which lets you connect to another computer through a COM port. For our installation, because we have a permanent broadband connection, we chose SSH1, SSH2, telnet, and rlogin.

4. Then the installation runs unattended; it finishes quickly.

The first time you run SecureCRT, you need to name a folder to store configuration data. SecureCRT gives you a default. Now you're ready to telnet, rlogin, or configure your client to use some nifty features.

Installing and configuring a secure server . . . telnet and more

The plain vanilla telnet server that came with the TCP/IP bundled with Linux starts automatically when the system starts. We didn't need to do any configuration at all.

First things first — finding out whether telnet services are running

If you're not sure whether your telnet server is started, you need to check your system for a process called telnetd, the telnet daemon (also known as server). There are lots of ways to see whether telnetd is running, and they vary with your operating system. With Linux, UNIX, and Mac OS X, you can run the ps command and look through the output for the telnetd process. Figure 14-5 shows an excerpt from the ps listing. Don't panic when you see a ton of raw data. You're simply looking at the end of the line for the name of the service.

You can also see ps information in graphical form on Mac OS X and most Linux and UNIX computers. From the Apple Menu on Mac OS X, choose Computer Settings⇨Network Manager and then click the Services tab. Figure 14-6 shows how we check our telnetd from the KDE control center. You can find KDE on Linux and UNIX.

If you don't see telnetd running, double-check for sshd. The sshd is the secure server that provides telnet services.

On Windows NT and 2000 Server, choose Start⇨Programs⇨Administrative Tools⇨Services.

Configuring a secure telnet server

Actually, most secure servers accept connections from more than just telnet. They also handle telnet, rsh, rlogin, and ftp functionality.

```
# ps  auxww
USER        PID   %CPU %MEM   SZ    RSS    TTY STAT    STIME    TIME COMMAND
root        1032  25.0  10.0    8   15400    -  A    12:09:24  243:15  kproc
root           0   0.0  10.0   12   15404    -  A    12:09:24   0:02   swapper
root        9034   0.0   0.0  108    140     -  A    12:12:11   0:00  / usr/sbin/biod 6
root        8796   0.0   0.0   44     52     -  A    12:12:24   0:00  / usr/sbin/uprintfd
root        7740   0.0   1.0 1072   1260     -  A    12:12:05   0:00  / usr/sbin/snmpd
root        7482   0.0   0.0  336    412     -  A    12:12:01   0:00  / usr/sbin/inetd
root        8278   0.0   0.0  140    192     -  A    12:12:18   0:00  / usr/sbin/rpc.lockd
marshall   12404   0.0   0.0  508    564  pts/0  A    16:12:04   0:00  - ksh
emily      12155   0.0   0.0  508    564  pts/0  A    16:12:08   0:00  - ksh
root       12184   0.0   1.0  876    812     -  A    16:11:54   0:00  telnetd -a
root       10066   0.0   0.0  448    520     -  A    12:12:24   0:00
/ usr/bin/AIXPowerMgtDaemon
candace     3256   0.0   0.0  212    256  pts/0  A    16:12:47   0:00  ps  auxww
root        4424   0.0   0.0  400    252     -  A    12:11:34   0:00  / usr/dt/bin/dtlogin
-daemon
root        6736   0.0   0.0  564    660     -  A    12:11:58   0:00  / usr/sbin/portmap
root        6994   0.0   0.0  324    372     -  A    12:11:55   0:00  / usr/sbin/syslogd
root        5426   0.0   0.0  512    416     -  A    12:11:35   0:00  dtlogin   <:0>
-daemon

#
```

Figure 14-5: The ps command shows the telnetd up and running.

```
# ps auxww
USER          PID   %CPU %MEM   SZ   RSS    TTY STAT    STIME    TIME COMMAND
root         1032   23.0 10.0     8 13400    -   A    14:09:24  142:13 kproc
root            0    0.0 10.0    14 13404    -   A    14:09:24   0:02 swapper
root         9034    0.0  0.0   108  140     -   A    14:14:11   0:00 / usr/sbin/biod 6
root         8696    0.0  0.0    44   32     -   A    14:14:24   0:00 / usr/sbin/uprintfd
root         6640    0.0  1.0  1062 1460     -   A    14:14:03   0:00 / usr/sbin/snmpd
root         6482    0.0  0.0   336  414     -   A    14:14:01   0:00 / usr/sbin/inetd
root         8268    0.0  0.0   140  192     -   A    14:14:18   0:00 / usr/sbin/rpc.lockd
marshall    14404    0.0  0.0   308  364   pts/0 A    16:14:04   0:00 - ksh
emily       14133    0.0  0.0   308   64   pts/0 A    16:14:08   0:00 - ksh
root        14184    0.0  1.0   866  814     -   A    16:11:34   0:00 sshd
root        10066    0.0  0.0   448  320     -   A    14:14:24   0:00
/ usr/bin/AIXPowerMgtDaemon
candace      3236    0.0  0.0   214  236   pts/0 A    16:14:46   0:00 ps  auxww
root         4424    0.0  0.0   400  232     -   A    14:11:34   0:00 / usr/dt/bin/dtlogin
-daemon
root         6636    0.0  0.0   364  660     -   A    14:11:38   0:00 / usr/sbin/portmap
root         6994    0.0  0.0   324  362     -   A    14:11:33   0:00 / usr/sbin/syslogd
root         3426    0.0  0.0   314  416     -   A    14:11:33   0:00 dtlogin    <:0>
-daemon

#
```

Figure 14-6:
A secure
telnet server
(sshd) is
running on
Linux.

Although our plain vanilla telnet server works just fine out of the box, it has no security features. So we chose to install a secure server named VShell from VanDyke Systems, Inc., the parent of SecureCRT. Installing a server is more involved than installing a client, and installing a secure server is more involved than installing a standard server. The server installation starts easily enough with a Setup Wizard that takes you through the following steps:

1. Selecting a directory to hold the VShell files.

2. Deciding whether you want a program group and shortcut on your desktop.

3. Generating the host key automatically.

   Read Chapter 20 for more information on host keys.

4. Setting the level of authentication.

   The choices are Password Only, Password & Public Key, Public Key Only If you choose Public Key, you need to check the Public Key LSA module box.

5. The Setup Wizard then tells you that it's copying files to the Windows `system32` directory. You must shut down and restart your computer to configure your VShell server.

When your computer restarts, the VShell configuration window opens. Unless you have some special reason to do otherwise, keep port 22 as the listening port. Selecting the Disconnect Idle Sessions check box is a good idea. Follow these steps to set up user security:

1. **Click Access Control in the Category list.**

   Figure 14-7 shows that the server, by default, allows everyone all access to all services except for remote port forwarding.

2. **To set access permissions for an individual user, click Add and type the person's username in the object name box.**

   Figure 14-8 shows that the Access Control window pulls in the username you type. No permissions are set for the user until you check the Allow or Deny boxes.

3. **Click Apply to assign the access rights.**

   Figure 14-9 shows that user candace has been added and now has all access rights.

4. **Click OK when you're done assigning access rights to users.**

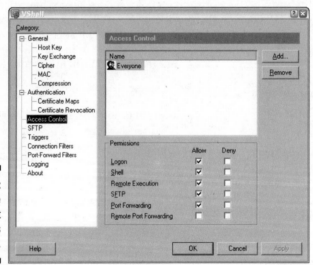

Figure 14-7:
Everyone
has almost
all access
by default.

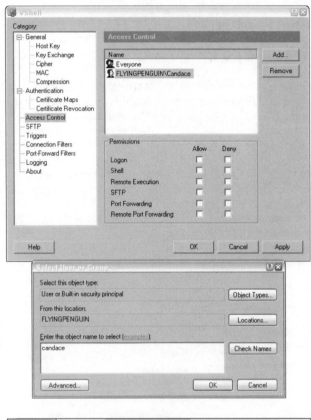

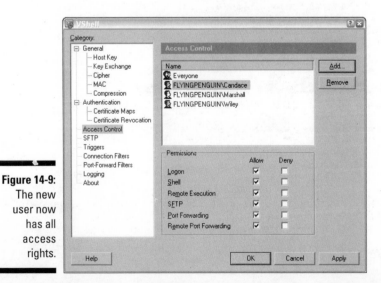

Figure 14-8:
By default, a new user has no access rights set.

Figure 14-9:
The new user now has all access rights.

Using a Secure telnet Client with a Secure Server

The secure client and secure server work together to guarantee that your username and password as well as your application data (for example, telnet, rlogin, ftp) cannot be stolen or interfered with. As an example, we use the SecureCRT client on Windows 98 and VShell server combination on Windows XP Professional in this section.

Be sure to use the SSH2 protocol to take advantage of the security features. The first time you use the SecureCRT client to access the secure VShell server, click the QuickConnect icon so that you can get SSH2 protocol. You need to fill in the protocol and the host you want to connect to. See Figure 14-10.

If you try to open a connection to a host without SSH2, you see the message shown in Figure 14-11.

Figure 14-10: Associate the SSH2 protocol with the host you want to connect to.

Quick Connect

Protocol: ssh2

Hostname: flyingpenguin

Port: 22 ☐ Use firewall to connect

Username:

Authentication
Primary: Password   Unsave Password
Secondary: <None>   Properties...

☐ Show quick connect on start up   ☑ Save session

Connect   Cancel

Figure 14-11: This user forgot to use the SSH2 protocol.

SecureCRT

⚠ The remote SSH server SSH-2.0-VShell_2_1_0_114 VShell requires SSH2. Please select SSH2 as the connection protocol.

OK

After you start the connection, you must enter your username and password — see Figure 14-12.

Figure 14-13 shows marshall connected to flyingpenguin and using the command-line interface.

Figure 14-12:
SecureCRTS
SH2-
UserPasswd
.bmp: Type
your
username
and
password.

Figure 14-13:
Marshall
steals some
cycles.

If you're not familiar with the command line in Windows, the first command you type should be **help**.

The Most Important telnet Tip for Servers

Turn off the telnet service if you don't need it. Services offer windows into computers that hackers can't resist.

The Second Most Important telnet Tip for Servers

Using a secure client gets rid of telnet security concerns. Use only plain vanilla telnet, rlogin, and rsh if you can't find a secure version for your operating system. Better yet, if you're buying a new computer and you plan to use these remote access services, make sure it comes with secure clients and/or servers already loaded. Our Linux came with the ssh daemon. Mac OS X 10 comes with a plain vanilla telnet server. Later versions use SSH instead . . . so upgrade.

Stealing Cycles on a Very Large Scale

Technologies, such as clusters and grid computing, build computers and storage systems into large pools of computing resources. A *cluster* is a group of computers that act like a single system to provide high availability, load balancing, and parallel processing. Grid computing allows multiple computers and storage systems across a network to act as one large pool of computing resources. Clusters are tightly coupled, meaning that the computers in the cluster form one administrative unit and are usually located in the same area. Computational grids are loosely coupled. Each computer in the grid may be separately managed, and the computers in the grid may be widely geographically distributed. In either case (grid or cluster), TCP/IP protocols bind the computers together.

Some clusters, for example, VMSclusters from Hewlett Packard, also use proprietary protocols for higher performance.

Using HTTP to help with SETI

SETI@home is a grid-like project that so far has borrowed over 1 million years of CPU cycles from Internet-connected computers in the Search for Extraterrestrial Intelligence (SETI). SETI@home uses the HTTP protocol.

Rather than using enormous supercomputers to analyze radio telescope data, SETI uses millions of small computers that work simultaneously to analyze different parts of the data. One of those small computers could be yours. SETI@home borrows idle cycles from computers that are sitting around running screen savers and using electricity. Millions of people have helped out SETI@home by downloading a special screen saver that gets data from SETI, analyzes the data, and reports the results to SETI. If you need to use your computer, the SETI screen saver stops and doesn't start up again until your computer sits idle again. If you would like to share your CPU cycles with SETI@home, you need to download and install the client software. You can download SETI clients for Windows 95/98/Me/NT/2000/XP, Mac OS, UNIX, Linux, OS/2, BeOS, and VMS at `http://setiathome.ssl.berkeley.edu/download.html`.

Chapter 15

Mobile IP, Dialup Networking, and IP Telephony

In This Chapter

▶ Understanding how to get mobile

▶ Networking by phone

▶ Securing mobile and dialup communications

▶ Using PPTP (Point-to-Point Tunneling Protocol) to implement a VPN (virtual private network)

▶ Reducing telephone charges by making phone calls over IP

You may have full network access from your office, but what about from your home or when you travel? Dialup networking and mobile computing give you access to remote computers, network services, and the entire Internet. You can even use your computer to make long-distance phone calls at local rates. We describe three recent developments for TCP/IP internetworking in this chapter:

✔ **Mobile IP:** Roam freely across the Internet without worrying about changing your IP address.

✔ **Dialup connections:** Dial the Internet or your corporate network from any telephone line.

✔ **IP telephony:** Telephone and fax without incurring any telephone company charges.

Mobile IP for Hassle-Free Travel

The Dynamic Host Configuration Protocol (DHCP, which we describe in Chapters 6 and 7) helps you connect your laptop to the corporate LAN during work hours and to the network in your house at night and on weekends without having to reconfigure your computer manually every time you change locations. Each time you start your laptop, the local DHCP server leases it an IP address. That's incredibly convenient, but sometimes it's not exactly what you need. Enter Mobile IP.

The original design of *Mobile IP* is an enhancement to IP that lets you use your wireless network-equipped device continuously, even while you are moving (but not while you are driving, please!), without changing its assigned IP address. Mobile IP allows you to use network applications on wearable computers, PDAs (personal digital assistants), palmtop computers, smart cellular telephones, two-way pagers, and other wireless devices.

This mobility support is similar to services from two providers you already know: cellular telephone companies and the postal service. Wherever you are, your cell phone has the same telephone number. Incoming and outgoing calls are handled automatically by the wireless network, even when you're moving.

The technical details of Mobile IP are similar to how the postal service forwards your mail when you go to your vacation house. You notify the post office staff of your temporary new address, and then they capture the mail that comes to your old address, paste new address labels over the old address, and forward the mail to your current location.

Mobile IP turns your computer into a *Mobile Host* (MH) that's supported by the cooperation of a *Home Agent* (HA) and a *Foreign Agent* (FA). (In IPv6, your Mobile Host is called a Mobile Node.) Whenever your MH is away from your *home network* — the one specified in your IP address (not the one in your house) — it tells an FA on the new network to notify your HA where you are. Even though you're on the move with your MH, packets still arrive for you on your home network. Your HA captures the packets, pastes new address labels over the old address (using the post-office analogy), and forwards them to the FA on the network you're currently on for delivery to your computer.

The cellular telephone companies don't have network coverage everywhere, so sometimes you can't make and receive calls, or your current call gets disconnected. The postal service occasionally has problems when you move — a letter may get lost in the process of forwarding it to your new home. Too bad they don't have Mobile IP working for them. As your MH moves, it constantly updates the HA with its latest address. Plus there's TCP to ensure that lost packets are resent.

The specifications for Mobile IP include RFC 3344, "IP Mobility Support for IPv4" and RFC 2977, "Mobile IP Authentication, Authorization, and Accounting Requirements."

Mobilizing security

Security is always an issue in computing and even more so when you're moving your computer all over the Internet. With Mobile IP, your home network needs advanced encryption and firewall technologies to protect your data wherever you go. Secure logon procedures and digital certificates for authentication (see Chapter 20) ensure that no one else can tell your Home Agent to send your packets to them.

Pervasive computing

Pervasive computing — access to network services anytime, anywhere, from any device you need to use — depends on mobile and wireless products and technologies, such as

- ✔ **WAP (Wireless Application Protocol)** — www.wapforum.org: In much the same way that HTTP carries HTML to your Web browser, WAP carries WML (Wireless Markup Language), or an equivalent data format, to your device's microbrowser or client application. WAP is not part of TCP/IP, but it can run over it.

- ✔ **Bluetooth** — www.bluetooth.com: Bluetooth is a low-cost radio frequency network for communicating over short distances.

- ✔ **802.11a and 802.11b** — grouper.ieee.org/groups/802/11: The IEEE working group for wireless LANs has published specifications for 11 Mbps networks (802.11b) and 45 Mbps networks (802.11a).

Connecting with Dialup Protocols

Your dialup choice depends on what you want to do from your "other" locations and what capabilities are available at the site you're dialing in to. Will you be connecting to a Linux system, a UNIX system, a Windows NT or 2000 system, or something else? Can you manage with limited services — just e-mail and Usenet news, for example? Or do you need all of the network services that you have at work (telnet, FTP, NFS, DNS, Web browsing)?

PPP, the pretty powerful protocol (see the following section), is the most popular dialup protocol. However, depending on what you're looking for, the answer may not be PPP. If you need to connect to your organization's private network via the Internet, you need PPTP. What do all these mean? We tell you in the next sections.

PPP (no, not "the bathroom protocol," silly!)

PPP, the Point-to-Point Protocol (pronounced by saying the letters P P P), is today's dialup network solution.

The point-to-point part of PPP's name is a little misleading because this connection method can be used to link one computer to another computer, one computer to a network, and/or one network to another network. With PPP, one computer can connect to another computer or to a whole network, or two networks can connect to one another with the help of a network device, such as a router (which we describe in Chapter 16). Microsoft Windows NT Server and Windows 2000 use PPP to implement Remote Access Service (RAS) Server.

Using PPTP to create virtual private networks

A *VPN* (virtual private network) is a restricted communications environment carried on the (very public) Internet. A VPN is secure because it runs through a private tunnel on the Internet. That tunnel uses a TCP/IP protocol, PPTP (Point-to-Point Tunneling Protocol).

PPTP lets you work remotely — at home or in a hotel room — and connect to your organization's intranet via the Internet. You dial and connect to a local Internet Service Provider (ISP). PPTP is the protocol that lets you connect (via a secure "tunnel") from the ISP to a private intranet. Why wouldn't you simply dial directly into your organization? Two main reasons involve cost. The third reason is security.

- ✔ **Telephone charges:** If it's a long distance call, you save your company a lot of money if you can dial a local number. If your organization consists of lots of telecommuters, local calls can be a big savings.

- ✔ **Easier (and cheaper) management:** In a VPN, the major investment is in modems for the telecommuters. Modems are cheap. Also, the network administrator at your site doesn't have to spend time configuring large dialup environments. The telecommuting employees use the Internet Service Provider's resources.

- ✔ **Security:** PPTP allows the network administrator to set up filtering. Filtering allows the administrator to say what kinds of network messages are allowed into the intranet, such as TCP only, IP only, UDP only, or some combination. The administrator can also deny all communications except through PPTP.

You can read more about VPNs in Chapter 20 and descriptions of the protocols that VPNs use in Chapters 4 and 5.

Dialup security

Protect your dialup communications in the same way that you protect your network. Some of the dialup security features that you may run into include

- **Username and password challenges:** When you dial in to your network, you should be challenged for a valid username and password before you're allowed to connect. Usernames and passwords are security controls that you may already be familiar with because you need them to log on to many computers.

- **Dial-back modems:** A modem is the device that connects your telephone and your computer (see Chapter 16). When you call your network, you go through the username/password challenge. If you're using a dial-back modem, the network disconnects you, and its modem calls you back at an authorized phone number that the network administrator set up. Even if an intruder has stolen your username and password, he or she can't get into your network (unless he or she can get into your home or remote office).

- **Encryption:** Is anyone listening in on your phone line? Encryption is standard with PPTP and optionally available for PPP. Encryption puts your data into a secret code before it goes over the wires. Eavesdroppers can't understand the code. Check out Chapter 20 for more information on encryption.

Understanding IP Telephony

Telephony refers to carrying voice, fax, videoconferences, and other information over connections that are traditionally provided by the public switched telephone network (PSTN) — what people usually call "the phone company." *IP telephony* is the same set of services carried as packets of data on the Internet — telephony without telephone lines! Internet Service Providers, telephone service providers, and cable TV companies are all entering the IP telephony market — and they must deliver the voice, fax, video, and other packets reliably, quickly, and with high quality.

VoIP — voice information in packets

Voice over IP (VoIP), pronounced Vee Oh Eye P, is a major part of IP telephony. To deliver voice using IP means sending voice information in packets over a data network (possibly even the Internet) rather than using the normal telephone lines. Like other forms of IP telephony (fax over IP, for example), VoIP avoids the charges of ordinary telephone service.

IP telephony and VoIP aren't just about individuals trying to save money — there are practical business uses, too. Some organizations use computer-to-phone IP telephony in managing customer relationships. When customers at a Web site click a particular icon, they're automatically connected to customer service representatives' phone lines.

The packets containing voice information must get to and from the users' computers quickly enough for the people to have a conversation. If there's too much delay, the people give up — not just on the conversation, but on VoIP as well. Ideally, the users would like to reserve some network bandwidth for their exclusive use in order to guarantee the quality of the service they get. That desire for good, predictable performance is true for other things besides IP telephony, such as streaming audio and video. That's why there are RFCs for the Resource ReSerVation Protocol (RSVP) and the topic of Quality of Service (QoS).

If you're interested in more details, here are some starting points:

- ✔ RFC 2990 — "Next Steps for the IP QoS Architecture"
- ✔ RFC 2386 — "A Framework for QoS-based Routing in the Internet"
- ✔ RFC 2210 — "The Use of RSVP with IETF Integrated Services"
- ✔ RFC 2208 — "Resource ReSerVation Protocol (RSVP) — Version 1 Applicability Statement Some Guidelines on Deployment"

How can 1 use VolP?

Using IP to send voice communications over the Internet gives you a lot of calling flexibility. Here are some of the services you can take advantage of:

- ✔ **Computer-to-computer calling:** If both you and the person you're calling have compatible software, you can speak to each other through the microphone connected to your computer.
- ✔ **Computer-to-phone calling:** You can start the call on the computer and make the phone ring at the other end. If the person you're calling is there, you have a conversation.
- ✔ **Phone-to-computer calling:** The person calling you can be on an ordinary phone. If you're not there, your computer can record a voicemail message.

All of these are available to you at no additional charge above the cost of your Internet service.

If you decide to move ahead with VoIP, make sure that you plan for the impact of the additional traffic on the network. Voice users and their QoS demands can slow down your e-mail, file transfers, access to remote computers, and Web traffic.

Part IV
Network Hardware and Security

The 5th Wave   By Rich Tennant

"We take network security very seriously here."

In this part . . .

Part IV really spices up TCP/IP with some advanced topics. We start with a look at hardware. You probably consider yourself to be a software person. We certainly think we are. But like it or not, software runs on hardware, and sometimes, to use software to its best advantage, you need to know a little about hardware. Chapter 16 describes how packets go through TCP/IP's software layers right down to the hardware before they go out onto a network to be handled by modems, switches, hubs, and routers on their way to their destinations. You also find out what kind of cable (or other connection medium) might suit your networking needs, depending on how far and how fast you want your network to go. After you get some hands-on tips for configuring routing, go ahead and look at our handy chart for deciding whether you need a router, switch, or hub.

Chapter 17 helps you troubleshoot some all-too-common TCP/IP and network problems, such as network congestion, unreachable computers, and network services that aren't running.

Part IV also includes three chapters on security. Chapter 18 is packed with practical security tips, including how to jump start your security plan in only four steps, and instructions for configuring firewalls. Chapter 19 helps you protect your e-mail and news and FTP applications. Chapter 20 is where we get into advanced security topics and discuss several security protocols, including S-HTTP, SSL, IPSec, and TLS. In Chapter 20, we also describe encryption, authentication, and digital signatures and certificates. You get hands-on advice for setting up a software firewall and the Kerberos authentication server. You also walk through a secure Internet credit card transaction and get started with virtual private networks.

Chapter 16

The Dreaded Hardware Chapter

*1*f you're reading this book, you're probably a software person (after all, network protocols are software). Or, you may be a hardware person who wants to see how the other half lives. If you're a hardware person, you probably already know what's in this chapter and can go on to some other one. If you're wondering why a software book includes a hardware chapter at all, remember that software runs on hardware. Software can't work without hardware, and there's no point in having hardware if there's no software for it.

Network administrators usually have to configure both the hardware and the software for a network. In this chapter, we cover the most commonly used network hardware devices — how they work to extend your network and enable it to communicate with other networks — and offer a little advice on making choices.

"It's a hardware problem"

Our personal favorite excuse when anything goes wrong is "It's a hardware problem." Try it. Say it over and over while you click your heels three times, and if you're wearing Dorothy's red shoes, maybe you can get by with it!

What's Hardware Got to Do with It?

Even though TCP/IP is software, it has to run over hardware. Like love and marriage, TCP/IP and hardware go together like a horse and carriage. And if you're responsible for a network, you can't be just "a software person" — no matter now hard you try. You need to pick up a little hardware knowledge and jargon to do your job right. Part of having a good marriage is understanding and appreciating each other's differences.

If you're asking "What has hardware got to do with doing a good job in network management?", our answer is this: Network cables (and other media), along with TCP/IP software, link computers together so that they can provide communication for and among your users. Computers are just hardware devices that happen to run some software — often, too slowly. If you're the network manager and the software runs too slowly, your users complain. And the problem may not be with the software. Your network needs some other hardware devices to create the infrastructure, too — unless it runs across the dining room table the way ours does.

Keep Layers in Mind

We list a major benefit of TCP/IP software in Chapter 5 — that it is independent of the underlying hardware. TCP/IP protocols do, however, work with hardware.

Some of the hardware that we discuss in this chapter communicates only with the physical (bottom) layer of the TCP/IP network layer cake, so protocols aren't an issue. Nevertheless, we have included information on these hardware devices. When designing or paying for a network, you may need to choose between a simple hardware device that has nothing to do with the middle (transport/internet) and upper (session/presentation/application) layers of the cake where TCP/IP is located and a more complicated solution, such as a packet filtering router, consisting of both hardware and TCP/IP software. We include descriptions of some physical layer devices so that you can compare their features to the devices that work with TCP/IP protocols.

Packets Chew through Network Layers

TCP/IP slices your network message into little bites called packets (see Chapter 2) and sends the packets out onto the network. When the packets arrive at the destination, TCP/IP reassembles them into your original message. We use the life of a packet to explain the layers in the network model.

A packet's life begins when an application creates it. Each packet travels down through the layers of the sending host, out across the network cables, up through the layers of the destination host, and into the appropriate application.

As the packets travel down through the layers of the sending host, headers containing control and formatting information and directions are added. When the packets reach the destination host, that information is read and stripped out as the packets move upward through each layer. For example, if you FTP a file from computer A to computer B, the data in the file is *packetized* at the application layer and sent through all the layers on computer A. By the time the packets are sent out across the wire, they have gained some weight — all that added network information. After the roly-poly packets reach the destination host, they start to slim down; when they arrive at the top layer and deposit your file, they're positively svelte again.

Figure 16-1 shows an FTP put operation: A packet travels from the application layer on computer A out onto the network wire and up to the application layer on computer B. You can see how the packet gains weight at each of computer A's layers and then goes on a diet as it moves up through computer B's layers. Yo-yo dieting may be unhealthy for humans, but it works great for packets on the network.

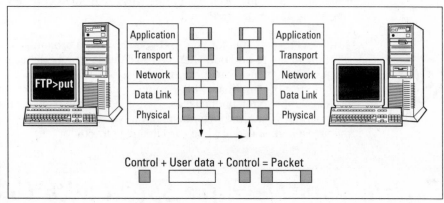

Figure 16-1:
Packets can eat TCP/IP wedding cake all day.

The rest of this chapter helps you understand some of the devices that you can use to extend your network, how they're different, and how to decide whether you need one on your network or internet.

Modems

A computer likes digital data. Your regular telephone line likes analog data. This is a Latin/Pig Latin communication problem. You need a translator. A *modem* translates a computer's digital data into analog signals that telephone lines understand. This process is called *modulation/demodulation — modem* for short. In the olden days (the early 1990s), the simplest way to connect to the Internet or any network was to connect a modem into your computer and dial the network's or the ISP's (Internet service provider's) telephone number. Your big decision was how fast you wanted the modem to transmit data versus how much you wanted to pay.

These days, you have a huge number of choices in modems that can communicate at many thousands of bits per second (Kbps), but consider yourself fortunate to be living in such speedy times. Both of your doddering authors have actually done work dialed in at a rate of 300 bps. Notice there's no K! (Windows hadn't even been invented yet, although UNIX had. And DOS was an IBM mainframe operating system.)

A "plain old" modem is still the simplest way to connect to a network, short of being permanently wired to it. The latest international standard for modems is known as V.92 (pronounced vee-dot-ninety-two) and it specifies data rates up to 56 Kbps. Your telephone wires may keep you from ever zooming along at top speed, though.

If V.92 still isn't fast enough for you, and you can't get a broadband connection, check with your ISP to find out whether you can use two modems and two phone lines simultaneously to increase your speed limit to 112 Kbps. (Ask them if they support "multilink PPP.") Some companies now make cards with two modems and two telephone jacks. That may be a good choice if you're going to upgrade your internal modem, but it isn't as appealing as if you already have a high-speed modem card inside your computer.

Satisfy Your Need for Speed with Other Things That People Call Modems

Some other connection devices, also commonly called modems, give you even more speed, although they add complexity, as well. Welcome to the wonderful world of *broadband* — the use of a *broad* range of transmission frequencies on the same cable to give you lots of *band*width. With broadband, you can watch cable TV and download files over the same coaxial cable, or you can make telephone calls and surf the Internet at the same time by using a single phone line.

Broadband gives you wide network pathways, lots of network capacity, and the speed you need to enjoy the most exciting new technologies available on the Web (real-time audio, audio-video phone calls, 3-D gaming, and Internet videoconferencing). It's not just the fancy new applications that benefit from the speed that broadband delivers; your day-to-day life on the Internet — such as downloading files and reading documents — is also much faster.

The leading broadband technologies (not really modems) are cable TV and DSL (Digital Subscriber Line). Why do we say their connection devices aren't really modems? The term *modem* comes from the modulating and demodulating of a digital signal into an analog one and vice versa. While cable "modems" and DSL "modems" connect you to a network, they don't do the same modulation/demodulation as conventional modems. Although they may seem to function like modems, electronically they do something else. Most people just call them modems. If you want another name, call them network devices or appliances.

Cable me up

A cable modem connects your computer to your coaxial TV cable which, in addition to letting you watch the sci-fi channel 'til all hours, becomes your Internet connection medium. Figure 16-2 shows how our computers share the cable modem's connection to the Internet. Accessing the Internet over cable TV cables is *fasssssssst,* up to 26 Mbps (million bits per second) for downloading. Uploading speed is up to 1.5 Mbps, depending on the capacity of the link between your ISP and the Internet and the number of other cable modem users in your neighborhood. That's still a lot faster than normal analog modem connections, and it's available 24 hours per day.

Before you buy a cable modem, make sure that your cable TV provider offers Internet access. Not all cable companies offer it. With a cable modem, your cable TV provider becomes your Internet service provider, as well. If you're planning to run a server for other people to use, check with your ISP to see whether it's okay and ask if you can have a permanently assigned TCP/IP address instead of the periodically changing DHCP address. (See Chapter 7 for the basics of DHCP and Chapter 6 for details on numeric addresses.)

DSL: Darn Speedy Linkage

DSL connects you to the Internet over a telephone line. "So what's the big deal?" you ask, "My modem does that now." We forgot to mention that the telephone line isn't a regular voice line. A *DSL line* is a special, super-speedy broadband phone line that gives you voice and data activity at the same time.

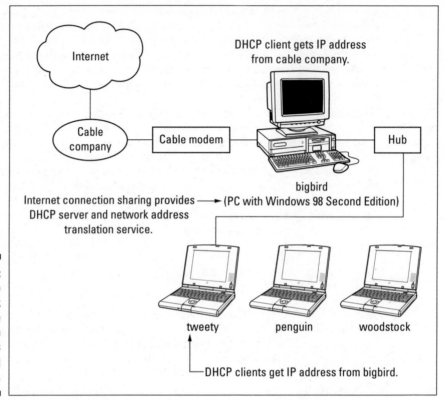

Figure 16-2:
Our home
network
with cable
modem
looks
something
like this.

DSL, pronounced by saying its letters, allows you to connect to the Internet or your organization's intranet almost as efficiently as if you were sitting on the LAN inside the building. You can use it to put your organization onto the Internet. Instead of transmitting data at modem speeds, you can use DSL to zoom along at speeds that start at 128 Kbps — more than twice as fast as 56 Kbps — and go up to 768 Kbps if you're willing to pay more. DSL is sometimes called ADSL (Asymmetric Digital Subscriber Line) because you receive data at the speed you pay for, but you transmit at something slower.

DSL is becoming more popular, but you may not be able to get service because

✔ Your telephone company and competing telephone service providers (if any) don't offer the service or don't offer it in your location.

✔ You may be too far away from a telephone service provider's central office. DSL has distance limitations.

✔ The equipment and service fees are more than you're willing or able to pay.

Try to get the telephone service provider to install your DSL connection at a special promotional rate. If the service provider says that it doesn't have one, ask whether a "sale" is planned for the near future and be sure to say that you're also asking competitors. These promotional rates are almost as common as cable TV's promotions. If your timing is right, you may get the modem for free.

How do you choose?

Not everyone gets a choice — certain areas have only one service available. If you have several choices available, consider the following before making your decision:

- ✔ **Cost:** Check the rates in your area because prices vary. Candace's brother can get DSL cheaper than she can. Price was a factor in your authors' decision to go with a cable modem. Our niece, Emily, can only get DSL. Her cable company isn't an ISP.

- ✔ **Hardware:** You need a special device (okay, call it a modem if you want) regardless of whether you select cable or DSL. Most types of DSL also require a splitter to keep the Internet separate from the voice. The service provider installs the splitter. If you get *DSL Lite* (also called *G.lite*) service, you don't need the splitter.

- ✔ **Crowds:** With DSL, your data transmission rate doesn't change regardless of how many people sign up for the same service that you have. With cable modems, you may notice that things slow down at peak times as more and more of your neighbors sign up and are surfing when you are.

Beam me down, Scotty!

Another high-speed connectivity option is a satellite dish. Now, don't start cutting down trees to make room for a concrete base underneath a huge earth station dish. We're talking about devices such as the Hughes Network Systems DirecPC dish. It's less than 36 inches across. You receive data from the satellite at 400 Kbps, but you transmit data over an ordinary modem connection. (So it's asymmetric, just like DSL.) If you want super high speed in both directions, you can get that, too — for more money. The incoming data gets a free trip into outer space and back (the satellite is in orbit 22,300 miles above the Earth), but the second half of the trip is downhill all the way. DirecPC is available in Europe, North America, Africa, and Asia.

Stretching the Network

Networks come in all sizes, shapes, and media. No matter what media your network runs on, each type has its own distance limitations. Take a look at Table 16-1 and examine Ethernet's cable limits. Chapter 2 tells you how Ethernet works and clues you in on Ethernet speeds.

Table 16-1	Ethernet Cable Maximums for Best Signal Transmission	
Cable Type	*Description*	*Maximum Limit, in Feet/Meters*
10Base5	Thick coaxial cable	1640/500 (Ethernet originally ran on this)
10Base2	Thinwire cable	606/185
10BaseT	Twisted-pair wire	328/100
10BaseF	Fiber-optic cable	6560/2000
100BaseT	Twisted-pair wire	328/100
1000BaseT	Twisted-pair wire	328/100
1000BaseLX	Fiber	16,400/5000
10GBASE-E	Fiber	131,200/40,000

You may be able to exceed these maximums (for example, by using thinwire cable that's 620 feet long) and get by; the limits usually have a small amount of play built in. But remember that your data is transmitted as an electronic signal across a cable. The longer that signal has to travel, the weaker it gets. The maximums in Table 16-1 indicate the point when the signal starts to weaken.

The hardware options for extending your network beyond the cabling limits in Table 16-1 include hubs, switches, routers, and gateways. We cover these options in the following sections.

Hubba, hubba

Suppose Table 16-1 shows that your twisted-pair wires, though cheap, aren't long enough to extend across your building as planned. Think twice before you throw away the wire and buy some expensive optical cable, which can extend your network not just across the building but across the county. Optical fiber may extend your network, but it also shrinks your budget.

Don't panic. There are other answers, including a device called a *hub* that ties multiple segments of wire or cable together. The hub also retransmits the signal so that it can travel longer distances, despite the limitations of the wires and cables. When you extend a cable with a hub, you can put more physical devices, such as computers, on the cable. Most people think hubs are the things under their desks for easily connecting multiple computers to the network — and they're right — but a hub also helps extend your network cable.

You can use hubs to extend a LAN by linking multiple network segments. These segments must be of the same type. In other words, all Ethernet is fine, but mixing Ethernet and token ring is not fine (see Chapter 2). The hub takes the electronic signals from one network segment and retransmits them on the other segments. It never thinks about packet formats or network protocols.

Although the hub can be a potential point of failure within the network configuration, a hub is a simple device and doesn't usually fail on its own. If you're thinking of using hubs to extend the distance your network wires span, be sure to consider the history of power outages in your area. Hubs don't have built-in power failure features, such as battery backup. They're simple, inexpensive, and they do the job — but they don't have a lot of advanced options.

Keep large animals away from your network wiring! Although hubs are durable and reliable network devices, if your pet elephant steps on one, it breaks. Our cats enjoy chewing our cables. If you have a hub under your desk, try not to kick it too often.

A switch in time saves intranet hassles

A *switch* is a network device that extends a LAN by linking multiple network segments. Gee, that sounds like a hub, doesn't it? Well, the two do share similarities but many differences as well, such as the following:

✔ A switch increases the available network bandwidth by connecting network segments together only when a packet needs to pass between them.

✔ A switch makes connection decisions based on address information inside the packet. The address information is either a NIC's hardware address (from Layer 2, the data link layer) or a numeric IP address (from Layer 3, the network layer). Flip to Chapter 5 for a discussion of TCP/IP's layers.

✔ A packet may pass through several switches on its journey from the sending computer to the receiving. Each switch must make its own connection decision because switches don't talk among themselves.

✔ Switches normally live in wiring closets and computer rooms rather than under desks.

Rowter or Rooter? Doesn't Matter

Routers connect networks. Routers range from someone's desktop PC running Internet sharing software to multimillion dollar systems of specialized hardware and software. In the original work on TCP/TP, the designers wanted to be able to move data across a network even if parts of the network became disrupted. For example, if a network link were taken out by enemy attack, the traffic on that link would automatically be rerouted to a different link. This reliable scheme is call *dynamic rerouting.* Your system doesn't have to be a victim of an enemy attack for dynamic rerouting to be valuable. If a forklift cuts a cable in a warehouse, for example, dynamic rerouting means that inventory data can still be sent across a network via a different route.

According to *Webster's,* a *router* (pronounced "rowter") is a woodworking tool. A *router* (pronounced "rooter") is a sports fan with a bet on the big game; it's also a horse that's trained for distance races. In network parlance, however, you can pronounce it any way you want, so pick a side and join the battle. People pronounce it both ways and some are willing to fight for their choice. We prefer to remain nootral.

A router extends a LAN by linking two or more network segments that may or may not use the same media type. The router permits each connected network to maintain its independent identity and address. Figure 16-3 shows a small intranet consisting of two subnets. The router connects the subnets and connects the entire intranet to the Internet.

When someone at address 130.103.2.1 sends e-mail to 130.103.2.4, the router is smart enough to see that the message is staying on the same subnet. There is no need to investigate any routes to the other subnet or to the Internet. When 130.103.2.1 sends e-mail to 130.103.1.4, however, the router forwards the message to the other subnet. When someone from anywhere within the intranet sends a message outside the 130.103 intranet, the router forwards the message out to the Internet.

What makes routers special is that they're intelligent enough to understand IP addresses. In fact, the decisions the router makes about directing the packets of your data are based on the network portion of the IP address. A router contains a network interface card for each segment of the network that it connects. Each network interface card has a different IP address because the router itself is a member of each network. The router gets most of its intelligence from routing tables. *Routing tables* are stored on the router and contain information about the following:

- Paths (routes) to particular networks
- How to handle special kinds of traffic
- Priorities for certain connections

On big fancy routers, routing tables also store statistics on which routes are fastest and shortest.

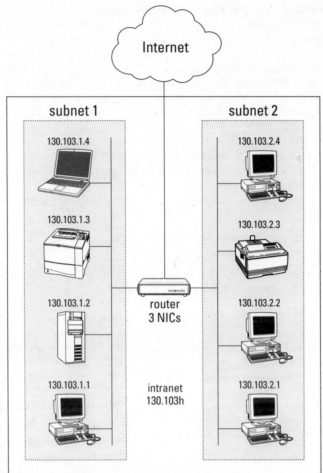

Internet

subnet 1

130.103.1.4

130.103.1.3

130.103.1.2

130.103.1.1

router
3 NICs

intranet
130.103h

subnet 2

130.103.2.4

130.103.2.3

130.103.2.2

130.103.2.1

Figure 16-3:
This router
connects
the subnets
to each
other and
the intranet
to the
Internet.

Understanding how routers work

Routers work at the internet, data link, and physical layers of the TCP/IP structure. A router resembles an octopus whose tentacles represent all of your cabling types. Routers are aware of the multiple paths that your data packets can take across the network to their final destination. The router knows about other routers on the network and can choose the most efficient path for the data to follow. This efficient path may change as network devices change and as traffic comes and goes.

For example, on Monday, the most efficient path may be from network A to network C to network B. On Tuesday, however, the most efficient path may be from network A to network D to network B because network C is broken. Because the router knows about any problems on the network path, it can detour your data when necessary. Not only are routers intelligent, they talk to each other and share knowledge, especially traffic reports: "Route A is jammed right now. Take route B instead. Route C has disappeared."

Routers use a routing protocol to find out information about the entire network and to determine the optimal path for sending a packet on to its destination. What's optimal? Is it the shortest path (fewest hops from one host to another)? Or the fastest path (more hops on speedier links)? Or the least congested path?

Suppose you want to go from Boston to New York City (NYC) to visit the Empire State Building. Your top three choices are probably these:

- ✔ Drive to NYC on Interstate 95 and use a city map to find the Empire State Building.

- ✔ Drive to Boston's Logan Airport. Fly to JFK Airport in NYC. Take a taxi to the Empire State Building.

- ✔ Drive to Boston's South Station. Take a train to Penn Station in NYC. Take the subway to the Empire State Building.

Which way do you think will get you there fastest? If you've never driven to Logan Airport during rush hour and through construction, you would guess that flying from Logan to JFK is the fastest route. However, depending on city traffic, flying may actually be the slowest way. (Trust us on this — we've had the experience to prove it over and over again.)

The shortest way isn't always the fastest way. Nor is the most direct route always the fastest way. And if you never go to New York City even once in your life, these facts are rules to live by on the network as well.

Switching to packet switching

Routers use *packet switching* to move messages from one place to another on a network. You already know that messages are divided into packets before they move out onto a network. During transmission, each packet is independent of the others. In fact, each packet in a message could take a different route to the destination. That's packet switching; the point is that all the packets in a message get to the destination, not how they get there.

Choosing a Router

Depending on the number of machines and networks you need to connect, you may not need special purpose hardware to be your router.

> ✔ **A router for a Small Office/Home Office:** If several networked computers share a connection to the Internet via cable or DSL, you can use the computer attached to the network device as your router. You need to add some kind of Internet sharing software to this computer. Microsoft's ICS (Internet Connection Sharing) is one example of Internet sharing software. Software packages are available for other operating systems as well. The routing software checks to see whether packets should stay on the local net or go out to the Internet. Because the routing software doesn't work too hard, it doesn't disturb other programs that are running on the computer.

> Be sure to protect your Internet connection with a firewall. See Chapter 18.

> ✔ **For larger companies:** Routers that do more than route: Companies that connect their subnets to the Internet need a more powerful, more intelligent router than a SOHO with a dozen computers. A special purpose router is the solution. A combination router/firewall is a good solution.

> ✔ **Really big routers for really big networks:** These are the routers that connect the networks of large worldwide corporations. Routers this large and complex handle millions of packets per second and cost millions of U.S. dollars. They form the backbone of the Internet itself.

Configuring a Router on Windows NT Server

While most routers are dedicated hardware devices running specialized software, you can use a general-purpose computer to perform the same function if you don't require complex routing. The computer must have two or more NICs and must be connected to two or more network segments. The TCP/IP implementation must include routing capabilities. Figures 16-4 and 16-5 show a Windows NT system that's in the process of being configured as a router. Notice that one NIC has already been installed and a second NIC is in the process of being installed.

Here's what you do:

1. **From the Start menu, choose Settings⇨Control Panel.**

2. **Click the Network icon.**

   This brings up the Network dialog box, shown in Figure 16-4.

3. **In the Network dialog box, click the Adapters tab to configure the NIC.**

4. **Click the Add button.**

   A list of Network Adapters appears in the Select Network Adapter dialog box.

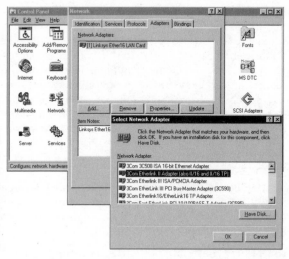

Figure 16-4:
Configure
your NICs
before
enabling
routing.

5. **Select your NIC from the list displayed, and then click OK.**

   If your NIC isn't on the list, you need a disk with the software driver for that NIC.

To configure a NIC for TCP/IP, follow these steps (which you need to do for each NIC installed in your router):

1. **After configuring your NIC, click the Protocols tab in the Network dialog box.**

2. **Click TCP/IP to open the Microsoft TCP/IP Properties dialog box.**

3. **Click the IP Address tab.**

4. **In the Adapter drop-down menu, fill in the address numbers, as shown in Figure 16-5 (on the left).**

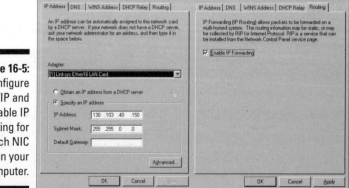

Figure 16-5:
Configure
TCP/IP and
enable IP
routing for
each NIC
in your
computer.

5. **Click the Routing tab, and then check the Enable IP Forwarding check box.**

   You're done!

Getting Started with Routing Protocols

When you buy a router, your purchase includes proprietary software that functions as a mini-operating system, which the network manager — probably you — must install and configure. The router also includes an installation guide. If you have to configure router software yourself, be sure to follow the instructions. Some routers load their "operating system" software from a server on the network via the BOOTP or TFTP protocols that we describe in Chapter 5.

When you configure the router, you also need to select the appropriate routing protocol(s); these protocols, too, come with the router. There are several, but the most prevalent routing protocols are as follows:

- **RIP (Routing Information Protocol):** RIP was developed by Xerox, which was way ahead of its time as a computer company — so ahead of its time, in fact, that it didn't catch on as a computer company. But the legacy of Xerox lives on in networking, especially in Ethernet. RIP has been part of UNIX TCP/IP since the beginning and is a part of every TCP/IP product on the market today. RFC 2453, "RIP Version 2" (also known as STD 56), specifies this standard protocol.

  Are you getting the point that RIP is old? Some people think it's old as in Old Reliable. Some people think it's old as in Rest In Peace. Although RIP is intelligent and routes your packets to their destinations just fine, it's a slow learner when it comes to network changes, such as the appearance of new routers and faster paths. RIP is one of the Interior Gateway Protocols, which means that, if it's in use at all, RIP is used within an organization and not on the wider Internet.

- **OSPF (Open Shortest Path First):** The "open" in OSPF isn't a verb; in this case, it's open as in open systems (see Chapter 1). OSPF is a descendant of and supersedes older protocols such as IS-IS (Intermediate System to Intermediate System). OSPF is built on the concept of *designated routers* — that is, all routers are created equal, but some get elected to positions of importance. OSPF is the most common Interior Gateway Protocol. RFC 2328 (STD 54) describes OSPF.

- **BGP (Border Gateway Protocol):** BGP is the protocol that the Internet's routers use to exchange routing table information. Because it is used between organizations, BGP is an Exterior Gateway Protocol — in fact, it replaced a protocol with that name.

✓ **CIDR (Classless Inter-Domain Routing):** CIDR is the key technology that has kept the world from running out of IP addresses, and it helps routers do their job as efficiently as possible. (Check out Chapter 7 for the essential information.) These days, every ISP uses CIDR. Because it isn't exactly a protocol itself, CIDR works with OSPF (for intranets) and with BGP (for the Internet).

Hungry for all the gory details of CIDR and the conservation of IP addresses? Check out RFC 2050, "Internet Registry IP Allocation Guidelines." It's also known as BCP (Best Current Practice) 12.

The CD-ROM that comes with this book contains all the RFCs that were available as of this writing.

Gateways: The Ultimate Interpreters

When the wine list is all French, most people need a knowledgeable *maître d'* or a *sommelier* to help out. Similarly, to do translations on the network, you need a gateway. *Gateways* work at all the TCP/IP layers, from the bottom physical layer right up to the top application layer, to move data across networks of any type. They translate and repackage information from one application to another — even from one protocol to another.

We describe the SMTP gateway, which sends and receives mail between non-SMTP sources and destinations, in Chapter 11. When a gateway does a translation, it looks at the addressing and routing information, as well as at the data being sent, and converts it all into the format of the protocols and data on the receiving network.

Because of all the translation involved, a gateway has more work to do than the other network devices in this chapter. You can go down to a computer store and buy a hub and then go home or to work and clamp it on your cables and put it right to work. A gateway, on the other hand, is usually a computer with two or more network interface cards, one for each different network being connected. And like most computers, a gateway has to be configured with an operating system and network protocols before you can put it to work.

A common gateway myth

Many people assume that a gateway extends the size of a network. Actually, a gateway extends the connectivity of the network by overcoming cultural and packet format differences between connected networks, including differences in protocols.

The Party's Over — It's Decision Time

To help you decide which network device(s) to use, we give you Table 16-2, in which we've summarized the capabilities and features of the network devices that we describe in this chapter.

Table 16-2	Comparing Network Devices			
	Hub	*Switch*	*Router*	*Gateway*
Intelligence	None	Moderate	High	Genius
Relative cost	Very low	Medium	High	Very high
Configuration	Simple	Average	High	High complexity
Network model layer	Physical	Physical, data link, internet	Physical, data link, internet	All
Addresses understood	N/A	Hardware, IP	Hardware, IP	Hardware, IP

Don't blindly add devices to the network without doing any planning. Suppose you decide that all you need is a hub. Before you write the check, consider whether that hub will still meet your needs in a month, in six months, or in a year. If your network is growing, in just a few months you may need to divide it with a switch or router. In that case, even though all you need today is a hub, you probably should go ahead and purchase a more complex device that will still work for you later.

Chapter 17

Troubleshooting Connectivity Problems Step by Step

*P*ing — pang — pung. Today we ping, yesterday we pang, and many times we have pung. In this chapter, we describe the most commonly used tools for basic troubleshooting and walk you through a troubleshooting exercise step by step. Depending on what operating system you run, you may be able to use additional tools for these information-gathering tasks. Microsoft Windows NT and 2000, for example, include the tools arp, finger, and ping, in addition to supplying a graphical monitor that tracks processes, such as daemons, and displays dozens of network utilization statistics. Other vendors, as well, support most of the basic lookup-style tools along with their own additions and extensions.

Getting Started with ping

The ping command, which we introduce in Chapter 8, is the first troubleshooting command most network administrators use when investigating network problems. ping lets you find out whether a remote computer is available by using the network "sonar" — the Internet Control Message Protocol (ICMP). ping bounces a message off a computer; if a reply comes back, the computer is alive — but not necessarily well.

The ping command only tests connectivity to a host's NIC. It doesn't test whether the operating system, the TCP/IP configuration, or services are working.

The ping command tells you whether a host is alive or dead. It also gives you a hint about network congestion and slow performance. When troubleshooting with ping, you may need to ping more than just one host. If ping doesn't return a response from the host that you're trying to contact, it doesn't necessarily mean that the host isn't available. Maybe it's the gateway or a DNS server that's not available. If either of them is down, the remote host may be fine, but there may be no way to get to it. You can ping to check the availability of a specific computer or of a domain. You can ping by name or IP address.

See Figure 17-1 where ping contacts an IPv4 domain. The time is the response time from the remote host. Hosts that are close to you should have faster response times than hosts farther away, unless there is network congestion on the route to the nearby host. If you suspect this type of congestion, run the traceroute command (which we describe in the next section) after ping. ping also displays summary statistics about packets sent, packets lost, and how long the ping round trip took. If you're using a Microsoft Windows system, you need the command prompt to type **ping**.

Figure 17-1:
Reach out and touch someone with ping.

```
Command Prompt
C:\Documents and Settings\Wiley>ping bbc.com

Pinging bbc.com [212.58.240.32] with 32 bytes of data:

Reply from 212.58.240.32: bytes=32 time=55ms TTL=242
Reply from 212.58.240.32: bytes=32 time=55ms TTL=242
Reply from 212.58.240.32: bytes=32 time=54ms TTL=242
Reply from 212.58.240.32: bytes=32 time=54ms TTL=242

Ping statistics for 212.58.240.32:
    Packets: Sent = 4, Received = 4, Lost = 0 (0% loss),
Approximate round trip times in milli-seconds:
    Minimum = 54ms, Maximum = 55ms, Average = 54ms

C:\Documents and Settings\Wiley>
```

Figure 17-2 shows pinging on an IPv6 network. This time we use the IPv6 address instead of the host name.

Figure 17-2:
Notice how long the IP addresses are.

```
% ping 5F00:2100:1024:9000:2490:800:2B37:7802
PING (5F00:2100:1024:9000:2490:800:2B37:7802): 56 data bytes
64 bytes from 5F00:2100:1024:9000:2490:800:2B37:7802: icmp6_seq=0 hlim=64 time=0 ms
64 bytes from 5F00:2100:1024:9000:2490:800:2B37:7802: icmp6_seq=1 hlim=64 time=0 ms
64 bytes from 5F00:2100:1024:9000:2490:800:2B37:7802: icmp6_seq=2 hlim=64 time=0 ms
5F00:2100:1024:9000:2490:800:2B37:7802 PING Statistics----
3 packets transmitted, 3 packets received, 0% packet loss
round-trip (ms)  min/avg/max = 0/0/0 ms
```

Did you notice that the IPv4 version of ping has TTL information, while the IPv6 version uses hlim instead? *TTL* means "time to live" — how long this packet should be allowed to survive before being discarded. TTL is measured not in time, but in hops from computer to computer across the network. *Hlim* means hop limit. Although hlim means about the same thing as TTL, it's a more accurate term.

Chasing Network Problems Step by Step

Imagine that you've tried to use a service on a remote host, maybe telnet or ftp or you're trying to browse a Web site, but you can't get there. There may be a dozen reasons why you can't do what you need to. A remote host may be unavailable because

- ✔ Your computer isn't properly configured for networking.
- ✔ The remote host is dead; that is, shut down, hung, doesn't exist any more.
- ✔ The network connection (yours or the remote host's) is dead, either by hardware or software.
- ✔ The network is so congested that it takes too long to get there. Requests time out.
- ✔ The system or network administrator has refused to allow you to get there.

Follow these steps to diagnose network problems:

1. **Check your local network configuration.**
2. **Check your hardware.**
3. **Check your gateway.**
4. **Check DNS on both sides (yours and the remote's).**
5. **Check for Internet problems.**

The following sections walk you through a network troubleshooting process so that you can find exactly where a problem exists. Naturally we start with `ping`.

pinging yourself and others

Follow the same steps whether you're on an IPv4 or IPv6 network. The figures in this section use IPv4.

1. **Use ping to test end-to-end connectivity between your local host and the remote destination. Refer to Figure 17-2 for an example.**

   A successful ping means that you can get to the remote host, but there must be a problem there with the network service you're trying to use. Go to Step 2 if the ping fails.

   If you cannot successfully ping a host, the host may actually be okay. Many firewalls ban requests from the ICMP protocol and the TCP/IP ports that ping uses.

2. **ping localhost as shown in Figure 17-3 to prove that your hosts file is available.**

   If this ping fails, TCP/IP may not be able to resolve names into addresses.

3. **If Step 2 works, ping your own IP address.**

   Don't know your IP address? Run ipconfig /all or winipcfg (Windows 95/ 98/Me only) to find out. See Figure 17-3.

4. **ping your host name (not the whole FQDN) to be sure that your resolver (see Chapter 10) understands how to expand your host name into an FQDN.**

   If this step fails, you may have trouble with DNS lookups. If this step succeeds, you know that your resolver is working properly. Continue to the next step.

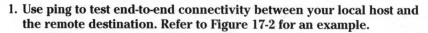

Figure 17-3:
ping
yourself.
Use ipconfig
to find out
who you
are.

```
Command Prompt                                                    _ |8| X

C:\Documents and Settings\Wiley>ping localhost

Pinging flyingpenguin.cardinalconsulting.com [127.0.0.1] with 32 bytes of data:

Reply from 127.0.0.1: bytes=32 time<1ms TTL=128
Reply from 127.0.0.1: bytes=32 time<1ms TTL=128
Reply from 127.0.0.1: bytes=32 time<1ms TTL=128
Reply from 127.0.0.1: bytes=32 time<1ms TTL=128

Ping statistics for 127.0.0.1:
    Packets: Sent = 4, Received = 4, Lost = 0 (0% loss),
Approximate round trip times in milli-seconds:
    Minimum = 0ms, Maximum = 0ms, Average = 0ms

C:\Documents and Settings\Wiley>ipconfig /all

Windows IP Configuration

        Host Name . . . . . . . . . . . . : flyingpenguin
        Primary Dns Suffix  . . . . . . . : cardinalconsulting.com
        Node Type . . . . . . . . . . . . : Unknown
        IP Routing Enabled. . . . . . . . : No
        WINS Proxy Enabled. . . . . . . . : No
        DNS Suffix Search List. . . . . . : cardinalconsulting.com

Ethernet adapter Local Area Connection:

        Connection-specific DNS Suffix  . :
        Description . . . . . . . . . . . : 3Com EtherLink III LAN PC Card (3C58
9D) (Ethernet)
        Physical Address. . . . . . . . . : 00-60-08-F5-27-09
        Dhcp Enabled. . . . . . . . . . . : Yes
        Autoconfiguration Enabled . . . . : Yes
        IP Address. . . . . . . . . . . . : 192.168.0.2
        Subnet Mask . . . . . . . . . . . : 255.255.255.0
        Default Gateway . . . . . . . . . : 192.168.0.1
        DHCP Server . . . . . . . . . . . : 192.168.0.1
        DNS Servers . . . . . . . . . . . : 192.168.0.1
        Lease Obtained. . . . . . . . . . : Sunday, August 25, 2002 3:22:22 PM
        Lease Expires . . . . . . . . . . : Monday, August 26, 2002 3:22:22 PM

C:\Documents and Settings\Wiley>ping 192.168.0.2

Pinging 192.168.0.2 with 32 bytes of data:

Reply from 192.168.0.2: bytes=32 time<1ms TTL=128
Reply from 192.168.0.2: bytes=32 time<1ms TTL=128
Reply from 192.168.0.2: bytes=32 time<1ms TTL=128
Reply from 192.168.0.2: bytes=32 time<1ms TTL=128

Ping statistics for 192.168.0.2:
    Packets: Sent = 4, Received = 4, Lost = 0 (0% loss),
Approximate round trip times in milli-seconds:
    Minimum = 0ms, Maximum = 0ms, Average = 0ms

C:\Documents and Settings\Wiley>_
```

5. **ping your FQDN to be sure that your DNS client is working.**

   At this point, you have proven that your computer is not the problem.

6. **ping your gateway to be sure that packets can leave your LAN.**

   Don't know where your gateway is? Use ipconfig or winipcfg to find out. (Refer to Figure 17-3.)

7. **If the gateway ping (Figure 17-4) doesn't work, check all your cables or other connection media (you might be on a wireless LAN but you still have connection media).**

   If a cable is loose or disconnected, the packets can't reach the gateway. Go back to Step 6.

8. **If your gateway ping is okay, ping the destination by IP address. Substitute the destination address for the address shown in Figure 17-3.**

   pinging by IP address bypasses the DNS. Although you know that DNS name resolution works on your local host, you need this step for two reasons. First, either the name and/or address of the remote destination may be missing or incorrect on the DNS server. Second, the DNS server might not be reachable.

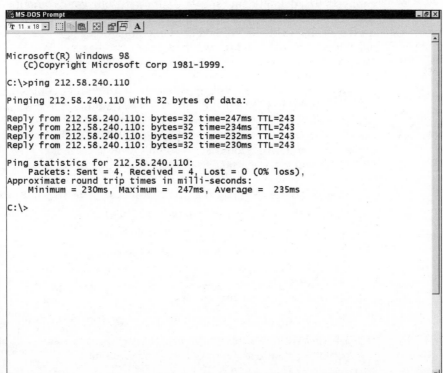

Figure 17-4: ping the gateway and the IP address.

Later, in Step 11, if nslookup displays a different address, redo this step using with that address.

9. **Try to reach the DNS server(s) by pinging the DNS server(s). (You can use ipconfig /all to find your DNS servers' IP addresses, too.)**

If the ping fails, either your DHCP server is giving you bad information or you've configured DNS manually on your client and made a mistake. For example, when you listed the DNS servers (refer to Figure 17-3), maybe you typed a number wrong. If your DNS server is sending wrong information, you need to contact the administrator. If you're the server administrator, now you know you've made a mistake. Go fix those IP addresses now!

If the ping in Step 9 works, you know that the DNS server is reachable, but you don't know whether it's working *properly*. Move on to Step 10.

10. **Switch to the nslookup program (see the following section) to see whether the DNS service is running on the remote server.**

Using nslookup to query a name server

When you start nslookup (ns for name server, lookup for, well, lookup), it connects to a default name server — the same one your computer normally uses for DNS queries. You can explicitly switch to another server anytime you need to by using the server and lserver commands. Figure 17-4 shows how to use the server command to switch to your DNS server — remember to use ipconfig if you don't know the address of your DNS server.

Be careful as you enter nslookup commands. Any typographical error is treated as a request for DNS information. For example, if you want to set a timeout value, but you type **sit timeout=5** instead of **set timeout=5**, nslookup asks the name server to find a computer named sit. If a computer named sit exists, you get information that you didn't want. If there is no computer named sit, you get a message to that effect — still not what you want.

11. **Run nslookup to verify that the IP address from Step 8 is correct.**

Figure 17-5 shows an nslookup query. If nslookup shows a different address, retry Step 8 with this new address.

12. **If you know for a fact (you've talked to the people at the remote host) that nslookup gave you the wrong IP address, add an entry to your local hosts file to override the DNS information. If you're in charge of the DNS server, fix the database.**

At this point, you can be sure the problem's on the Internet.

13. **Use traceroute or tracert (in the next section) to figure out how far a packet gets before running into the problem.**

```
tsg11 - SecureCRT
# nslookup
Default Server:  wtf-ns1.lotus.com
Address:  9.33.10.20

> set type=any
>
> bbc.co.uk
Server:  wtf-ns1.lotus.com
Address:  9.33.10.20

Non-authoritative answer:
bbc.co.uk
        origin = ns.bbc.co.uk
        mail address = hostmaster.bbc.co.uk
        serial = 200206280
        refresh = 1800 (30M)
        retry  = 1800 (30M)
        expire = 86400 (1D)
        minimum ttl = 1800 (30M)
bbc.co.uk           nameserver = ns1.thdo.bbc.co.uk
bbc.co.uk           nameserver = ns1.thny.bbc.co.uk
bbc.co.uk           nameserver = ns.bbc.co.uk
bbc.co.uk           nameserver = ns1.bbc.co.uk
bbc.co.uk           nameserver = ns.reith.bbc.co.uk

Authoritative answers can be found from:
bbc.co.uk           nameserver = ns1.thdo.bbc.co.uk
bbc.co.uk           nameserver = ns1.thny.bbc.co.uk
bbc.co.uk           nameserver = ns.bbc.co.uk
bbc.co.uk           nameserver = ns1.bbc.co.uk
bbc.co.uk           nameserver = ns.reith.bbc.co.uk
ns1.thdo.bbc.co.uk      internet address = 212.58.224.21
ns1.thny.bbc.co.uk      internet address = 38.160.150.21
ns.bbc.co.uk    internet address = 132.185.132.21
>
```

Figure 17-5: For inquiring minds: "set type=any" returns all available information.

```
Start    8:22 - AT&T Net Client   tsg11 - SecureCRT   100%         8:26 AM
```

Using traceroute to find network problems

Traceroute is a program that helps you identify where problems exist on a network. Traceroute displays both the route that packets follow on their way to a destination and the time in milliseconds for each round-trip hop. Each place a packet goes through is a *hop*. Traceroute tests each hop along the way three times and displays the minimum, average, and maximum time for a round trip in milliseconds.

Figure 17-6 shows a successful traceroute. Notice that traceroute tries to show both the name and the IP address of the router. When traceroute goes out onto the Internet, the router is a fully qualified domain name. The tricky bit about analyzing traceroute output is to know what a slow response time is. For example, 220 milliseconds is a long time between Boston and New York, but it is normal between Ottawa and Tokyo. Hops between local links should be no more than a few milliseconds.

14. **Run traceroute (Figure 17-6) to see whether packets make it to the destination.**

    If the traceroute is successful, the problem is with the service on the remote computer. Perhaps the service is stopped or hung or simply misconfigured.

Most operating systems spell the command traceroute. When using a Microsoft Windows operating system, you spell the command tracert , as shown in Figure 17-6.

If a trace ends with timeouts and never gets to the destination, you've found the host or network connection that's the obstacle.

15. **If you're running traceroute on a private intranet, you should let the administrator know where the problem is. If the problem is on the Internet, you can either contact the administrator where traceroute identified a blockage, or you can wait for it to be fixed.**

Of course, if you've read this far, you probably are the administrator of the intranet. Aren't you relieved to know where to look on your network to solve the problem?

Figure 17-6: Traceroute helps you find slowdowns in your packet's path.

There's one exception to this step. A timeout line (like the one following) usually means that the firewall at the destination is blocking ICMP requests. In other words, you've gotten to the destination's firewall, and the firewall won't let the trace in. You can't find out anything else from here without contacting the system or network administrator at the last point in the trace.

```
16   *   *   *    Request timed out.
```

Don't add all the times to find the total time to the traceroute destination. The time for the last hop is actually the total round-trip time.

Using ps to Diagnose Network Services

The ps command on Mac OS X and Linux/UNIX shows process information, including the network daemons that implement TCP/IP services. For example, when you disable the rwho daemon, use ps to prove that it's no longer running. Figure 17-7 shows ps output from a host with lots of network processes. If someone who's followed the troubleshooting steps in this chapter calls to tell you that you have a problem with a network service, ps is where you start. Use ps to see whether the problem service is running. Look in the far right COMMAND column for the service.

You can identify network services by looking for the name of the service followed by the letter "d" for daemon. For example, in Figure 17-7, you can see telnet running. This is not the network service. This is someone running the telnet application. Look a little farther down the ps output and you see telnetd. That's the telnet service. Another clue for distinguishing a service from an application comes in the first column, labeled USER. Services run under the privileged username, root (the administrative user). Applications run under a username such as "sylvan" or "ellend".

You can use the ps command to check services on remote computers if you have access rights. Use your favorite remote access application, such as telnet, rlogin, or rsh, to log on and then run ps on the remote system.

```
$ ps auwx                                                          Neat! The
USER      PID %CPU %MEM   VSZ  RSS TT  STAT STARTED  TIME COMMAND   rwho
leiden  20113  3.0  0.0   348  172 p3  R+   3:06PM   0:00.04 ps auwx daemon is
root       65  0.0  0.0  1160  992 ??  Ss   Thu12PM  1:31.58 named   running.
root       68  0.0  0.0    52  108 ??  Ss   Thu12PM  0:08.83 rwhod ───┘
root       70  0.0  0.0    60  108 ??  Is   Thu12PM  0:00.09 portmap
root       76  0.0  0.0    56   16 ??  S    Thu12PM  5:13.29 nfsiod 4  Users
root       77  0.0  0.0    56   16 ??  I    Thu12PM  1:47.96 nfsiod 4  might
root       78  0.0  0.0    56   16 ??  I    Thu12PM  0:48.53 nfsiod 4  come in
root       79  0.0  0.0    56   16 ??  I    Thu12PM  0:20.84 nfsiod 4  via
root       80  0.0  0.0   444  132 ??  Ss   Thu12PM  0:39.04 sendmail: rlogin.
accepting connections (sendmail)
root       83  0.0  0.0    76  100 ??  Ss   Thu12PM  0:17.39 inetd        /
root    22947  0.0  0.0    96   72 ??  I    10:28PM  0:00.48 rlogind
patt    22948  0.0  0.0   468   76 p1  Is+  10:28PM  0:00.53 -bash (bash)
WiseGuy 27152  0.0  0.0   312   72 r6  I+   12:36AM  0:01.55 ncftp ───Looks
root     5542  0.0  0.0    96   88 ??  I    8:26AM   0:23.60 rlogind   like a
sylvan   6137  0.0  0.0   148  112 r0  I+   8:36AM   0:30.77 telnet    version
netcom.com                                                            of ftp.
anmary   6792  0.0  0.0   568  476 p6  S+   8:52AM   0:35.11 irc (irc-2.6)
root     7004  0.0  0.0    84   88 ??  S    8:58AM   0:38.18 rlogind
root    15491  0.0  0.0   120  172 ??  I    1:00PM   0:00.35 telnetd
Bryant  16380  0.0  0.0   452  480 p2  S+   1:23PM   0:21.04 irc (irc-2.6)
root    16444  0.0  0.0    84  196 ??  S    1:26PM   0:15.52 rlogind
ellend  16534  0.0  0.0   156  260 q0  S+   1:29PM   0:07.03 telnet
realms.dorsai.org 1501      They're both using IRC to chat, but probably not to each other. ─┘
root    16936  0.0  0.0   120  200 ??  I    1:41PM   0:03.15 telnetd
shepherd 17449 0.0  0.0  2940  372 qc  I+   1:53PM   0:18.34 tin
ellend  17573  0.0  0.0   156  260 q0  T    1:56PM   0:00.47 telnet main.com
4444                                                                   |
root    17891  0.0  0.0    28  196 ??  S    2:05PM   0:00.46 comsat      |
deepwatr 18126 0.0  0.0  5408  592 s3  I+   2:11PM   1:08.44 trn      Someone's
root    18127  0.0  0.0    96  216 ??  I    2:12PM   0:04.62 rlogind  using
shift   18943  0.0  0.0   276  372 p7  S+   2:34PM   0:02.70 ftp      telnet.
rdf     19827  0.0  0.0   152  260 s8  I+   2:58PM   0:00.13 mail
batsoid@xx.netcom.com
root    19833  0.0  0.0   484  168 ??  I    2:58PM   0:00.06 sendmail:
server relay3.UU,NET cmd read (sendmail)
whitehed 20008 0.0  0.0   224  556 ??  S    3:03PM   0:00.40 ftpd:    Someone's
dip27n8.drc.com: whitehd: RETR pgp262.zip\r\n (ftpd)                  getting a file
root    20033  0.0  0.0    28  232 ??  S    3:03PM   0:00.07 ntalkd   via FTP.
mlspeake 20060 0.0  0.0   440  356 pf  I+   3:04PM   0:00.42 gopher ──┘
```

Figure 17-7:
With ps, you find that this computer has several TCP/IP services running.

Chapter 18

Protecting and Monitoring Network Security

*B*eing connected to a network, especially the Internet, comes with some security risks. Is it worth it? For most people and organizations, the answer is yes, but a few important precautions are usually necessary.

This whole chapter is about security, but you won't be seeing any other security icons after this one. We suggest you use the extra free space in the margins to jot down reminders to check the security of your computers.

Before you even think about securing network protocols and services, you must secure the computers on the network. As classic wisdom says, "A chain is only as strong as its weakest link." Often a single computer and/or its user is the weakest link.

This chapter contains information that is valuable for everyone from end user to security administrator. However, the bulk of the chapter is intended for system, network, and security administrators. Chapter 19 is full of tips for securing popular applications. Chapter 20 gets into more advanced security topics, such as using encryption and authentication to secure a network.

The *TCP/IP For Dummies,* 5th Edition, CD-ROM contains lots of useful security information and software, including

- ✔ "The CERT Coordination Center FAQ" from the CERT Coordination Center
- ✔ "Is There an Intruder in My Computer?" by Larry Rogers, CERT Coordination Center

To find out more about specific security problems and solutions, we recommend visiting the Web site for the U.S. Department of Energy Computer Incident Advisory Capability (CIAC) at `www.ciac.org/ciac`. You can read all about security problems. While at CIAC, you can also find out about Internet hoaxes — as if real computer viruses aren't enough to worry about. Nowadays, some strange people think it's funny to circulate warnings about viruses that don't even exist.

Looking Back at Early Security

Twenty years ago, the precursor of the Internet was the U.S. Department of Defense ARPANET. ARPANET security depended on the physical isolation of the network and the fact that the hosts and users were trustworthy. IP didn't have much in the way of built-in security. Back then, the concepts of encryption, authentication, and secure transactions were totally alien. As the network grew into the Internet, minimal security features were bolted onto TCP/IP. The world isn't such a friendly place now, and most sites need more than those early minimal security features.

Today's technology can't guarantee that your network and all the hosts and devices on it will be 100 percent secure all the time. Even if the technology were available, adding users always adds vulnerability. If you want a 100 percent guarantee, turn off your computer, remove all the cables, and bury your computer on the Moon. Short of burying your computer on the Moon, this chapter gives you basic, practical tips for protecting your network, its computers, and the files on hard disks. Chapter 19 helps you protect the application data you send and receive across networks.

What's Involved in Network Security?

Network security involves everything:

- ✔ **Hardware:** The computers and other devices on the network.
- ✔ **Operating systems:** The security features, such as user accounts and passwords.

✔ **Software:** The applications themselves.

✔ **File systems:** The mechanisms for protecting directories and files.

✔ **Network design:** The whole kit and caboodle.

✔ **Organizational policies and procedures:** Codes of conduct for acceptable uses of the computers and the network, and consequences for actions that jeopardize security.

✔ **Training and education:** Teaching the users what you expect of them and the right way to do things.

✔ **Rules and regulations:** This includes punishments for breaking the rules.

✔ **Physical security:** This includes locks on computer room doors and security cables for laptops.

Everyone involved in setting up security must consider a variety of questions. What are you protecting and from whom? Are the regular users on your network a greater threat than outsiders trying to break in? How much are you willing to pay, and for how much protection? How much inconvenience will legitimate users tolerate?

The following RFCs may be helpful to you:

✔ RFC 3365, "Strong Security Requirements for Internet Engineering Task Force Standard Protocols" (also known as BCP 61), describes the IETF's position that the standard protocols must provide the best and most appropriate security possible.

✔ RFC 2196, "Site Security Handbook" (also known as FYI 8), contains good information to help your organization establish security policies and about the security risks of connecting to the Internet.

✔ RFC 2828, "Internet Security Glossary" (also known as FYI 36), is the place to go when you need definitions of security terms.

✔ RFC 2350, "Expectations for Computer Security Incident Response" (also known as BCP 21), describes what to expect if you report a problem to a Computer Security Incident Response Team (CSIRT) and what to provide if you're creating a team for your users.

✔ RFC 2504, "Users' Security Handbook" (FYI 34), works with the Site Security Handbook (RFC 2196) to show network users and administrators how to keep their systems and networks secure.

✔ RFC 2179, "Network Security for Trade Shows," provides a list of things to watch out for if you host or just participate in a trade show that provides a network, especially if that network is connected to the Internet.

The CD that comes with this book contains all the RFCs available at the time of publication.

Who's responsible for network security?

Everyone is responsible for network security:

- ✔ Users, who must not reveal their passwords
- ✔ System administrators, who configure and monitor the services
- ✔ Network administrators, who manage the network connections
- ✔ Organization management, which establishes policies and procedures regarding unacceptable behavior as well as punishments for breaking the rules (We could tell you what these are, but then we'd have to kill you!)
- ✔ Information management security staff, who enforce everything

Don't practice *security by obscurity;* that is, don't assume that users are stupid. Some users are smarter than your assumptions; others make the most amazing mistakes.

Here's an example: Leo configures his organization's Anonymous FTP server so that it is publicly writeable and assumes that no one will find out simply because he doesn't announce the change. Leo is attempting to practice security by obscurity.

What's the worst that can happen?

There are seven major kinds of security attacks to worry about:

- ✔ **Theft:** Scoundrels break onto networks or into hosts to steal computing resources and/or information.
- ✔ **Spoof:** Scoundrels pretend to be other people without permission in order to send fake e-mail or use someone else's access rights, or they make a host assume the identity of another host to get users to the wrong machine. For example, it's very easy to use telnet to spoof e-mail.
- ✔ **Denial of service:** Scoundrels send so much traffic to hosts that authorized users can't perform normal activities because the hosts are too busy or insufficient network bandwidth remains.
- ✔ **Replaying:** Scoundrels record and repeat legitimate network traffic that should have happened only once.
- ✔ **Password cracking:** Scoundrels break into authorized users' accounts by systematically guessing their passwords. Another technique is to use a sniffer to capture plain text passwords as they float across the Internet.

✔ **Break encryption:** Scoundrels steal and/or guess encryption keys and decrypt protected data if you don't use the right keys.

✔ **Viruses, worms, Trojan horses, and zombies:** Scoundrels deploy malevolent applications to destroy data, create chaos, open secret passages into hosts, and prepare for future denial-of-service attacks.

Are you worried yet? We hope so, but don't abandon hope. You have many tools and techniques to help protect yourself, your family and friends, your colleagues, and your users. You can and should use the following protections in various combinations:

✔ **Encryption:** Strongly encrypt data and network traffic to prevent scoundrels (and even authorized users) from seeing data that they're not supposed to see. See Chapter 20 for more information on encryption.

✔ **Passwords:** Require users to choose good passwords and to change them regularly to make it more difficult for scoundrels to guess the passwords.

✔ **Digital certificates:** Use digital certificates to be sure that users are who they say they are. See Chapter 20 for more about digital certificates.

✔ **Digital signatures:** Use digital signatures and other integrity checks to be sure that messages and data haven't been altered during transmission. See Chapter 20 for more information on digital signatures.

✔ **Firewalls:** Use firewalls to filter out evil traffic and hide the addresses of internal hosts so that scoundrels won't know they're there. See the "Introducing Firewalls" section, later in this chapter.

Jump-starting Security in Only Four Steps

 If you're really in a hurry and don't want to read this whole chapter, here are the bare minimum steps (which you *need* to know) for securing your network:

1. **Disable all unnecessary services.**

   Do you really need finger? Disable the service.

2. **Run antivirus software on all computers in the network.**

3. **Keep your operating system, your antivirus software, and all network services updated and patched.**

4. **Set up a firewall (at least one) to keep unfriendly traffic out.**

Now that you've looked at the steps, don't you want to know how and why to follow them? Read on.

Sweating the Small Stuff!

Don't get so involved in security complexities that you forget the basics. Without the following simple practices, all the fancy network security tips in the world are useless:

- **Require users to change their passwords on a regular basis.** Use a password-checking program to discover whether users have selected passwords that are too easy for scoundrels to guess. Users who share their passwords are the weakest link in a secure environment.

- **Deploy virus-scanning applications widely and use them regularly.** Keep them updated so that they know about the latest viruses, worms, and Trojan horses.

- **Back up your systems regularly.** And remember to store the backup media (tapes, disks, floppies, CDs, or whatever) *offsite*.

Using Built-in Security Tools

Every server class operating system includes a set of built-in tools for monitoring security related events. An *event* is some action that may affect the system security. Event-based auditing systems write records to log files whenever an audited event occurs. Auditing systems come ready to log a set of default events. The system or security administrator can add to or remove events from the defaults based on site-specific needs.

With most operating systems, the system or security administrator needs to start the auditing system. The Microsoft Event Logger is a *hybrid*: It automatically audits system and application events, but you must start security auditing yourself. Most security tools write to binary format event logs, which means the computer can read the log files, but you can't. You use an event viewer program, such as the Microsoft Event Viewer, to read the security logs. After you've set up security auditing, you can review the log files. For example, the Windows 2000/NT/XP Event Viewer displays various security violations and attempted break-ins.

One way to run the Microsoft Event Viewer is from the Start menu. Choose Start➪Programs➪Administrative Tools➪Event Viewer. By default, the Event Viewer displays activity in three log files: Application, Security, and System. Double-click the log you want to view. The Event Viewer displays a list of events, including the date and time the event occurred and how serious the event is. If you want more details, double-click a single record in the list. Figure 18-1 shows a TCP/IP event from the System Log — a computer connected to the network.

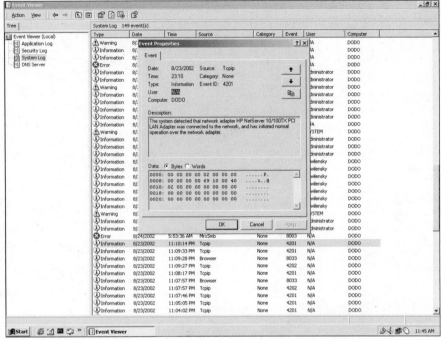

Figure 18-1:
Not all
events are
cause for
concern —
this is an
informa-
tional
message.

Before you can see any security events in the Windows Event Viewer, you must enable security auditing. Follow these steps to turn on security logging. Figure 18-2 shows what's happening in Steps 1 through 4. Figure 18-3 shows Steps 5 through 8.

1. **Choose Start⇨Run, type** mmc /a, **and then click OK.**

2. **On the Console menu, click Add/Remove Snap-in, and then click Add.**

3. **Under Snap-in, click Group Policy, and then click Add.**

4. **In the Select Group Policy Object dialog box, choose Local Computer, click Finish, click Close, and then click OK.**

5. **In Local Computer Policy, click Audit Policy.**

6. **In the details pane, highlight the attribute or event you want to audit.**

7. **Choose Action⇨Security.**

8. **In the Local Security Policy Setting dialog box, select the options you want, and then click OK.**

Look in all three Microsoft log files to find information about break-ins and attempted break-ins.

Figure 18-2:
You must turn on security logging to view security events on Windows NT/2000/XP.

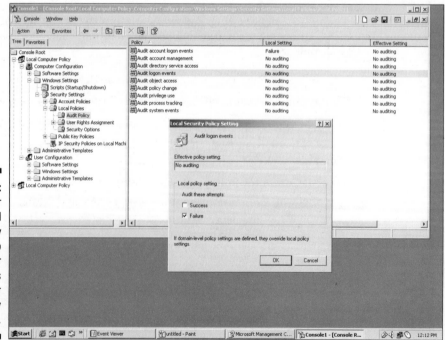

Figure 18-3:
Set up your Local Security Policy to monitor Windows server security events.

In addition to providing security auditing and viewing tools, Linux, UNIX, and Mac OS X also include the `syslog` event logging daemon. The `syslog` daemon reads the `/etc/syslog.conf` file to see which events to log and where to log those events. You can use the default `syslog.conf` file, or you can edit it with your favorite text editor to tell the event logger which files to use for logging various events.

When you add an entry to `/etc/syslog.conf`, you name the facility — for example, `authpriv` (for security) or `mail` — and specify the level of severity you want to log. Separate the facility from the level with a "." (period). Using the "*" (asterisk) wildcard means log everything; for example, `*.emerg` means log everything that happens at the emergency level. `Auth.*` means log security events at every level. Then name the file you want those errors logged to. Table 18-1 lists the security levels from the most severe to the least. An excerpt from a `syslog.conf` file follows:

```
# Everything that starts with # is a comment.
#Format is
#facility.severity    file
# Log everything of level info or higher into the messages file
*.info                /var/log/messages
# Log security events of all levels.
authpriv.*            /var/log/secure
# Log messages from ipfw (IP Firewall)
security.*            /var/log/ipfw
# Log every ftp event of level warning or higher
ftp.info              /var/log/ftpmsg
# Log all the mail messages of all levels in one place.
mail.*                /var/log/mail
# Log all the news messages in one place.
news.*                /var/log/news
# Log all emergencies to the computer on this network named logger.
#*.emerg              @logger
```

Table 18-1	Syslog Severity Levels (Mac OS X, UNIX, Linux)
Category	*Description*
emerg	Time to panic. Events have caused the system to become unstable, in danger of crashing.
alert	Take care of these events immediately. You may need to shut down the system.
crit	Critical errors, such as running out of disk space. If this happens on the disk where you're logging security information, you need to stop the system and get more space. Maybe someone deliberately filled up the logging disk in order to damage the system without purposely leaving a trace.

(continued)

Table 18-1 *(continued)*

Category	Description
err	Miscellaneous errors.
warning	Miscellaneous warnings.
info	General system information.
debug	Sometimes used by programmers for finding errors in code, may contain information that invades user privacy.
—	Don't log anything.

Protecting Your Network

When you think about securing your network, you need to look at it from the bottom up, in this order:

- ✔ Connection media
- ✔ Computers and network devices
- ✔ Users

Protecting the cables

Are you the person who decides which devices are and are not attached to your network? Could someone illicitly "tap in" to your network?

The security of your network depends primarily on the network design and physical installation. The efforts you make to keep illegal devices off the network will vary with the media you employ. (If you need to know more about networks in general, flip to Chapter 2.) Here are some things to keep in mind:

- ✔ The cable on a traditional token ring network is shielded twisted-pair. The cable and connectors, plus the circular nature of the network, make it difficult to tap in illicitly.
- ✔ Traditional Ethernet coaxial cable (10Base5) can be tapped without cutting through it, with special tools and a transceiver to make the illicit connection.

✔ Thinwire Ethernet cable (10Base2) is extremely easy to tap, especially at the tee connectors and terminators. Preventing someone from simply making additional connections on active network segments is virtually impossible.

✔ Twisted-pair Ethernet (10BaseT and 100BaseT) cable is regular wire that you can buy in any hardware store. So to make your wiring secure, be sure to run the wires into locked communications closets.

✔ In all wiring closets, unused ports on hubs should be deactivated, as should the jacks in unused offices.

✔ Fiber-optic cable is extremely difficult to tap. The network fails completely when the cable is cut, so illicit taps announce themselves pretty clearly.

✔ You need to encrypt the data that goes across all wireless links — infrared, radio frequency, lasers, microwaves, and satellite dishes — because they're all interceptible broadcasts. How do you know if someone is eavesdropping on your transmissions? You don't — you need to encrypt the data so that eavesdroppers can't use it.

How promiscuous is your NIC?

Normally, your network interface card (NIC) is interested only in looking for packets addressed to it and ignores all the rest. Some network monitoring and management software, however, is able to place the NIC in *promiscuous mode,* making it keep and display every packet. These kinds of tools (sometimes called *protocol analyzers* or *packet sniffers*) are useful for debugging network problems, but they should be available to and used by authorized network administrators only.

Anyone using this software, or any network analyzer, can see the contents of any packet including an unencrypted password or e-mail message. This network monitoring and management software is easy to get for personal computers — perhaps too easy. It is extremely difficult to detect the presence of any of these tools. You may have difficulty protecting yourself and your network.

Detecting unauthorized hosts or devices on a network

You can find unauthorized hosts with the built-in security auditing tools that come with your operating system. Take another look at Figure 18-1. It shows a TCP/IP event in the Microsoft Event Viewer's System Log: A new network adapter has been added to the network. It's up to you, the administrator, to decide whether that event is okay or whether someone added a computer to your network without authorization.

Besides hosts, some other network devices, such as wiring hubs, may have built-in management and auditing controls. For many devices, you need a real network management solution based on TCP/IP's SNMP (the Simple Network Management Protocol; pronounced by saying the letters S N M P). Here are a few SNMP network management products:

✔ Computer Associate's Unicenter

✔ Hewlett-Packard's OpenView

✔ IBM's Tivoli NetView

You can also get free (public domain) SNMP-based network management software from the following locations (to name just two):

✔ SourceForge.net: `sourceforge.net/projects/net-snmp`

✔ SNMPWorld: `www.snmpworld.com/`

Detecting unauthorized users on a network

If you use the Microsoft Event Viewer to find possible break-in attempts, be sure to look in both the System and Security logs. Compare the information about a user trying to log on with Administrative privileges. Figure 18-4 shows the information in the Security Log. Figure 18-5 shows the same event in the System Log. Both entries show the date and time the attempt occurred, the user name that was used, and the reason the attempt failed. If you look carefully, you'll see that the first is a direct attempt to log on as Administrator while the second is an attempt to get in via FTP.

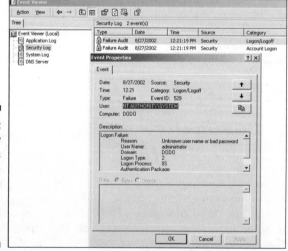

Figure 18-4:
The Security Log shows a possible break-in attempt to a privileged account.

Figure 18-5:
The System
Log shows
the same
unauthorized
user.

With UNIX, Linux, and Mac OS X operating systems, the syslog daemon logs unauthorized user attempts. The log file is the one you specify in the /etc/syslog.conf file. In the example in the "Using Built-in Security Tools" section, the file is /var/log/secure. All you need to do is read the text file. The following bit of code shows a user trying to log on to an account with a user id (UID) of 0. Any account with UID 0 has full privileges. The information in the file is similar to the information in the Windows Security and System logs. This privileged user, miss_scarlett, tried to get in by using FTP. The entry also shows the IP address of the computer she used in her attempt to access dodo.

```
Sep  1 19:51:54 dodo ftpd[1226]: PAM-listfile: Refused user
           root for service ftp
Sep  1 19:52:17 dodo in.ftpd[1230]: connect from 192.168.0.3
Sep  1 19:52:28 dodo PAM_pwdb[1230]: authentication failure;
           (uid=0) -> miss_scarlett for ftp service
```

Introducing Firewalls

You need to understand how routers work before diving into this section, so be sure to read about routers in Chapter 16.

Webster's Ninth New Collegiate Dictionary defines a firewall as "a wall constructed to prevent the spread of fire." Notice it doesn't say anything about putting out the fire. A real firewall actually only slows the fire's movement through a building.

In network terminology, a *firewall* is more like a dam with a hydroelectric power plant. The dam has a specific number of very carefully built openings and spillways that allow some of the water through in a controlled way. And "damn!" is what you might say while you try to set up a network firewall — and what your users might say when they try to do work through one. We can also compare a network firewall to passport control and customs at an international airport. Before you're allowed into or out of a country, you must pass a series of checkpoints. Similarly, in a network firewall, each packet has to pass certain checkpoints before it's allowed to continue on its way.

In terms of network traffic, you're more concerned with *inbound* traffic (from the Internet to your network and computers) than with *outbound*. There's no easy way to look in every packet and find out what the heck it's for. You have to use what's there — the source address, the destination address, and the port (the service that's being used) — to determine which services are allowed through the firewall and which aren't. If you decide to look at the actual data within the packets, be prepared for slow performance. When we talk about firewalls, the term *inside* means inside on your private intranet's side of the firewall; *outside* means on the Internet's side of the firewall.

Choosing a firewall: The must-haves

So many firewall products are out there. How do you choose? To help you, we've put together a list of *must-haves* — the basic features a firewall must have to protect your network and the devices on it from attacks. Here's the list:

- ✔ Access control that allows you to define friendly traffic and unfriendly (unwanted) traffic. The firewall should allow friendlies to pass through while blocking unfriendlies.

- ✔ Alerting and logging that lists all intruder attempts to access your network. The audit log should be thorough enough so that you can track down the source of the attack.

- ✔ The capability to quickly block all traffic in an emergency.

- ✔ Efficient performance that doesn't devour system resources.

For more on firewalls

Firewall protection any more sophisticated than what we cover in this section is beyond the scope of this book. For additional solutions, consult your Internet Service Provider. For more information, look at the following resources:

- ✔ The Internet firewalls mailing list. To subscribe, send an e-mail message to majordomo@greatcircle.com. The subject doesn't matter, but the body must contain subscribe firewalls. You can get back issues by Anonymous FTP from ftp.greatcircle.com.

- ✔ The newsgroup comp.security. firewalls.

Understanding how a firewall works

The firewall examines every packet and decides whether it's allowed in or out. If the firewall refuses to let it pass, the packet is thrown away. The outside system gets the idea when there's no response. Most applications take the lack of response as bad news; they may try again or give up and go away. (What does a caller do if you don't answer your phone when it rings?) Chapter 17 shows an example where a firewall blocks traceroute from finishing.

A firewall lets you control how users inside an intranet can get to the Internet and how to handle requests to enter your intranet from the Internet. Firewalls come with a set of default rules for protecting your computer(s) and/or network. You also get to set up your own rules. For example, you may want only one FTP server to be available to people from the Internet. You make a rule that declares which computer on your intranet can receive FTP requests. The firewall blocks other FTP requests heading to your intranet.

A firewall's rules are called *packet filters*. They train the router to drop certain packets on purpose.

The four fields that can trigger the filters are the source address, the destination address, the port number, and possibly specific words inside the packet itself:

- ✔ **The source address:** Answers the question "Where did this packet come from?" Remember that Ms. Suspicious Scoundrel can set her computer's IP address to anything she wants. Depending on how her computer is attached to the network and how its packets reach your computer, you can't necessarily trust the validity of that source address. The DNS helps her by telling her what IP address to use for spoofing attacks. But your filter can say, "I don't trust this computer at all and will not talk to it."

- ✔ **The destination address:** Answers the question "Where is this packet going?" When the destination is one of your computers, you can decide whether any packet is allowed to go there at all. Your filter can say, "Look, this computer doesn't receive packets directly from outside. Forget it. No way." Sometimes you may choose to redirect the packet to a special server. In this case, your filter can say, "The packet is okay, but send it over there instead."

E-mail is a good example of a service that you may want to redirect. You can disallow receipt of e-mail directly from outside, arranging for all e-mail to be routed instead through a single point of contact. The DNS mail exchange records, known as *MX records,* are designed specifically for this purpose.

- **The port number:** Answers the question "What service is this packet destined for?" If you're not running a particular server, why should you accept any packets of that protocol? For example, if you're not running a World Wide Web server, you can freely and safely ignore any HTTP packets. Your filter can say, "I refuse to talk about that subject."

- **Specific words:** Answer the question "What words and phrases should cause a packet to be blocked?" You can instruct some firewalls to sniff through each packet looking for an exact match for the text you're filtering. Overusing this option slows down your network, so use it sparingly.

If you're connected to the Internet via a commercial ISP, ask your provider about its own security precautions and firewall(s).

Identifying different types of firewalls

You can look at firewalls in two ways: personal versus network and software versus hardware:

- **Personal:** A personal firewall is software that you run on a single computer to protect it from attacks.

- **Network:** A network firewall protects all the computers on a network at once. If a company has more than one connection to the Internet, a firewall should sit at each network access point. If even one LAN is unprotected, crackers may be able to sneak onto your network. (A network firewall can be either software or hardware.)

- **Software:** You run firewall software on a computer that you want to protect or on a computer that will provide protection to other computers on the network. Software firewalls are usually easy to configure and fairly inexpensive, even free in the case of personal firewalls. A software firewall competes for system resources (CPU, memory, and disk space) with the other applications running on that computer.

- **Hardware:** You can run firewall software on a computer that you dedicate to that purpose, or you can use a special purpose device that's specifically designed to be a firewall. The first (and still most popular) hardware firewalls are routers with packet filtering controls. The newest devices are often referred to as firewall *appliances* and typically include other features you might find useful, such as Network Address Translation (NAT) and Virtual Private Network (VPN) tunneling.

  Hardware firewalls often allow more custom filtering rules than software firewalls. As a result, hardware firewalls are usually harder to configure. Hardware firewalls don't use system resources on any of the users' computers in your network. Hardware firewalls cost more than software firewalls.

Protecting yourself with a personal firewall

In addition to the two firewalls that we've included on the CD, you can find many free personal firewalls available for download from the Internet. If an unknown source tries to connect to your computer, a pop-up window, shown in Figure 18-6, alerts you to the intrusion and prompts you to choose whether to grant access. The firewall software also writes the details of the access into a log file so that you can review it later. The pop-up in Figure 18-6 is from a laptop running the ZoneAlarm personal firewall.

Figure 18-6:
Personal firewalls also protect you from inside intruders.

ZoneAlarm Alert
Protected

The firewall has blocked Internet access to your computer (NetBIOS Session) from 192.168.0.2 [TCP Port 3751] [TCP Flags: S].

Time: 8/28/02 12:33:20 AM

1st of 6 alerts

AlertAdvisor   [More Info]

☐ Don't show this dialog again

[OK]

Personal firewalls protect you not only from outside attacks but also from inside attacks. The attack shown in Figure 18-6 did not come from the Internet. It came from another computer on the same intranet trying to break into unshared files.

Examining a software firewall's log

The sample network for this book uses ZoneAlarm Pro, a bigger version of the personal ZoneAlarm. You have to pay for this firewall, but you get more features to protect your entire network. Figure 18-7 shows entries in a piece of ZoneAlarm Pro's log file. The log file lists the alerts sorted by time, beginning with the most recent. To get more information about an alert, right-click it and then click More Info.

When you ask for more information, ZoneAlarm Pro starts AlertAdvisor, featuring four tabs in the upper-right corner. Figure 18-8 shows the detailed information on the Technical Info tab.

The system and network administrators should review what ports and services the intranet needs on which computers and shut down any unneeded ports and services, such as port 53 for DNS access.

Figure 18-7:
We need
more
information
about this
log entry.

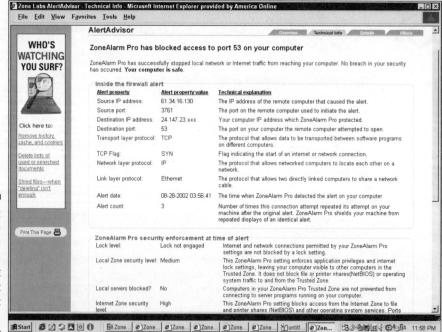

Figure 18-8:
Is someone
probing
through the
DNS port
53? Not
once, but
three times.

The next step in tracking down where this attempted access came from is to use the WhoIs tab (Figure 18-9) to translate the IP address into a name. If your firewall doesn't have a neat WhoIs feature, you can go to a public whois server, such as `www.internic.net`, and type in the address. The server returns the network name and country and other details. Whether your firewall does this for you or you do it yourself, you now have contact information for where this alert began.

Installing Windows XP Internet Connection Firewall

If you run the Windows XP operating system, you get the Internet Connection Firewall (ICF) built in. ICF is designed to protect a SOHO network or single computer connected to the Internet with a dialup modem, cable modem, or DSL modem.

To use ICF, you must follow these steps to enable it:

1. **On the Control Panel, double-click Network Connections.**

2. **Click the Dial-up, LAN, or High-Speed Internet connection that you want to protect. Under Network Tasks, select the Change Settings of This Connection option.**

3. **Under Internet Connection Firewall, click the Advanced tab, and then select the Protect My Computer and Network by Limiting or Preventing Access to This Computer from the Internet check box.**

   Now that you've enabled ICF, you need to configure it.

4. **Click the Settings box to set the firewall's properties.**

5. **Click the Security Logging tab and make sure that the Log Dropped Packets option is checked.**

6. **Click OK to close the dialog boxes.**

One firewall is good, but two are better

If you haven't set up a separate firewall for your intranet, you're relying solely on your ISP's firewall for protection. Because you have no control over the rules for your ISP's firewall, you may be concerned that it doesn't give you the protection you need. And you'd probably be right. Figure 18-10 shows a small network that depends on an ISP's hardware firewall for protection. If a threat gets through the ISP's firewall, you can see in Figure 18-10 that the intranet is left unprotected and attacked also. Such a situation might keep you up nights.

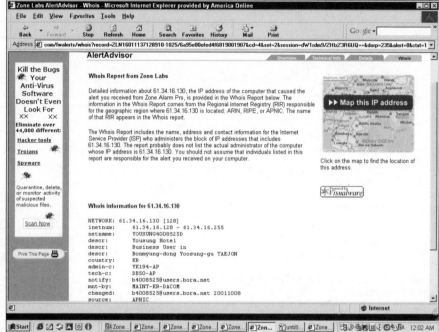

Figure 18-9:
Was
someone in
a Korean
hotel room
probing our
network?

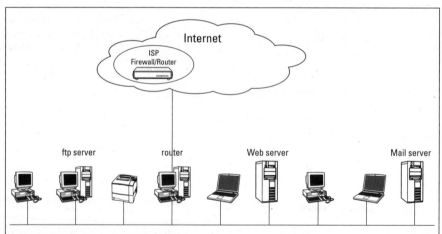

Figure 18-10:
Does your
network
depend on
an ISP's
firewall?

So that you can rest easy, your intranet needs its own firewall. When you set up your firewall, you can create a *demilitarized zone* (DMZ) between your intranet and the Internet; see Figure 18-11. The DMZ is a separate network between the two firewalls. This setup helps when attacks get through your

ISP's firewall. If your ISP lets an attack through, the attacking packets still have to deal with your firewall — another line of defense. Hopefully, your firewall has better rules than your ISP's firewall and discards the packets so that the attack never reaches your intranet.

In the worst case, the attack penetrates both firewalls. Disconnecting your intranet from your firewall stops the attack and gives you time to repair the damage. However, suppose that you're a business and you don't want customers to think you've gone away. Figure 18-11 shows that you put a couple of other computers in the DMZ. With a DMZ, the outside world sees that you still exist on the Internet because some of your computers are still active, even though no traffic can get all the way in. The central mail server stores e-mail for later forwarding and delivery inside. External users can still get to the Anonymous FTP server and can still browse the World Wide Web server.

Keep the computers in the DMZ dedicated to specific tasks. In other words, if you're low on disk space on your laptop, don't put any of your personal files on the hard drive of a computer in the DMZ, even temporarily.

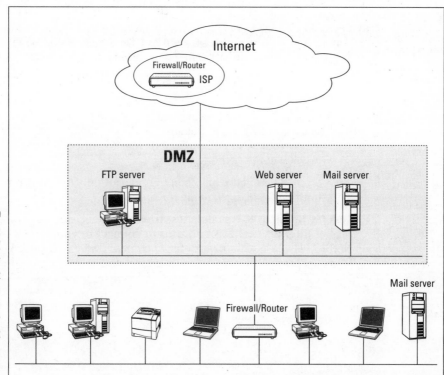

Figure 18-11:
The DMZ keeps your Internet presence even when your intranet is disconnected.

Protecting against internal attacks

Suppose your organization is protected from outside intruders. That's good, but is it protected from an inside attack, as well? Your firewall may well keep the bad guys out, but are you sure there aren't any scoundrels inside the organization — perhaps a disgruntled employee or just an ignorant one? Do you need to prevent salespeople from browsing engineering data? Do you need to protect data, such as salary and medical information? If so, you need internal firewalls as well as external ones.

Analyzing Windows Internet Security

Now that you think you've protected your system from cracking, go ahead and test it out. The free online service ShieldsUP!, from Gibson Research Corp. (www.grc.com), probes computers running various Microsoft Windows operating systems from the Internet to see what information you've left public. There are two tests: Probe My Ports and Test My Shields.

- ✔ **Probe My Ports:** Port testing tries to establish TCP connections to common ports and services, such as FTP, telnet, finger, HTTP, and POP3. The results can be stealth, closed, or open:

    - *Stealth:* The stealth result (see Figure 18-12) is the most secure — outsiders can't even *see* your ports.

    - *Closed:* The closed result means that the port is visible to outsiders, but they can't use it. Because you're giving intruders information about your system, however, a closed result does mean that system privacy could be better.

    - *Open:* The open result is not good. Not only are your ports visible, but they're also available for break-ins.

- ✔ **Test My Shields:** The shields test tries to connect to your computer, probes Internet port 139, and tries to connect to your NetBIOS protocol. NetBIOS is a Windows proprietary protocol that can expose your system to crackers.

Port	Service	Status	Security Implications
21	FTP	Stealth!	There is NO EVIDENCE WHATSOEVER that a port (or even any computer) exists at this IP address!
23	Telnet	Stealth!	There is NO EVIDENCE WHATSOEVER that a port (or even any computer) exists at this IP address!
25	SMTP	Stealth!	There is NO EVIDENCE WHATSOEVER that a port (or even any computer) exists at this IP address!
79	Finger	Stealth!	There is NO EVIDENCE WHATSOEVER that a port (or even any computer) exists at this IP address!
110	POP3	Stealth!	There is NO EVIDENCE WHATSOEVER that a port (or even any computer) exists at this IP address!
113	IDENT	Stealth!	There is NO EVIDENCE WHATSOEVER that a port (or even any computer) exists at this IP address!
135	RPC	Stealth!	There is NO EVIDENCE WHATSOEVER that a port (or even any computer) exists at this IP address!
139	Net BIOS	Stealth!	There is NO EVIDENCE WHATSOEVER that a port (or even any computer) exists at this IP address!
143	IMAP	Stealth!	There is NO EVIDENCE WHATSOEVER that a port (or even any computer) exists at this IP address!
443	HTTPS	Stealth!	There is NO EVIDENCE WHATSOEVER that a port (or even any computer) exists at this IP address!
445	MSFT DS	Stealth!	There is NO EVIDENCE WHATSOEVER that a port (or even any computer) exists at this IP address!
5000	UPnP	Stealth!	There is NO EVIDENCE WHATSOEVER that a port (or even any computer) exists at this IP address!

Note: Several of the "Service" names shown above link directly to items on the ShieldsUP! FAQ Page to provide specific

Figure 18-12: The ports on this computer are very well protected by its firewall.

For your consideration . . .

The following rhetorical questions are intended to get you thinking about the security issues in your environment:

✔ Do you have to know in advance who's allowed to talk to you and how? Or are you willing to talk to anyone, anytime? If the latter is true, how do you do that in a secure manner?

✔ Can you add security to what's currently happening on the network?

✔ Can you build new applications that are aware and secure?

✔ Can you identify who the sender really is?

✔ Is the sender trustworthy?

We don't have all the answers, but we want you to understand that there are *lots* of questions.

Chapter 19

Securing E-Mail and Other TCP/IP Applications

In This Chapter

▶ Becoming aware of all the dirty tricks people may play on your e-mail

▶ Finding out how to secure your e-mail client (MUA)

▶ Avoiding bombing, spamming, and spoofing by adding security to your e-mail servers (MTAs)

▶ Making Usenet news more secure on both the client and server side

▶ Being careful with Anonymous FTP

▶ Looking for suspicious NFS mounts

▶ Figuring out "Who Do You Trust?"

S ome of your favorite Internet applications may be the biggest threats to your host and intranet security. This chapter is full of tips for adding security to popular applications.

Don't Believe Everything You Read, Part One: E-Mail

Do you think you have nothing to hide? Maybe you don't, but e-mail security is always a personal privacy issue even if you aren't mailing credit card numbers or secret formulas for eternal youth. Don't think that using S/MIME for security can completely protect you. E-mail security involves three concepts:

▶ **Confidentiality:** An e-mail message should only be seen by the sender and recipient(s).

✔ **Authenticity:** As a recipient, you should know that e-mail really comes from the sender, not someone claiming to be the sender. As a sender, your e-mail should go only to the recipient(s), not someone claiming to be the recipient.

✔ **Integrity:** No unauthorized person should be able to modify an e-mail message.

If you use the tips and techniques that follow, and teach them to others, you can gain some comfort about the confidentiality, authenticity, and integrity of your e-mail. But you must always stay alert and at least a little suspicious.

Be suspicious of your e-mail messages

You can never be sure that an e-mail message came from the person it says it's from. Anyone who wants to send fraudulent e-mail messages can change the name of his or her computer — and even his or her username. When the message goes through, SMTP doesn't verify the username, computer name, or even the sender's e-mail address. It just passes the message through with the counterfeit information. Figure 19-1 shows the SMTP dialog between the sending and receiving computers.

On many computers, you can't change your username or the computer's name (unless you're the system administrator), but on a personal computer you don't have such limitations. It's your machine and you can call it anything you want — even `whitehouse.gov`!

Figure 19-1:
The receiving SMTP computer believes what the sending computer tells it.

```
% mail -iv mwilensky@lotus.com
Subject: file to put on floopy
~rtools.txt
"tools.txt" 623/34384
                .
Cc: leiden
leiden... Sent
mwilensky@lotus.com... Connecting to crd.lotus.com. (smtp)...
mwilensky@lotus.com... Connecting to lotus.com. (smtp)...
220 lotus.com Sendmail 4.1/SMI-4.10801.1994 ready at Wed, 31 May 95 09:49:27 EDT

>>> HELO max.tiac.net ───────────────── SMTP trusts that you are who you say you are.
250 lotus.com Hello max.tiac.net, pleased to meet you
>>> MAIL From:<leiden@max.tiac.net>
250 <leiden@max.tiac.net>... Sender ok ─────── SMTP doesn't ask to see your ID.
>>> RCPT To:<mwilensky@lotus.com>
250 <mwilensky@lotus.com>... Recipient ok
>>> DATA
354 Enter mail, end with "." on a line by itself
>>> .
250 Mail accepted
mwilensky@lotus.com... Sent (Mail accepted)
Closing connection to lotus.com.
>>> QUIT
221 lotus.com delivering mail
You have mail in /usr/spool/mail/leiden
%
```

Microsoft Outlook and Outlook Express have been favorite "tools" of many scoundrels. They write malicious code that executes in the e-mail client and automatically sends itself to everyone in your Address Book. Protecting yourself completely is difficult, but you can spare your family, friends, and correspondents by running an up-to-date antivirus product and keeping your Address Book empty! It may not be practical, but it does help limit the spread of these attacks.

Don't let people eavesdrop on your mail

Imagine that you're having a wonderful time in Tahiti. But you run out of money. What do you do? Send a letter to Mum asking for money. This letter moves from the post office in Tahiti to Australia to Singapore to Bombay to Cairo and finally reaches good old Mum in Dublin. Suppose that in each post office, an employee reads your mail before forwarding it. How rude! "If only I'd e-mailed to Mum instead, so no one would have known I was in debt."

Your mail message goes through more computers than just yours and your recipient's. Take a look at Figure 11-2, which shows mail being stored briefly and forwarded through several computers on its way to its intergalactic destination. A hacker doesn't even have to be very good to snoop on your mail. All the busybody has to do is use a packet sniffer to intercept passing mail messages. A *packet sniffer* is a program that a network administrator uses to record and analyze network traffic, but the bad guys use them, too. Dozens of free packet sniffers are available on the Internet. Packet sniffers capture data from packets as they travel over a network. That data may be clear text, usernames, passwords, and confidential information, such as medical records and industrial secrets.

Wall up your network to keep out shady characters

If you receive mail from people outside your network, be sure that a firewall protects your network. The *firewall* is a computer that prevents unauthorized data from reaching or leaving your network. For example, if you don't want anything from snoopers.com to penetrate your net, put your net behind a firewall. The firewall can block out all snoopers.com messages. Refer to Figure 11-2 (yes, you read that right — Figure 11-2, back in Chapter 11), which shows our favorite Vulcan's network defended by a firewall. (If you're interested in firewalls, Chapter 18 is for you.)

Avoid getting bombed, spammed, or spoofed

Have you ever been bombed, spammed, or spoofed? If you're an e-mail user, it has probably happened to you.

- ✔ *Bombing* **happens when nasty people continually send the same message to an e-mail address.** This doesn't mean that someone who accidentally sends you the same message twice is a criminal. However, if you reside in the United States and a person maliciously sends you 200 copies of the same message, you can report the cyber-pest to the FBI. Seriously, the FBI has a National Computer Crime Squad in Washington, D.C. (phone 202-324-9164 or e-mail them at `nccs-sf@fbi.gov`).

- ✔ *Spamming* **is a variation of bombing.** A spammer sends junk mail to many users (hundreds and more) of users. It's easy to be an accidental spammer. If you choose your e-mail's Reply All function and you send a reply to a worldwide distribution list, you're a spammer.

  If you go on vacation and set up an automatic mail responder program, be careful not to let the information wind up in the hands of spammers. You might incorrectly set up your autoresponder message to read, "I'm out of the office on vacation for ten days." This message goes out to all mailing list messages you receive, including those of spammers. A thief could use this information to rob your house.

- ✔ *Spoofing* **happens when someone sends you e-mail from a fake address.** If spoofing doesn't seem like it could be a major problem for you, think about this: You get e-mail from a system administrator telling you that you should immediately change your password to a new, administrator-defined password for security reasons. Most people will comply because the system administrator knows best, right? Imagine the consequences, however, if a spoofer sent this e-mail, faking the system administrator's e-mail address, to all the users on a computer. All of a sudden, the spoofer knows everyone's passwords and has access to private and potentially sensitive or secret data.

  Spoofing is possible because plain-vanilla SMTP doesn't have authentication capabilities. Without authentication features, SMTP can't be sure that incoming mail is really from the address it says it is. In Chapter 20, we explain authentication in more detail. If your mail server allows connections to the SMTP port, anyone with a little knowledge of the internal workings of SMTP can telnet to that port and send you e-mail that appears to be from a spoofed address. Besides connecting to the SMTP port of a site, a user can send spoofed e-mail by modifying Web browser interfaces.

Set up your e-mail servers for safety

An *e-mail server* is a computer that runs MTA (mail transfer agent) software to route mail across a TCP/IP network. It uses various TCP/IP mail protocols including SMTP, POP3, and IMAP4. Keep the number of computers vulnerable to SMTP-based attacks to a minimum by having only a few centralized e-mail servers, depending on the size of your organization.

Only allow SMTP connections that come from outside your firewall to go to those few central e-mail servers. This policy protects the other computers on your network. If your site gets spammed, you have to clean up the central e-mail servers, but the rest of your networked computers will be okay. We describe what firewalls do and how they work in Chapter 18.

Take a look at Figure 19-2. An SMTP connection from an MTA somewhere on the Internet, transporting an e-mail message to Marshall, is blocked by the firewall from going directly to his actual e-mail server, Neptunium. Instead, the connection is diverted to his organization's central mail server sitting in a *DMZ* (demilitarized zone).

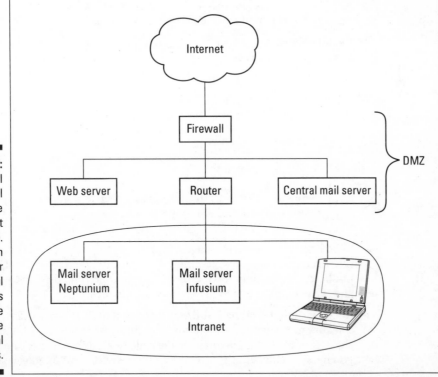

Figure 19-2:
The central e-mail server is like a main post office. Neptunium and other e-mail servers inside the intranet are like postal substations.

The central e-mail server runs an MTA that accepts mail on behalf of all of the organization's internal mail servers and also maintains a directory of users within the corporate intranet. The directory can be something as simple as a list of e-mail aliases, including `mwilensky@lotus.com`, which really means `marshall_wilensky@us.ibm.com` or something as complicated as Microsoft Windows 2000 Active Directory. The directory means that when you send mail to Marshall, you never need to know exactly which computer is serving his mail — how very convenient! The mail message passes through the firewall to the central mail server and is stored and forwarded through the router to the MTA on Neptunium, which serves up mail to lots of users at Marshall's company. Neptunium notifies Marshall that he has new mail, which he finally reads with the MUA (mail user agent).

Make sure your MTA serves up security

In the trusting, friendly past, the essential service an MTA performed was to route e-mail. Today, if moving mail is the main course, your MTA really needs to serve up security as a side dish while it moves mail. Be sure that your MTA can provide security services such as the following (for a more complete explanation of these terms, see Chapter 20):

- SMTP authentication, proving that incoming mail is coming from the server that the mail says it's coming from — no spoofing allowed

- E-mail encryption (PGP); that is, encoding e-mails so that only you and the recipient can read them

- The ability to add on software for virus and spam checking

- A log of incoming traffic so that the network administrator can track down potential bombers, spammers, and spoofers

Use secure MUAs (mail clients)

Use an MUA that allows you to

- **Prove your identity with digital ids:** A *digital id* consists of a public key/private key pair and a digital signature. Read about these in Chapter 20. You must have a digital id to digitally sign or encrypt mail.

- **Send encrypted mail messages:** The body of the message is encrypted (changed from plain text to cipher text with the recipient's freely available public key. Since only the recipient has the matching private key, he or she is the only person who can decrypt the message.

- **Receive digitally signed and/or encrypted mail messages:** If you receive a secure message that was tampered with or that has a problem with the signature, your MUA displays a message describing the problem. Then you must decide whether to take a chance and read the message.

Figure 19-3 shows an Outlook Express user encrypting and digitally signing a mail message. Write the message and, before sending it, open the Tools menu and check the Encrypt and Digitally Sign options.

Some MUAs, mutt for example, add in additional security goodies, such as an advanced IMAP client that supports Kerberos authentication. Kerberos is coming up in Chapter 20. For now, take our word for it: Kerberos is a very strict and reliable authentication. No one will be able to spoof Kerberos. Eudora is another MUA that builds in security features. Eudora supports SSL (Secure Socket Layer) in order to give your Internet mail messages encryption and authentication.

SSL (RFC 3207) protects you from bad guys intercepting and modifying your Internet data, including your e-mail messages.

If you use packet filtering, you need to configure only your e-mail servers. *Packet filtering* analyzes packets based on the source and destination addresses. The analysis decides whether to accept the packets and pass them through to your networks or to reject them as being unsafe. Firewalls often use packet-filtering techniques (which we cover in Chapter 18).

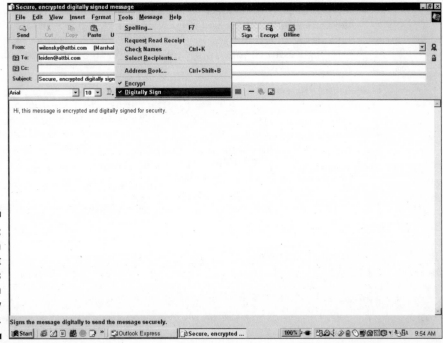

Figure 19-3:
Use an e-mail client that has built-in security features.

Protect yourself

You can protect your data and configure your mail system to make mail fraud more difficult. Some simple things you can do to prevent mail fraud include the following:

- ✔ **Don't forward or respond to spam.** Forwarding junk mail only adds to the problem. Responding confirms your e-mail address and means you'll get even more spam.

- ✔ **Never send unencrypted passwords across a network.** Cryptography isn't just for secret agents. Many e-mail products allow your messages to be encrypted (coded in a secret pattern) so that only you and your recipient can read them. Make sure that everyone understands that they should not respond to requests for sensitive information through the e-mail system.

- ✔ **Learn how your ISP communicates with you.** Our niece had a problem because she followed instructions she received from AOL, except the message wasn't really from AOL. She was only 12 and didn't realize that AOL has a special format for Official AOL Mail. (See keyword Official AOL Mail if you're an AOL subscriber.) Whatever your ISP, be sure to know how to recognize official messages.

- ✔ **Try to identify the source of the e-mail bomb/spam.** The system or network administrator can usually do this by reading through the e-mail headers to determine the origin of the e-mail. The system or network administrator can then configure the router to prevent incoming packets from that address.

- ✔ **Report if someone invades your mail system to the Computer Emergency Response Team (CERT).** Letting CERT know about attacks helps them correlate intruder activities all over the world. You can send e-mail to cert@cert.org to report an incident. You can also phone or fax CERT. The numbers are on the Web site at www.cert.org. See Chapters 20 and 22 for more information about what CERT does and how it can help you.

The CD with this book contains a bundle of security tips and hints from CERT.

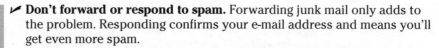

Don't Believe Everything You Read, Part Two: Usenet News

When you're reading Usenet news articles, you have the same lack of assurance about their authors as you do about e-mail senders. It's not impossible for a clever villain to generate deceitful news articles. To help you here, NNTP, the Network News Transfer Protocol (see Chapter 11), provides some optional features, such as certificate-based authentication and SSL encryption.

The NNTP server can be configured so that it only accepts news articles if it can authenticate the source computer and author and only if the article is encrypted during delivery. For this to work, both the NNTP server and the client must use the authentication and encryption features. Most servers today aren't using them, so users don't either — even though their clients (such as Microsoft Outlook Express and Netscape Messenger) could.

To configure enhanced security for the Microsoft Windows 2000 NNTP Service, obtain and install an SSL server certificate. Then follow these steps:

1. **Launch the Microsoft Management Console (MMC) by choosing Start⇨Settings⇨Control Panel⇨Administrative Tools⇨Computer Management.**

   The Microsoft NNTP server depends on Internet Information Server (IIS), which appears in the left window at the bottom of the Services and Applications list.

2. **Click the plus sign (+) next to Internet Information Services to expand it.**

3. **Click Default NNTP Virtual Server to highlight it.**

4. **From the Action menu, choose Properties.**

5. **On the Access tab, in the Access control section, click the Authentication button.**

6. **In the message box (Figure 19-4) that appears:**

   a. Clear the check box for Allow Anonymous.

   b. Clear the check box for Basic Authentication (Password Is Sent in Clear Text).

   c. Make sure that Windows Security Package is selected.

   d. Select Enable SSL Client Authentication (Requires Server Certificate).

   e. Select Require SSL Client Authentication.

   f. If your users have Windows user accounts, select Enable Client Certificate Mapping to Windows User Accounts.

   g. Then click the Client Mappings button to establish either 1-to-1 associations of X.509v3 client certificates to specific user accounts or Many-to-1 to share a user account among many certificates.

      For more detailed instructions for this, read the online help and the IIS documentation.

   h. Click the OK button.

   i. Click this OK button, too.

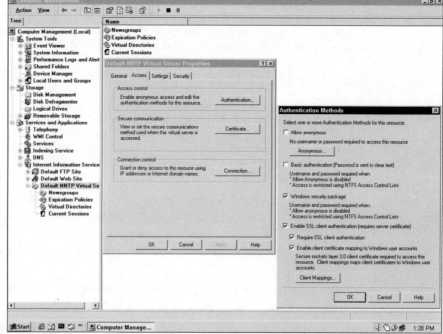

Figure 19-4:
You can completely tighten down access to your NNTP server's newsgroups.

7. **Click the plus sign (+) next to Default NNTP Virtual Server to expand the list of subcomponents.**

8. **Click Virtual Directories to highlight it and, in the right window, click Default to highlight it.**

   You're setting the security controls for normal newsgroups.

9. **From the Action menu, choose Properties.**

10. **In the message box that appears, in the Secure Communications section, click the Secure button and then select Require Secure Channel and Require 128-bit Encryption.**

11. **Click the OK button.**

12. **Click this OK button, too.**

   Repeat Steps 8 through 12 for *control* (rather than *default*) to set the security controls for NNTP control messages. (They do things like automatically create new newsgroups.)

Because NNTP authentication works only with the cooperation of the users (at properly configured NNTP clients), it ensures only that the good guys are who they say they are. The villains aren't going to use software that inhibits their misdeeds — at least, not voluntarily.

Usenet news articles can be trusted only if all the authentication pieces are properly coordinated.

Passwords May Not Be As Safe As You Think

At the top of the TCP/IP layer cake, in the application/presentation/session layer, the applications can have their own security features.

In addition to e-mail, other network applications (FTP, telnet, rexec) employ passwords, which seem like a good safeguard, but most of the basic FTP, telnet, and rexec applications send passwords unencrypted — that is, in clear text. By now you know how vulnerable these passwords are.

The good news is that security-enhanced versions of these applications are available. (Check out www.ssh.com.) *Ssh* is a protocol for encrypted communication between clients and servers. The secure shell-based (ssh) applications, for example, are a more secure alternative to telnet, ftp, rlogin, rsh, and rcp because ssh encrypts the data in a remote logon session. However, ssh doesn't encrypt everything in the TCP/IP packet — for example, the packet header. Ssh encrypts the passwords, too, so that snoopers can't grab and read the packets that contain your password (as they can with telnet or rlogin sessions). Ssh is not an Internet Standard yet, but there are ten Internet Drafts on various aspects of it. Use the RFC Editor's Internet Draft Index Search Engine (www.rfc-editor.org/idsearch.html) to find them.

The *TCP/IP For Dummies,* 5th Edition, CD-ROM includes SecureCRT from VanDyke Software, Inc.

Be Aware of Security Pitfalls in Your Applications and Services

In this section, we look at some of the additional security precautions that you can apply to specific applications, protocols, and services. The most important tip: Don't run services you don't need! That way no scoundrels can exploit them.

Put limits on TFTP

The Trivial File Transfer Protocol, TFTP, provides downline loading and remote booting. Imagine the damage if people were using TFTP not just to download an operating system to a diskless computer but also to grab your password file. So make a careful decision about whether you really need TFTP. If you do, configure it properly and carefully so that you limit which files can be fetched and by whom.

Test TFTP yourself — but only on your own computers. Testing other people's systems is probably illegal. Try fetching your system's critical files and other things you shouldn't be able to get. If you've secured things properly, the transfers fail.

If your users don't need TFTP, be sure your servers don't run the daemon that enables it. If they do need it, make the TFTP directory (usually called "tftpboot") top-level with no subdirectories. If your TFTP server supports accept and deny controls, use them to limit the computers that can download files.

Be careful of what's anonymous

Because anyone from anywhere can use Anonymous FTP, configure it carefully so that you limit the files that can be fetched. As with TFTP, Anonymous FTP could be used by a scoundrel to grab your password file.

When you configure Anonymous FTP, you specify the topmost directory holding the files that you're offering. But that makes any subdirectories under the specified directory automatically accessible (normal file and directory permissions should still apply). So after you configure Anonymous FTP, test it to make sure that you aren't making critical files available. You also need to make sure that users aren't able to change to a directory outside the tree you specify.

Consider dedicating a computer to Anonymous FTP and not putting anything on it that you're not willing to share. If you can't use a dedicated FTP server, make all your Anonymous FTP directories top-level with no subdirectories. It's more administration, but it's harder for security holes to get past you.

The CD that comes with this book includes SAINT (the Security Administrator's Integrated Network Tool) from World Wide Digital Security, Inc.

We trust only Johnny Carson and Walter Cronkite

Before his famous chat show, Johnny Carson hosted a game show, "Who Do You Trust?" Candace remembers watching it after school. Do the math. She's getting old. Walter Cronkite, after many years in the new business, still tops the list as America's most trusted broadcaster. We dedicate this section to them.

The trust-based services (rsh, rcp, rlogin) know which computers and which users to trust, but only because of the contents of a text file. Protect these files and their directories so that only authorized users can change the contents. (On UNIX systems, these include /etc/hosts.equiv and the .rhosts files in users' home directories.)

The security of your trusted TCP/IP network services is, in reality, a function of operating system security. Any user of rsh, rcp, and rlogin, including the system administrator, can open holes in security — accidentally or on purpose.

When you set up a trust relationship with another computer, always specify the fully qualified domain name (FQDN — see Chapter 10). Otherwise, if you say you trust lotus, you're trusting every computer named lotus everywhere on the Internet.

NFS = No File Stealing!

On UNIX systems, the file named /etc/exports lists the disk space that your NFS (Network File System) server is willing to share. It also allows you to limit access to only the NFS clients you name, as well as to restrict the actions of the privileged users on those NFS clients.

Here are some tips for keeping your NFS servers safe and secure:

- **Be specific about the disk space you're sharing.** Only list the directories that need to be shared.

- **Be specific about the NFS clients you support.** Put their FQDNs in the file.

- **Don't allow privileged users on NFS clients to have privileged access to your disk space.** State (in /etc/exports) that those clients aren't allowed privileged access.

To see which NFS clients have mounted shared disk space from an NFS server, run the showmount command on the NFS server. Showmount is an important tool for system managers and network administrators who are responsible for network security. Here's an example:

```
% showmount -a
frodo.lotus.com:/var/spool/mail
frodo.lotus.com:/usr1/emacs
bilbo.lotus.com:/var/spool/mail
bilbo.lotus.com:/usr2/netscape
```

If you ever see a numeric IP address instead of the name of the NFS client, it could indicate a security problem. It means the NFS server was unable to look up the name of the client in the local hosts file, the DNS, or in NIS. Maybe a client has tapped into your NFS system.

We explain DNS (Domain Name System) in Chapter 10. If you want to review NIS or NFS, take a look at the bonus chapters on the CD.

Chapter 20

Advanced Security

*T*he Computer Emergency Response Team (CERT) has been collecting statistics on computer security since 1988, when it reported six incidents. CERT statistics include incidents such as denial of service (DoS) attacks, attacks by malicious insiders on intranets, and viruses and Trojan horses. One incident may involve one site or thousands of sites. CERT reported 3,734 incidents in 1998 and 43,136 in the first half of 2002. These statistics certainly raise security consciousness. This chapter works with Chapters 18 and 19 to provide guidelines and techniques for building secure systems and networks. The information in this chapter is aimed at system, network, and security administrators.

Visit www.cert.org/stats/ to see CERT's incident statistics as well as other security statistics that CERT collects.

Visit www.guardiandigital.com/products/software to see Guardian Digital, Inc.'s En Garde Secure Linux. It is a special version of Linux that has extensive built-in security features such as intrusion detection and a gateway firewall.

The *TCP/IP For Dummies,* 5th Edition, CD-ROM contains lots of useful security information and software, including

✔ Various secure clients and servers

✔ A bundle of white papers and technical incident reports from CERT

This whole chapter is about security, but you won't be seeing any other security icons after this one. We suggest you use the extra free space in the margins to jot down reminders to check the security of your computers.

Getting Started with Encryption and Authentication

Every layer in the TCP/IP layer cake offers (and needs) different security components. (Take a look at Chapter 5 to find out about layers.) The following sections explore some layer-specific security steps.

Defining encryption

At the bottom of the TCP/IP structure, in the physical and data link layers, you can encrypt the data on the wire. This is one of the most common security techniques used in communications. Encryption and some of the other terminology used for computer security come straight out of the world of secret agents. Here are definitions of some of these concepts.

- ✔ **Cryptography:** This is the process of scrambling *(encrypting)* and deciphering *(decrypting)* messages in secret code. (We've seen some authors use the term *cryptology,* but as far as we know, that's the study of crypts.)

- ✔ **Encryption:** *Encryption* is the process of scrambling a message into code to conceal its meaning. A common method of encryption is to use a pair of keys — a public key and a private key — to encode data so that only the person who is intended to see it can read it. If Marshall sends a message to Helen, Candace's mother, he encodes the message with Helen's public key. She decodes the message with her private key. Only Helen's private key can decode the message. Candace can't peek at what Marshall and Helen are saying about her.

- ✔ **Encryption key:** The *encryption key* ("the key" for short) is the essential piece of information — a word or number or combination — used in encrypting and decrypting the message, but it isn't the algorithm (process) used for encryption.

  IPv6 allows applications to encrypt an entire packet (maximum security) or just the data portion using various mathematical methods (more on IPv6 in Chapter 9).

- ✔ **Public key/private key cryptography:** In the public key/private key coding process, one encryption key is used to encrypt the message and another key is used to decrypt the message. There's a mathematical relationship between the two keys. The public and private keys are long prime numbers that are numerically related (factors of another, larger number). Possession of one isn't enough to translate the message because anything encrypted with one can only be decrypted with the other.

Every user gets a unique pair of keys — one key is made public and the other is kept secret. Public keys are stored in common areas, mailed among users, and may even be printed in newspapers. Private keys must be stored in a safe place and protected. Anyone can have your public key, but only you should have your private key. It works something like this: "You talkin' to me? I won't listen unless you encrypt the message using my public key so that I know no one else is eavesdropping. Only my private key, which no one else has, can decrypt the message, so I know no one else can read it. I don't care that lots of other people have my public key because it can't be used to decrypt the message."

PGP, which stands for Pretty Good Privacy, is an exportable, public-domain (free) software package for public key/private key cryptography. It's the most widely used privacy program. PGP is the technical underpinning for adding security to applications. PGP encrypts and decrypts Internet e-mail. It can also be used to send an encrypted digital signature (more on this in the next section) to guarantee the sender's identity and that no one changed the message en route. The best answers (plural!) to "Where can I get PGP?" are at `www.faqs.org/faqs/pgp-faq/where-is-PGP`. PGP is available for all the major operating systems. Some e-mail clients, including mutt, exmh, and PMMail2000, have PGP built in to them.

Peering into authentication

In the middle of the layer cake, in the internet and transport layers, there's a security measure for authentication of computer names and addresses that an application may use. Authentication goes beyond identifying yourself. You have to prove that you are who you say you are.

> *"Knock, knock."*
>
> *"Who's there?"*
>
> *"Special agent Fox Mulder, FBI."*

Do you believe the breathy voice on the other side of the door and open up? Or do you authenticate him by looking at his ID? Can you really believe his ID? Do you even know what a real FBI ID looks like? Do you call the Federal Bureau of Investigation headquarters and try to verify his identity? What if he's really a space alien in disguise?

In TCP/IP, the process of authentication must be built into the applications. For example, an Anonymous FTP server does only very basic authentication. To interact with the FTP server, you need an FTP client program, a user account name (anonymous), and a password (just your e-mail address).

Username/password authentication is the easiest kind to crack. Encrypting the username and password makes cracking them much more difficult. Certain applications, such as VanDyke Software's SecureCRT/VShell Secure Server, Lotus Notes, and electronic commerce Web sites, use much more stringent authentication controls, such as *digital certificates* and *digital signatures.*

Do you have any ID? A digital certificate will do

Just as your passport proves that you are who you say you are to an immigration official, network authentication proves that you are who you say you are to an application or server. Sometimes your passport is sufficient to allow you to enter a country, but not always. Some countries require a visa — an additional piece of identification — for security purposes. Network and computer security works the same way. Sometimes an application or server accepts your simple authentication by itself, and you're then allowed to access the application and server resources. Sometimes, however, the application or server requires additional electronic identification for security purposes. That "electronic visa" is called a *digital certificate* and it contains your encryption keys.

In real life, you have separate forms of identification for specific purposes: passport, driver's license, employee ID, and so on. For these identification papers to be trustworthy, they must come from a recognized authority, such as the government or your employer. On a network, you may need a separate digital certificate for each application or server that you need to use. For these certificates to be trustworthy, they must come from a *Certification Authority* (CA) — an organization that issues certificates. Sometimes it's called simply a *Certificate Authority.*

Your passport connects your identity (your photograph) with your identification (name, age, birthplace, citizenship). A digital certificate is an encrypted, password-protected file that connects the identity of a person or a server with its identification, including the following:

- ✔ The name of the certificate holder
- ✔ The private key for encryption/decryption and verifying the digital signature of a message sender by matching the sender's public key
- ✔ The name of the issuing CA, for example, Verisign or RSA Certificate Services
- ✔ The certificate's validity period

The CA digitally "signs" and guarantees the file (certificate).

How to get a digital certificate

Your organization acts as its own CA when it issues the certificate you need to access intranet resources. The Internet has trusted third-party CAs that issue electronic IDs only after verifying the identities of the requesters. You can get a personal certificate to use with your Web browser or e-mail client by completing an application at Verisign (www.verisign.com), Thawte (www.thawte.com), GlobalSign (www.globalsign.net), Digital Signature Trust (www.digsigtrust.com), and others. Some applications and software are responsible for creating certificates. For example, when you're registered as a Lotus Notes user, you get a user ID that contains your certificate and public key/private key pair.

The CD that accompanies this book includes VanDyke Software's secure client, SecureCRT.

Here's how to get a signed digital certificate from a trusted third-party CA:

1. **Decide what kind of certificate you need:**

   - *Personal certificates* let you send and receive encrypted e-mail and digitally sign documents.

   - *Server certificates* enable 128-bit SSL encryption so that users have secure communication. There are versions of server certificates for Web servers, wireless servers, and other purposes.

   - *Developer certificates* digitally shrinkwrap your applications and Web content so that an ActiveX control, VBA file, Office 2000 macro, Java applet, dynamic link library, .cab file, .jar file, HTML page, or channel content is safe.

2. **Submit a request to a CA (a company that checks that your server and organization are who they say they are).**

3. **Pay the service fee to defray their costs for verifying that all requesters are who they claim to be.**

How digital certificates are used

Organizations on the Internet use digital certificates to establish mutual trust so that the participants can trust each other's identity during transactions, such as

- ✔ Internet credit card purchases

- ✔ Internet banking and investing

- ✔ Enrolling and checking benefits with healthcare organizations

- ✔ Communication between employees on private corporate information

The certificate request and validation protect you and your organization. A server certificate provides these protections:

- ✔ People who communicate with your server are sure that it really belongs to your organization, not to an imposter's.

- ✔ Your e-commerce server is set up to conduct transactions on the Internet.

✔ Your Web server is able to establish secure SSL connections with Web browsers.

✔ Your e-mail server is able to establish secure connections with other e-mail servers and with e-mail clients by using S/MIME (Security-enhanced Multipurpose Internet Mail Extensions).

RFC 2312, "S/MIME Version 2 Certificate Handling," describes how certificates and S/MIME work together.

Kerberos — Guardian or Fiend?

Big benefit: Your password doesn't travel across the network.

Kerberos is an authentication service, application, and protocol. Project Athena at the Massachusetts Institute of Technology (MIT) was dedicated to researching very large computing environments — "very large" meant thousands of computers. Kerberos was the security part of that research. Kerberos is also a protocol used by the component parts of a secured computing environment. It's a client/server environment — but isn't everything these days? See Chapter 3 for more on client/server.

The Kerberos master server — there's only one in your secure network — provides an authentication service used for security in an Internet environment. Encrypted user-account information is stored in a database on the Kerberos master server rather than in a local password file or an NIS map.

The secured computing environment needs coordinated time services so that all computers synchronize their ticket expirations properly. (Aha, that's a new piece of the pie: tickets. More about tickets shortly.)

RFC 1510 describes the Kerberos Network Authentication Service.

Playing at Casino Kerberos

Suppose we walk through what happens when you're running under Kerberos. Meet Barry, who likes to play roulette:

1. One fine day, Barry knocks on the special door at the back of Casino Kerberos. (Barry types his username at a Kerberos-enabled computer.)

2. Barry asks the bouncer for permission to enter the secret inner casino. (Barry's computer asks the Kerberos master server for a *ticket-granting ticket,* which is permission to talk to the ticket-granting server.)

3. The bouncer then asks Barry for the casino password. Barry gives the right response and is allowed in. (Barry's computer asks him for his password and uses it to verify the response from the Kerberos master server.)

4. Barry is happy. He goes to the cashier window and buys some gaming chips. He has a choice; the casino games all require different chips. The chips are only valid for a short time. When that time is up, his chips are worthless. (Barry's computer sends a request to the ticket-granting server requesting an *application service ticket,* which has a limited lifetime.)

5. Barry is ready to play. He can now lose money at the casino game of his choice, as long as he uses the correct chips at the gaming table he chooses. If he wants to move to a different gaming table, he must have the correct chips or return to the cashier window to get them. (Barry's computer can now present the application service ticket to an application server as permission to use the service.)

6. By the way, everyone in the casino speaks Pig Latin. (All communications — between Barry's computer and the Kerberos master server, between Barry's computer and the ticket-granting server, and between Barry's computer and the desired application — are encrypted.)

7. When all of this is in place and operating properly, Barry can be sure he's at the right table and that everyone else standing around the table is playing by the rules. (Barry knows he's talking to the computers and services that he wants to talk to, and the computers and services can be sure that Barry is who he says he is.) Everybody's happy, right?

Training the dog — one step per head

In Greek mythology, Kerberos was a three-headed dog with the tail of a snake and snakes wrapped around his neck; he guarded the entrance to Hades. If you got past Kerberos, you were in hell. We have to wonder if this is what MIT intended.

Kerberos includes a framework, a set of command-line tools, the Kerberos management application, and a Kerberos logon authenticator. A system or network administrator has a lot of work to do before Kerberos is ready to protect a network. Here are the basic steps necessary to configure (or *Kerberize*) the computers and applications on your network:

1. **Start the Kerberos server.**

   Attention network administrators! Forget about sleep and regular meals until you finish this step. You have to install software, edit files, create a database, and insert records for people and computers.

2. **Register principals.**

   A *Kerberos principal* works like a regular computer account. The name of the principal looks like this:

   ```
   You choose this part@YOUR.REALM
   ```

   If you love chocolate, you probably love chocolate brownies frosted with more dark chocolate. If you love security, you will love the idea of a Kerberos principal. The encrypted principal is the frosting on the Kerberos security brownie. A principal looks something like an e-mail address, but the resemblance ends there. Kerberos knows just how to use it in a secure environment. You get to choose the part before the @. A typical choice is your regular account name. The part after the @ is the name of the realm — it may look like your computer name for convenience. Each principal is encrypted with a Kerberos master key so that not just anyone can examine it and is stored in the Kerberos database. The principal includes the name, password, and some techie stuff.

3. **Get programmers to Kerberize applications.**

   Kerberizing involves checking to see who is using the application, validating that user's identity, checking to make sure that the user has the right ticket, and getting the user the appropriate ticket.

Guarding the "Gates" of Microsoft

Microsoft Windows 2000 and XP have built-in Kerberos support. Some of the ways that Microsoft Windows 2000 uses Kerberos for authentication include

✔ Print spooling

✔ Distributed file-system management

✔ Certificate requests to the Microsoft Certificate Server for domain users and computers

✔ IPSec security authentication

✔ Intranet authentication for Internet Information Server

Why Windows?

The reasons Microsoft did so much work to make Kerberos its Windows 2000/XP network authentication protocol is that Kerberos, in addition to being so secure, offers some other benefits as well:

✔ **Interoperability with non-Windows Kerberos realms is possible.** Computers with a Windows 2000 operating system can participate in Kerberos realms that aren't Windows 2000 domains and vice versa.

The Windows 2000 `ksetup.exe` program helps network administrators configure clients to participate in non-Windows Kerberos realms.

✔ **Trust relationships are simpler to manage.** The Kerberos protocol allows two-way trust. This bidirectionality makes life easier for a network administrator who manages large networks made up of several domains.

✔ **Network overhead can be reduced.** We're talking about more efficient authentication. Instead of a server connecting to a domain controller each time a client needs authentication, Kerberos skips the step of going to a domain controller. It authenticates the client by examining the client's ticket, reducing network requests.

Adding more heads to the dog

Windows 2000 mostly follows RFCs 1510 ("The Kerberos Network Authentication Service (V5)") and 1964 ("The Kerberos Version 5 GSS-API Mechanism").

Microsoft has gone beyond the RFC specifications and extended the Kerberos protocol by using public key certificates instead of shared keys. Microsoft created this extension to the protocol defined by the RFCs to allow logons with smart cards.

Where do the keys come from?

Windows 2000 has a new domain service called the KDC (Key Distribution Center). The KDC automatically starts on every domain controller and gives birth to two subservices:

✔ **The AS (Authentication Service):** Gives you a ticket to get a ticket. In the "Playing at Casino Kerberos" section earlier in this chapter, Barry had to ask the bouncer for permission to enter Casino Kerberos. The AS is the technical implementation of the bouncer.

✔ **The TGS (Ticket Granting Service):** Gives you the ticket you need to use the services you need to do your work. After the bouncer let Barry in to Casino Kerberos, Barry had to get chips to play. The TGS is the technical implementation of those chips.

Just as the Casino has rules you must follow if you want to play, Windows 2000 has Kerberos policies that must be followed, such as how long your ticket can remain valid and whether you can log on from anywhere in the network or just from a local computer.

Kerberos is a protocol for authentication, not authorization. Kerberos verifies that computers, networks, and people are who they say they are. Kerberos doesn't protect access to files and directories. You need to rely on your applications' and operating system's access control mechanisms for permission to use files and directories.

Some popular Mac CFM-based applications, such as Eudora and Fetch (a Kerberized FTP) won't work with Mac OS X Kerberos. Kerberos does not currently include CFM (Code Fragment Manager) support. To use the Mac OS X Kerberos with Eudora and Fetch, you must install Mac OS X 10.2 Kerberos Extras.

Guarding the gates of Linux and UNIX

To get Kerberos running on Linux and UNIX, you need to install the software packages, configure your realm and database, register an administrator principal, and start the services. The following section steps you through this process on Red Hat Linux.

Setting up a Kerberos server step by step

In this section, we describe the basic steps you need to follow to install and configure Kerberos server software on Linux or UNIX. The following steps are specific to Red Hat Linux running the Gnome user interface. Your flavor of Linux/UNIX may vary slightly.

1. **Decide which computer will be your Key Distribution Center (KDC).**

2. **Install these packages on the KDC:**

   - **krb5-libs:** shared libraries

   - **krb5-server:** Kerberos server programs

   - **krb5-workstation:** Kerberos client programs

   - **gnome-kerberos:** GUI tools including krb5, for managing tickets, and gkadmin, for managing realms

   Note: You need krb5-workstation on every client computer, too.

3. **Name your Kerberos realm (in UPPERCASE) and domain-to-realm mappings by editing the files** /etc/krb5.conf **and** /var/kerberos/krb5kdc/kdc.conf.

   Remember to enter DNS domain names and host names in lowercase. If you just need a simple configuration:

   - Change *EXAMPLE.COM* and *example.com* to your DNS domain name. Be sure to use the same case as the text you're replacing.

   - Change *kerberos.example.com* to the fully qualified domain name of your KDC.

4. **Create the Kerberos database that stores the keys for your realm by typing this command:**

   ```
   /usr/kerberos/sbin/kdb5_util create -s
   ```

5. **Control which principals have the right to administer the database by editing this file:**

```
/var/kerberos/krb5kdc/kadm5.acl
```

For the simple configuration, simply change *EXAMPLE.COM* to your DNS domain name in the line */admin@EXAMPLE.COM *.

6. **Register a username as an administrator principal.**

The following command registers user marshall as an administrator principal:

```
/usr/kerberos/sbin/kadmin.local -q addprinc marshall/admin
```

7. **Enter these commands to start Kerberos:**

```
krb5kdc start
kadmin start
krb524 start
```

8. **Add principals with your choice of kadmin's add_principal command, or gkadmin's menu** Principal .. Add.

9. **Test your environment by entering these commands:**

```
kinit
klist
kdestroy
```

Your Kerberos server is running!

Setting up a Kerberos client step by step

In this section, we describe the basic steps you need to follow to install and configure Kerberos client software on Linux or UNIX. The following steps are specific to Red Hat Linux running the Gnome user interface. Your flavor of Linux/UNIX may vary slightly.

1. **Install these packages on every client:**

```
krb5-libs
krb5-workstation
```

2. **Copy the** /etc/krb5.conf **file from the KDC.**

3. **Run kadmin and enter these commands (substitute the computer's fully qualified domain name for** myhost.example.com**):**

```
add_principal -randkey host/myhost.example.com
ktadd -k /etc/krb5.keytab host/myhost.example.com
```

4. **Using kadmin, add a host principal for the workstation.**

The instance in this case will be the hostname of the workstation. Because you'll never need to type the password for this principal again, and you probably don't want to bother with coming up with a good password, you can use the -randkey option to kadmin's addprinc command to create the principal and assign it a random key.

5. **After you create the principal, run kadmin on the workstation, and enter the following ktadd command:**

```
ktadd -k /etc/krb5.keytab host/blah.example.com
```

This extracts the keys for the workstation and installs them.

Setting up a Kerberos 5 client is less involved than setting up a server. At minimum, you need to install the client packages and provide clients with a `krb5.conf` configuration file. Kerberized versions of rsh and rlogin also require some configuration changes.

There are a few more steps you need to follow to run kerberized applications:

✔ Before a particular client in your realm can allow users to connect using kerberized rsh and rlogin, that workstation must have the xinetd package installed and have its own host principal in the Kerberos database. The kshd and klogind server programs must have access to the keys for their service's principal.

✔ In order to use the kerberized versions of rsh and rlogin, you need to run either ntsysv or chkconfig to enable klogin, eklogin, and kshell.

✔ To use kerberized telnet, use ntsysv or chkconfig to enable ktelnet.

✔ If you want to provide FTP access as well, you must create and extract a key for a principal with a root of ftp, and the instance set to the hostname of the FTP server. Then use ntsysv or chkconfig to enable gssftp or another kerberized FTP application.

That's all you need to do to set up a simple Kerberos realm.

Using Secure Protocols for Secure Internet Transactions

Secure Sockets Layer (SSL) and Secure HTTP (S-HTTP) provide the encryption and authentication needed to guarantee secure shopping on the Web. But they're not just for shopping. You can use them to protect your own network applications as well.

Understanding S-HTTP protocol basics

Secure HTTP (S-HTTP) is HTTP with security enhancements; it addresses the issue of moving data securely across a public environment, such as the Web. HTTP is the HyperText Transfer Protocol (check out Chapter 12), which is how browsers communicate with servers on the Web.

RFC 2617, "HTTP Authentication: Basic and Digest Access Authentication," describes S-HTTP.

S-HTTP provides transaction security services and confidentiality as well as authentication. It builds encryption into the application level before you even get to the Web server. HTTP, on the other hand, makes the client try to access the Web server before issuing a username and password challenge, if needed. Secure HTTP doesn't require any changes to HTML, the language that makes the Web's pages look so good. (Although HTML is also getting new features, they're driven by other requirements.)

By the way, S-HTTP also supports Kerberos security. (For more on Kerberos, flip to the "Kerberos — Guardian or Fiend?" section.)

URLs that begin with `https://` use SSL to protect information (think of the "s" as meaning "secure").

Understanding SSL protocol basics

When Netscape introduced SSL in 1995, it made online information, including credit card information, as secure as handing a credit card to a salesperson in a store — maybe even more secure. Don't shop at a site that does not use SSL. Check your browser's status bar for the lock icon that's shown in Figure 20-1.

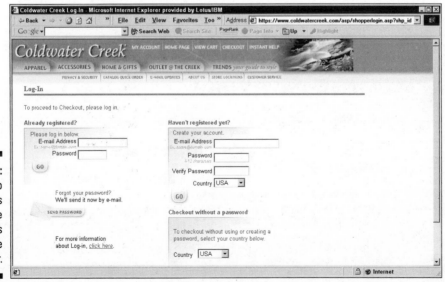

Figure 20-1: Web browsers mark secure transactions in the status bar.

The SSL protocol ensures privacy between a client and server by using certificates to authenticate the server (and optionally, the client) and ensures confidentiality by encrypting the data they exchange. No one can put a computer on the network and fool SSL into believing the spoofing server should receive the client's confidential credit card information. If you're shopping on the Web, you want the commerce server to prove that it is who it claims to be. Did you read about the alien impersonating Fox Mulder in the earlier section, "Peering into authentication"? Well, SSL won't let that happen. SSL also has an option to authenticate the client so that a server can be sure you are who you claim to be. SSL requires a reliable protocol for the transport — TCP, not UDP.

SSL isn't tied to a particular application. This is a great advantage. You can layer any application or protocol, such as HTTP or FTP, over SSL. SSL sits on top of TCP/IP, taking care of encryption, security keys, authenticating the server, and — possibly — authenticating the client before the application sends or receives any data.

Understanding TLS protocol basics

The goal of the TLS (Transport Layer Security) protocol is for client/server applications to operate without danger of anyone eavesdropping or tampering with their networks or forging either personal or computer identities. TLS sits on top of the TCP protocol in the transport layer, and the applications sit on top of TLS. Although TLS is based on Netscape's patented SSL protocol, the two protocols don't operate together. Contrast TLS with the IPSec protocols, which provide security one layer down, closer to hardware and farther from applications at the network layer, where the IP protocol is. Chapter 5 describes the TCP/IP network layer cake.

RFC 2246, "The TLS Protocol Version 1.0," describes the Transport Layer Security (TLS) protocol.

SSL is available from many vendors

Netscape invented SSL and still owns it. If you're wondering how its proprietary network protocol got into this book, the reason is that SSL filled a hole that international standards had left open. TLS, the Transport Layer Security protocol, is on the IETF standards track with its first version. The goal of this protocol is like the goal of SSL — to enable client/server applications to operate without danger of anyone eavesdropping or tampering with their networks or forging either personal or computer identities. In fact, TLS is patterned after SSL, and Netscape is helping the IETF to create a standard protocol.

Understanding e-commerce essentials

E-commerce, electronic commerce, is high-volume and (hopefully) high-speed shopping over the Internet's Web. It can also be over an intranet's web.

If you want to provide electronic shopping and ordering services, you need servers with the following Internet capabilities:

 ✔ **Continuous availability:** You don't have to close your store because the front door of the mall is broken.

 ✔ **High reliability:** If Marshall buys a new Lamborghini over the Internet, he may be upset if he receives a Kia. By the way, is that for Candace's birthday?

 ✔ **Secure transactions that use appropriate encryption and authentication:** When Marshall purchases the car, the "store" has a responsibility to protect the credit card information.

TLS and SSL secure your network connections. Don't forget that both the client and server computers and applications must also be secured if you want to keep the cyber-criminals away. To get SSL working, you need a digital certificate from a trusted third-party source. See the "How to get a digital certificate" section, earlier in this chapter.

Getting technical with an SSL transaction

Here are the technical details of an SSL transaction, such as sending your credit card number over the Internet:

1. The client program, such as a Web browser, indicates that it wants to send a document using the `https://` protocol.

2. The server program sends its certificate to the client program.

3. The client program checks to see whether the certificate has been issued by a trusted authority (CA).

   If not, the server sends a message to the user: "Do you want to continue without a certificate or end the transaction?" Sometimes you see a "Certificate Expired" message at this point.

4. The client program compares the information in the certificate with the authentication key.

   If they match, the client program knows that the site is secure — that is, that the site is who it says it is.

5. The client program tells the server what encryption algorithms it can understand.

6. The server program chooses the strongest encryption algorithms that it has in common with the client program. The server program tells the client what encryption algorithm they're going to use to communicate.

7. The client program generates a key using the agreed-upon encryption.

8. The client program encrypts the key and sends it to the server program.

9. The server program receives the encrypted key from the client and decodes it.

10. The client and server programs continue to use the key throughout the transaction's back and forth communication.

Security software that's based on SSL or TLS can't protect you from disreputable people. In TCP/IP, as in life, security makes you less vulnerable to the bad guys, but in networking (as in real life), you have to trust someone. Even special agent Mulder trusts his partner, Scully. For example, when you buy something over the telephone, you trust the person who takes your order with your credit card information. When you buy something over the Internet, you trust the server administrator at the site with your credit card information. The server administrator maintains the security software, the physical security of the computers, and the security of passwords and private keys.

IPSec (IP Security Protocol)

IPSec is especially useful for building VPNs (virtual private networks) and for setting up secure remote access to private intranets through dialup modems. A big advantage of IPsec is that the security does not require you to change anything, such as your IP address, on your computer

IPSec gives you two levels of security services:

- ✔ **Authenticating the sender of a network message, called Authentication Header (AH):** The AH ensures that the message sender is the person that he/she claims to be and that the data wasn't changed during transmission. However, if the data is clear text, nothing guarantees that snoopers won't see it as it crosses the network.

- ✔ **Authenticating the sender and also encrypting the message, called Encapsulating Security Payload (ESP):** ESP makes the data unreadable by snoopers.

IPSec information gets stuffed into the packet before the data and after the IP packet header.

The IETF IP Security Protocol Working Group (www.ietf.org/html.charters/ipsec-charter.html) has so far produced 24 Internet drafts and 17 RFCs on the way to creating a security standard for all of TCP/IP. See Chapter 4 to review what the Internet Engineering Task Force does.

There's shopping and then there's SHOPPING!

The country of Singapore is an example of e-commerce on a grand scale. Singapore is setting up an Electronic Procurement System (EPS) for all government purchasing agencies. The Singapore government plans EPS to be an e-commerce system that manages all procurements from more than 10,000 suppliers and distributors. By coordinating their activities through EPS, all government departments combine their buying power to get the best possible service and prices. Singapore expects tremendous savings in manpower and time.

RFC 2411, "IP Security Document Roadmap," describes how the multiple documents that describe the IPSec protocols are interrelated. If you're interested in IPSec, RFC 2411 helps you decide where to start reading. It explains what you can find in each IPSec RFC.

Getting Started with VPNs (Virtual Private Networks)

People away from the office have a couple of ways to telecommute:

- ✔ The office builds a bank of dialup modems (very expensive) so that users can dial in and connect over PPP (Point-to-Point Protocol; see Chapter 15).

- ✔ Each user connects to an ISP and runs a VPN client that connects to a VPN server at the office and establishes a secure tunnel that runs through the Internet. The tunnel can run between one user's computer and the LAN or between two LANs. VPNs use either IPSec or a combination of PPTP and Layer Two Tunneling Protocol (L2TP). Both the client and the server must run the same protocol(s).

A *VPN* (see Chapter 4) is a private network that runs across a public network (usually the Internet). The company in Figure 20-2 uses the VPN connections across the Internet to connect a main office with its branches.

The tunnels you see in Figure 20-2 are not physical cables or other connection media. The term *tunnel* refers to the data that's crossing the VPN. After the data is first encrypted for privacy, it is *encapsulated,* or wrapped, with a special header that says where the data is going. The part of the connection where the data is encapsulated is called the tunnel.

The VPN in Figure 20-2 consists of three LANs and mobile dialup users. The goal of the VPN is to connect those three LANs so that they look like one network to users — and to do it cheaply and securely. Of course, the corporation in Figure 20-2 could connect all three LANs with private lines or satellite links, but that's too expensive.

Here's where the Internet comes in. The Internet already has worldwide backbones and connection media to carry your VPN traffic cheaply. On the downside, you can't get any more public than the Internet. So here's where VPN comes in: VPN security lets you be private on the Internet. To build a private network that runs through the Internet, you need to use the security technologies that we describe in this book:

- ✔ Access control including passwords and hardware security tokens
- ✔ Firewalls (see Chapter 18)
- ✔ Authentication
- ✔ Encryption

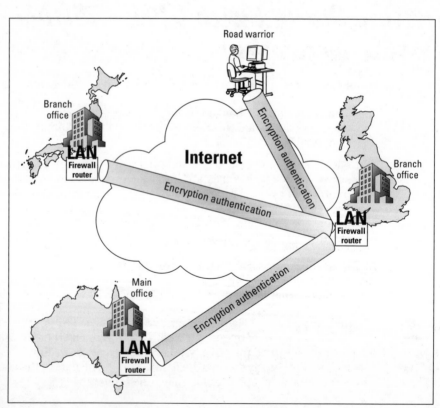

Figure 20-2:
This VPN runs through the Internet.

Part V
The Part of Tens

The 5th Wave   By Rich Tennant

"Good news, honey! No one's registered our last name as a domain name yet! Hellooo Haffassoralsurgery.com!"

In this part . . .

These chapters are TCP/IP nuggets. We even give you a Web refrigerator to keep them fresh. If you're ready for some fun, look at Chapter 21. We had to call Australia to find out what kole beer is (it's not what you think). And if you need some recreation, you can play with model trains or water an online garden — no kidding! When you're in a more serious mood, Chapter 22 gives you some quick security tips and tells you where to go to keep up on the latest viruses, worms, Trojan horses, and other nasty intrusions. Chapter 23 helps you get all those RFCs that define the protocols and gives you some hints and tips as to how to read them.

As you work through this part, you may notice that "ten" doesn't always equal 10 — that's computer math for you. Are we talking decimal numbers or binary? Hex, maybe? In octal, 10 means 8. In binary, it means 2; and in hexadecimal, it means 16. We reserve the right to count in whatever base we like!

Chapter 21

Ten Strange but Real TCP/IP Network Devices (No Kidding!)

*I*n this chapter, we tell you about some fun things on the Internet — a few of which are just plain silly. You can access the devices in this chapter with any Web browser, so start yours and play around.

To get to the appropriate Web page, just type in the URL. Don't forget that things change rapidly on the Internet, so some of these devices may have taken a powder or may be hanging out elsewhere.

This chapter gets harder to write with each new edition of this book. When we wrote the original chapter, lots of Internet devices were amazing. Now such devices — for example, wireless devices that connect to the Internet and that can track where you are on the Earth or show you a map of where you're going — are common. Pagers can trade on the stock market while they play a tune. All these everyday uses of the Internet make amazing devices a lot harder to find.

Soda Machines

When we wrote the first edition of this book, college students connected soda and candy machines to IP networks so that they could control them from their computers and check to see whether their favorite soda brands were available. Those wacky soda machines were the inspiration for this chapter. Now they're serious business. Isochron Data Corporation built the VendCast system, a wireless vending system that monitors and controls vending machines attached to the Internet. The delivery person needn't drive to soda machine sites to check inventory. He or she can get the information over the Internet. If you still want to see college kids and what they can do to a soda machine, you'll find lots of sites on the Internet for that.

For example, computer science students at the University of Western Australia are a thirsty bunch. By looking at the University's soda machine online (`www.ucc.gu.uwa.edu.au/services/drink.html`), you can see that cola is popular, but nothing beats kole beer. To get the most up-to-date info on who's drinking what, click the finger link in the Machine Status and Drink Dispensing section. The results are shown in Figure 21-1.

Toasters

Network toasters are a favorite device of vendors for showing the capabilities of their *SNMP* management stations. (We discuss SNMP, the Simple Network Management Protocol, in Chapter 18.) With the right connections between the host and the toaster, you can easily control the darkness of the toast and the amount of time your bread or muffin is inside.

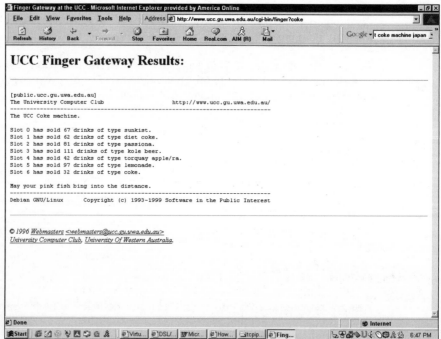

Figure 21-1:
You can satisfy your caffeine and sugar cravings and more in Western Australia.

You Better Watch Out, You Better Not Pout

Webcams are all over the Internet, but we like this one from the North Pole, `www.arctic.noaa.gov/gallery_np.html`. We're hoping to see Santa fly by. This, the first webcam at the North Pole, tracks the North Pole snow cover, weather conditions, and the status of the meteorological and ice sensors.

From the North Pole to the South Pole

Weather data is collected constantly by instrument packages around the world. We considered telling you about the one at the University of Washington so that you could decide whether or not to take that drive around downtown Seattle. But instead, check out the automatic weather station at Mawson in Antarctica. As we write this chapter, the air temperature is –24.6°C and the humidity is 34 percent — lovely weather for penguins. Mawson updates (`www.antdiv.gov.au/stations/mawson/mawson_aws.html`) roughly every ten minutes. Too cold for you at Mawson? Browse the Web to see real-time weather all around the world.

A Telescope in California

You can look at the night sky by using the telescope at UCSB. Browse to `www.deepspace.ucsb.edu/rot.htm` and click the Image box. They aim the telescope for you, and you see your piece of the sky.

The Refrigerator

You can find several refrigerators on the Web, but *the* state-of-the-art fridge is in Germany at `www.electrolux.com/screenfridge/`. This refrigerator is TCP/IP powered to support audio and video messaging, radio, and TV. It even keeps track of the food inside and creates recipes for what you have on hand. As soon as it figures out how to cook the food, we'll be first in line to get one.

The Streets of Seattle (for Anne Marie)

This one is for our good friend, Anne Marie Schanz, who lives near Seattle. The city of Seattle, Washington, has electronic sensors embedded in the roads and video cameras mounted on lampposts in order to monitor the flow of traffic in and around the area. The sensor information is linked to a map in order to display the traffic in a user-friendly format. Before she goes to work each day, A.M. can check the traffic in the Seattle/Bellevue area at `www.wsdot.wa.gov/PugetSoundTraffic/cameras/`.

An Interactive Model Railroad

Didn't you want to be a train engineer when you were a kid? You don't need to build your own model railroad. Just get on the Web and operate the model trains at the University of Ulm in Germany at `http://rr-vs.informatik.uni-ulm.de/rr/`. This site also has a co-browser window so that you can communicate with other model railroaders at this site. Go to the Gallery page to see all the crashes that have occurred at this site — some model railroaders are out of control.

Tend a Garden Even If You Have No Land

You can tour the garden 24 hours a day at `www.usc.edu/dept/garden/`. If you register at the site (at no charge), you can actually command a robot to plant seeds and water the garden.

Space: The Final Frontier on the Web?

It's just like being there. You can watch live what goes on at the Kennedy Space Center `http://science.ksc.nasa.gov/shuttle/countdown/video/video.html`. When the space shuttle launches, you can watch live. Try some of the links on this page. They can be fascinating on a busy day. On a slow day, well . . . try another link.

Chapter 22

Watch Your Back —
Ten Practical Security Tips

Remember the old saying, "The Internet protects those who protect themselves"? Okay, you caught us. We made it up. As you chew your way across the Internet and Web, try saying it over and over. Protect yourself. Protect your business. This chapter provides a smorgasbord of tasty delights that protect you from being eaten alive by security breaches.

Protecting Your Business

If you're doing business over the Internet, be sure that you protect your customers with encryption, authentication, and digital certificates — the major concepts that we discuss in Chapter 20. If you're a business owner and send confidential documents through e-mail, try an electronic postmark from the U.S. Postal Service. The USPS Electronic Postmark can detect e-mail tampering and helps you find out who did the tampering. The service is only available to businesses and organizations. Go to www.usps.com/electronic postmark to find out more.

The digital *sealing wax* of the postmark includes public key/private key cryptography, a digital certificate, and a lot of math.

Take a Free "Snoop Test"

Surf to www.anonymizer.com to take a free snoop test. Anonymizer looks at your computer across the Internet and lets you know what it finds. If Anonymizer can find it, so can crackers. When Candace took the snoop test on her client ("practice what you preach"), her score was pretty good. Six of the seven tests indicated good security. When it came to her browser, Anonymizer was able to see the browser, including the version she uses, her operating system, how many pages she browsed today so far, and the fact that Java and VBScript are enabled. When a cracker knows what browser and operating system you're using, it helps them decide what hacks and exploits will work best against you.

Browse Anonymously

If you don't want anyone finding out about you and what you do on the Web, surf anonymously. Anonymizer Private Surfing (www.anonymizer.com) is one (there are others) commercial anonymous browsing service that protects your identity. Anonymizer also provides a free service. The free service doesn't include SSL and pop-up ad blocking, but it's a good way to try the service to see it it's right for you. Free or paid, it's a handy service if you want to travel the Internet incognito. Both services work with Internet Explorer 5.5 and higher.

Use Secure Clients

Use secure clients to replace the telnet, ftp, rsh, rlogin, and other insecure applications and services that come with TCP/IP. Secure clients, such as VanDyke Software's SecureCRT (included on the CD) and the publicly down-loadable Secure Shell (ftp://ftp.ssh.com/pub/ssh), encrypt usernames and passwords and may encrypt your data as well, depending on how you use them. Look for clients that also provide authentication so that you can be sure no one is spoofing you. SSH also has a version to protect wireless communications. Secure clients are just as easy to use as their non-secure counterparts, sometimes easier if you like graphical interfaces. A free, non-commercial version of SSH is available for download; go to www.ssh.com/products.

SecureCRT, from VanDyke Software (www.vandyke.com), is one of many Windows 95/98/NT/XP/2000 terminal emulators that provide ftp, telnet, and rlogin functionality and supports the Secure Shell (SSH1 and SSH2) protocol.

Use Secure Servers

Use secure servers to replace non-secure services, such as telnet and ftp, that come with TCP/IP. In order to take advantage of all the features of a secure client, you need a secure server that supports authentication, certificates, and encryption.

Try out the Systems Secure Network Client & Server and the FTP server from GoodTech Systems.

Be CERTain You Know the Dangers

Internet-savvy folks get themselves on the CERT (Computer Emergency Response Team) mailing list. CERT keeps you up-to-date on the latest security vulnerabilities and virus alerts, and shows you how to solve or work around them. To get on CERT's mailing list, send e-mail to majordomo@cert.org. Put "subscribe cert-advisory" in the subject line.

Be sure to investigate the CERT techtips and practices. This collection of documents helps you design and implement network security policies.

Know What Your Browser Is Doing

Before you submit a credit card number or other private information via a Web form, check for the visual indication — a closed padlock icon — to be sure that the communication is encrypted.

Figure 22-1 shows the information that you receive when you click the Security icon (the open padlock) on Netscape Navigator's toolbar. (You can also press Ctrl+Shift+I, which is the shortcut for Communicator➪Tools➪ Security Info.) Figure 22-2 shows the Microsoft Internet Explorer security options that you can control after you choose Tools➪Internet Options and click the Advanced tab.

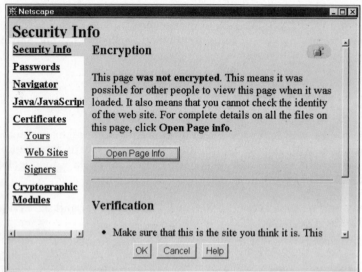

Figure 22-1:
Check
Navigator's
security
settings.

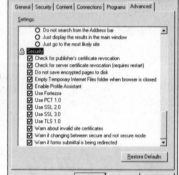

Figure 22-2:
Check
Internet
Explorer's
security
settings.

Keep Security Up-to-Date

When software vendors find security holes or bugs in their products (and they do, unfortunately), they publish *patches* that you can download to fix the problem. In addition to keeping up-to-date on browser patches, you need to keep track of operating system, protocol, service, and application patches. Internet Explorer security patches are part of Windows Update (http://windowsupdate.microsoft.com). Microsoft updates its site often, so be sure to check frequently. For Netscape fixes, head to http://home.netscape.com/security. The major operating system vendors have built-in tools, such as Red Hat's UP2DATE tool, that check for security updates, automatically download the patches, and then install them. PatchManager (`https://sunsolve.sun.com/patchpro/patchpro.html`) from Sun Microsystems is a UNIX example.

If you have a choice of download sites for patches, try to use sites that provide digitally signed patches. Signed patches guarantee that no one can tamper with the patch as it downloads across the Internet.

Clear the Browser Cache

Your browser's *cache* is an area on your hard disk that keeps a copy of every page you access. You may not even be aware that the browser cache exists because the browser copies Web pages to your cache without notifying you. If you leave your computer unattended, some nosy person can check your cache to see what you've been browsing. Clear the cache so that inquiring minds don't find out anything about your browsing habits. Different browsers provide different methods for managing the cache.

When a browser displays an encrypted page, it leaves a clear text copy of the page in your disk cache.

Parents who have no idea where their kids go on the Internet can look at the pages in the cache. Some parents consider this invading their children's privacy. Others feel it is necessary supervision. We couldn't possibly comment.

To empty your Internet Explorer cache, choose Tools⇨Internet Options. On the General tab, click the Delete Files button. You can set the security options to empty your disk cache when you exit a browser. Refer to Figure 22-2. To empty your Netscape Navigator disk cache, choose Edit⇨Preferences, click the "+" next to Advanced to expand it, click Cache, and then click the Clear Disk Cache button.

Cover Your Browser's Tracks in the Windows Registry

This tip is for you only if you're totally paranoid. If you type URLs directly into Internet Explorer's Address bar, you can reuse them later from that drop-down list. Those URLs have to be stored somewhere to offer you the pull-down convenience. That place is the *Windows Registry*. Some nosy people know that they can look there to see where you've been browsing. Cleaning up those URLs is an exception to the rule "Don't mess with the Registry!" If you're worried about touching the Registry, back it up first with your favorite backup software.

Here's how to wipe out those URLs with the Registry Editor:

1. **Close Internet Explorer.**

2. **Choose Start➪Run, type** regedit, **and then click the OK button.**

3. **Expand in turn the Registry keys** HKEY_CURRENT_USER, Software, Microsoft, **and** Internet Explorer **on the left side of the display; click** Typed URLs **once to select it.**

4. **Examine the list of URLs in the Data column on the right side of the display.**

5. **Edit an existing entry by double-clicking the** *url#* **in the Name column and updating the Value Data in the Edit String dialog box that appears.**

6. **Delete entries by selecting the** *url#* **in the Name column and choosing Edit➪Delete or by pressing the Delete key.**

Netscape Navigator's Location bar works the same way, but the URLs aren't stored in the Windows Registry. Look on your computer for a file called prefs.js (start in C:\Program Files\Netscape\Users). Open it with a text editor or word processor and edit and/or delete the lines that follow the one that starts with user_pref("browser.url_history.URL_1".

If you delete only some of the URLs, be sure that the entries in the Name column for those you keep are in a consistent sequence. Be careful because they're listed in alphabetical order rather than numerical order — that means that 10 appears between 1 and 2, rather than after 9. If there are gaps in the sequence, the pull-down list stops at the first gap.

Chapter 23

Ten Ways to Get RFCs

The most common and easiest way to get an RFC (Request for Comments) is to find it online on the World Wide Web. (You can read it online, or save it to your hard disk if you need to keep a copy.) Anonymous FTP is another way to read and download RFCs. If you have no access to either a Web browser or an FTP client, you can still get an RFC via e-mail. RFCs are available from many sites around the world. The Internet Society's RFC Editor (www.rfc-editor.org) publishes the RFCs. The RFC Editor also includes the master list of RFCs, the RFC Index.

Think about this before you retrieve the whole RFC Index. It is over 900Kb in size.

You can find the entire collection (as of this writing) of RFCs from the IETF on the CD included with this book. Because the list of RFCs grows almost every week, however, go to www.rfc-editor.org/rfc-index.html to access the most recent list.

Making Friends with the Editor

The RFC Editor isn't just one person, it's a small group of people: the Networking Division of the USC Information Sciences Institute (ISI) in Marina del Rey, California. The Internet Society funds ISI to function as the RFC Editor.

You can always count on the RFC Editor to have a complete list of Internet documents and lots of different ways to get to them. Figure 23-1 shows the RFC Editor's home page. Later in this chapter, in the "Using the Web to Get an RFC (And More)" section, you can see other Web sites that contain RFCs and other Internet documents that you may find easier to chew through than the RFC Editor.

The RFC Editor lets you search for RFCs in different ways, including the following:

✔ The fastest way to find an RFC is to search the RFC database by type (RFC, STD, FYI, or BCP) and number.

✔ If you don't know the document number, you can search the RFC database by author, title, and/or keywords. Click the All Fields pull-down menu to select your search criteria. When you find the ones you want, you can retrieve RFCs as text or PDF (the Adobe Acrobat Portable Document Format).

✔ You can head straight to the FTP archive of RFCs at `ftp://ftp.rfc-editor.org/in-notes` (for the text versions) or `ftp://ftp.rfc-editor.org/in-notes` (for the PDF versions). You can also download the entire RFC Index via FTP.

Figure 23-1:
The RFC Editor keeps the complete set of RFCs, FYIs, STDs, and BCPs.

✔ Download the weekly updated collection of all RFCs in various compressed formats.

✔ Search through the contents of the entire RFC database. This content search taxes the RFC Editor's computer, however, so try to avoid searching this way.

All RFCs have titles, but their numbers are the key to finding the documents, especially if you use Anonymous FTP. After you find the number of the RFC you want, you can just go after it. (Skip ahead to either "Using the Web to Get an RFC (And More)" or "Using Anonymous FTP to Get an RFC" if you know the number of the RFC you want.) Unless you've memorized all the RFCs by number — there are more than 3,300 as of this writing! — your first task is finding an RFC Index.

Finding the RFC Index

The RFC Index is a list of all the RFCs, usually with both their numbers and their names. Several RFC Indexes are available on the Web in HTML and as text files that you can copy with Anonymous FTP.

See the "Using Anonymous FTP to Get an RFC" section later in this chapter to find out how to get your own copy of the RFC Index. If you prefer to download the index from a Web browser, surf to the RFC Editor and follow the link for the RFC Database. There's also a link to download the index.

Understanding entries in an RFC Index

The entries in the RFC Index contain the following information:

✔ RFC number

✔ Title

✔ Author

✔ Date issued

✔ Format — text (.txt), PostScript (.ps), PDF (.pdf) — and size in bytes

✔ Type — whether the RFC is also an FYI (For Your Information), STD (Internet Standard), or BCP (Best Common Practice)

✔ Relationship of this RFC to any others — whether this RFC is an update of an existing RFC, has made a previous RFC obsolete, or has been rendered obsolete by another RFC

For example, the entry for RFC 3000 contains the following information:

```
3000 Internet Official Protocol Standards. J. Reynolds, R.
         Braden, S. Ginoza, L. Shiota. [ November 2001 ]
         (TXT=115207 bytes)(Obsoletes RFC2900) (Also STD1)
```

This entry tells you that J. Reynolds, R. Braden, S. Ginoza, and L. Shiota wrote RFC 3000 in November 2001. The RFC is a text file of 115,207 bytes. It has made a previous RFC obsolete. RFC 3000 replaces RFC 2900. This RFC is also an STD. (Remember that this is an example. Things may have changed by the time you read this.)

RFC name format

RFC filenames use these naming conventions, where the #### represents the RFC number without leading zeros:

```
rfc####.txt
rfc####.ps
rfc####.pdf
```

The .txt extension indicates a text file; the .ps extension indicates a PostScript file, and the .pdf extension indicates a PDF file. The PostScript version often contains figures and graphics that can't be represented in plain text, so you need a PostScript printer or PostScript previewer software to use the file. You need Adobe Acrobat Reader to view PDF files.

When you fetch a copy of an RFC with Anonymous FTP, make sure that you copy the file that's in the format you want.

Using the Web to Get an RFC (And More)

When you read an RFC on the Web, you don't have to worry about the file format because HTML takes care of everything. Reading RFCs on the World Wide Web is easy. Besides the RFC Editor, there are various sites around the world in different languages, maintained by organizations and private citizens.

RFCs are stored on many Web servers around the world. To find a server near you, use www.rfc-editor.org/repositories.html, the list that the RFC Editor maintains. Or use a Web search engine to find the sites that have the RFC Index or the specific RFC that you want.

Other people and organizations have Web sites that hold RFCs. Figure 23-2 shows a favorite of ours, www.faqs.org/rfcs, from the Internet FAQ

Archives site, `www.faqs.org`. Besides being easy to navigate through the RFCs, this site includes such tasty tidbits as the following:

✔ A brief overview of the RFC process, filled with links to other sites for more detailed information

✔ Where and how to get new RFCs

✔ How to get RFCs via e-mail

✔ How to publish an RFC

✔ Instructions for RFC authors

✔ A link to the RFC Editor home page

Besides the "official sites," some hardworking, knowledgeable people maintain Web sites where you can find RFCs and more, such as Lynn Wheeler's site at `www.garlic.com/~lynn/rfcietff.htm`. In addition to the RFCs, this site links to a useful set of references about TCP/IP and the Internet. Then there are the language sites:

✔ Spanish: `www.rfc-es.org`

✔ Russian: `www.protocols.ru/iso/rfc.shtml`

✔ Italian: `www.napolihak.it/pagine/rfc_it.htm`

✔ Japanese: `www.se.hiroshima-u.ac.jp/~isaki/rfc/`

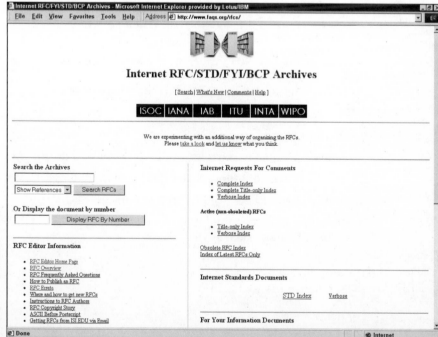

Figure 23-2:
The Internet
FAQ
Archives
include an
easy-to-use
RFC section.

Using Anonymous FTP to Get an RFC

The RFC Editor helps you get an RFC text file by number from an FTP directory by linking you to an FTP directory at `ftp://ftp.rfc-editor.org/ in-notes/`. This FTP archive has the files plus separate directories for RFCs, STDs, FYIs, and BCPs. (There's also a directory, `pdfrfc`, just for PDF versions.) The document files are named after their numbers. Luckily, for those who order by name, not number, each directory has an index that lists the names and numbers. For example, if you need an RFC and you know the name but not the number, click `rfc-index.txt` in the RFC Editor directory. After you find the number, click the Back button on your browser and then click the RFC you want to read.

In these examples, we look up the Next Hop Resolution Protocol (NHRP) that VPNs (virtual private networks) use:

1. **Go to the ftp site for the RFC Index,** `ftp://ftp.rfc-editor.org/ in-notes/rfc-index.txt`.

   Going to the Web to find FTP archives may sound a little strange, but believe us, it's worth it to get a comprehensive list.

2. **Search or scroll through the index until you find the RFC for NHRP.**

   Figure 23-3 shows how we found it by searching.

3. **Go a level up in your browser to** `ftp://ftp.rfc-editor.org/ in-notes`.

4. **Search or scroll through the list. When you reach** `rfc2735.txt`, **click it.**

5. **To download the RFC, use your browser's File⇨Save As menu.**

If you don't want to bother with a browser, you can use FTP directly. Follow these steps:

1. **Fire up FTP and connect to** `ftp.rfc-editor.org`.

2. **Type** cd in-notes **to see a list of RFC indexes and documents.**

3. **Display the list of indexes, and then type** dir *index* **(Figure 23-4).**

4. **To download the RFC Index, type** get rfc-index.txt.

5. **Check the number of the RFC you want and type** get **again followed by the filename, such as** rfc2735.txt.

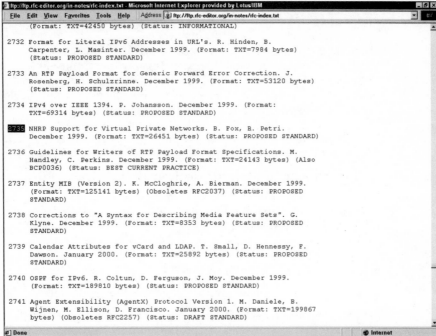

```
ftp://ftp.rfc-editor.org/in-notes/rfc-index.txt - Microsoft Internet Explorer provided by Lotus/IBM
File   Edit   View   Favorites   Tools   Help    Address  ftp://ftp.rfc-editor.org/in-notes/rfc-index.txt
     (Format: TXT=42450 bytes) (Status: INFORMATIONAL)

2732 Format for Literal IPv6 Addresses in URL's. R. Hinden, B.
     Carpenter, L. Masinter. December 1999. (Format: TXT=7984 bytes)
     (Status: PROPOSED STANDARD)

2733 An RTP Payload Format for Generic Forward Error Correction. J.
     Rosenberg, H. Schulzrinne. December 1999. (Format: TXT=53120 bytes)
     (Status: PROPOSED STANDARD)

2734 IPv4 over IEEE 1394. P. Johansson. December 1999. (Format:
     TXT=69314 bytes) (Status: PROPOSED STANDARD)

2735 NHRP Support for Virtual Private Networks. B. Fox, B. Petri.
     December 1999. (Format: TXT=26451 bytes) (Status: PROPOSED STANDARD)

2736 Guidelines for Writers of RTP Payload Format Specifications. M.
     Handley, C. Perkins. December 1999. (Format: TXT=24143 bytes) (Also
     BCP0036) (Status: BEST CURRENT PRACTICE)

2737 Entity MIB (Version 2). K. McCloghrie, A. Bierman. December 1999.
     (Format: TXT=125141 bytes) (Obsoletes RFC2037) (Status: PROPOSED
     STANDARD)

2738 Corrections to "A Syntax for Describing Media Feature Sets". G.
     Klyne. December 1999. (Format: TXT=8353 bytes) (Status: PROPOSED
     STANDARD)

2739 Calendar Attributes for vCard and LDAP. T. Small, D. Hennessy, F.
     Dawson. January 2000. (Format: TXT=25892 bytes) (Status: PROPOSED
     STANDARD)

2740 OSPF for IPv6. R. Coltun, D. Ferguson, J. Moy. December 1999.
     (Format: TXT=189810 bytes) (Status: PROPOSED STANDARD)

2741 Agent Extensibility (AgentX) Protocol Version 1. M. Daniele, B.
     Wijnen, M. Ellison, D. Francisco. January 2000. (Format: TXT=199867
     bytes) (Obsoletes RFC2257) (Status: DRAFT STANDARD)

Done                                                             Internet
```

Figure 23-3:
The RFC
Index
shows that
we want
RFC 2735.

```
FTP
 12 x 16
C:\>ftp ftp.rfc-editor.org
Connected to ftp.rfc-editor.org.
220 ftp.isi.edu NcFTPd Server (free educational license) ready.
User (ftp.rfc-editor.org:(none)): anonymous
331 Guest login ok, send your complete e-mail address as password.
Password:
230-You are user #21 of 550 simultaneous users allowed.
230-
230-If you have problems downloading and are seeing "Access denied" or
230-"Permission denied", please make sure that you started your FTP client in
230-a directory to which you have write permission.
230-
230-If your FTP client crashes or hangs shortly after login please try using
230-a dash (-) as the first character of your password.  This will turn off
230-the informational messages that may be confusing your FTP client.
230-
230-All transfers and commands to and from this host are logged.
230-
230-If you experience any problems using ftp, please report them via
230-e-mail to Action@isi.edu.
230-
230 Logged in anonymously.
ftp> cd in-notes
250-"/in-notes" is new cwd.
250-
250-*==============================================================*
250-*                                                              *
250-* This directory is maintained by the RFC Editor.  If you experience *
250-* any problems, please report them to rfc-editor@rfc-editor.org. *
250-*                                                              *
250-*==============================================================*
250
ftp> dir *index*
200 PORT command successful.
150 Opening ASCII mode data connection for /bin/ls.
-rw-r--r--   1 ftpuser   ftpusers      11204 Jul 30 13:58 bcp-index.txt
-rw-r--r--   1 ftpuser   ftpusers       8024 Jul 30 13:58 fyi-index.txt
-rw-r--r--   1 ftpuser   ftpusers       3991 Aug  2 02:30 rfc-index-latest.txt
-rw-r--r--   1 ftpuser   ftpusers     513246 Jul 30 13:58 rfc-index.txt
-rw-r--r--   1 ftpuser   ftpusers       9521 Jul 30 13:58 std-index.txt
226 Listing completed.
ftp: 362 bytes received in 0.05Seconds 7.24Kbytes/sec.
ftp>
For Help, click Help Topics on the Help Menu.
```

Figure 23-4:
Use
Anonymous
FTP to
conect to
ftp.rfc-
editor.org
and display
the indexes.

Getting an RFC via E-Mail

What! You don't have a Web browser? And no FTP client? It may sound strange, in this connected age, but it happens. Don't worry. If you can get e-mail, you can get an RFC. You use the RFC-Info services by sending an e-mail message to RFC-INFO@ISI.EDU. The contents of your e-mail determine what RFC-Info sends back to you:

1. **If you need help using RFC-Info, type** HELP: help **or** HELP: topics **as your e-mail message.**

2. **If you want RFC-Info to e-mail you the index of all RFCs, type** HELP: rfc_index **as your e-mail message.**

3. **If you know the number of the RFC you want, send a message with the following information:**

   - The keyword **retrieve**

   - The RFC type, such as RFC, FYI, BCP, STD

   - The document number, such as RFC2735, FYI0004

4. **If you want a list of RFCs that match a certain search criteria, type** LIST: RFC **in your message, followed by a keyword.**

   For example, if you phrase your message as **LIST: RFC gateway**, RFC-Info responds with a list of RFCs with the word "gateway" in the title.

5. **If you don't like any of the ways that we list in Steps 1 through 4, use the following phrases in the body of your e-mail message:**

   - HELP: ways_to_get_rfcs

   - HELP: ways_to_get_fyis

   - HELP: ways_to_get_stds

Appendix

About the CD

The *TCP/IP For Dummies,* 5th Edition, CD contains bonus chapters, reference information, and software that you may find useful. We've included programs for Windows (95, 98, NT, XP, and 2000), Mac OS X, UNIX, and Linux — but not everything is provided for every operating system.

Here's what you'll find on the CD:

✔ The entire collection of RFCs — as of the time of writing this book

✔ Messaging tools and Web browsers

✔ FTP shareware utilities

✔ Networking utilities

✔ A secure Linux operating system

✔ Security applications

✔ Security white papers, incident notes, and advisories

System Requirements

Make sure that your computer meets the minimum system requirements listed in this section. If your computer doesn't match up to most of these requirements, you may have problems using the contents of the CD. Most new computers come with a network interface card (NIC). If your computer did not come with a NIC, you need one for all the systems that we list in this section.

Microsoft Windows 95, 98:

- ✔ PC with a processor running at 200 MHz or faster.

- ✔ At least 32MB of RAM installed on your computer. For best performance, we recommend more.

- ✔ A network interface card (NIC) or a modem with a speed of at least 28,800 bps.

- ✔ A CD-ROM or DVD drive.

Microsoft Windows NT 4.0, XP, or 2000:

- ✔ PC with a processor running at 200 MHz or faster.

- ✔ At least 64MB of RAM installed on your computer. For best performance, we recommend more.

- ✔ A network interface card (NIC) or a modem with a speed of at least 28,800 bps.

- ✔ A CD-ROM or DVD drive.

Linux or UNIX:

- ✔ At least 32MB of RAM installed on your computer. For best performance, we recommend more.

- ✔ A network interface card (NIC) or a modem with a speed of at least 28,800 bps.

- ✔ A CD-ROM or DVD drive.

Mac OS:

- ✔ A Mac running Mac OS 7.6.1 or later. Most Mac tools on the CD are for Mac OS X and higher.

- ✔ At least 32MB of total RAM installed on your computer; for best performance, we recommend at least 64MB.

- ✔ A network interface card (NIC) or modem with a speed of at least 28,800 bps.

- ✔ A CD-ROM or DVD drive.

Using the CD with Microsoft Windows

To install the items from the CD to your hard drive, follow these steps:

1. **Insert the CD into your computer's CD-ROM or DVD drive.**

2. **Start Windows Explorer and navigate to the CD.**

3. **Double-click the file called** License.txt.

This file contains the end-user license that you agree to by using the CD. When you're done reading the license, close the program, most likely Notepad, that displayed the file.

4. **Double-click the file called** `Readme.txt`.

This file contains instructions about installing the software from this CD. It might be helpful to leave this text file open while you're using the CD.

5. **Double-click the folder for the software you are interested in.**

Be sure to read the descriptions of the programs in the next section of this appendix (much of this information also shows up in the Readme file). These descriptions will give you more precise information about the programs' folder names, and about finding and running the installer program.

6. **Find the file called** `Setup.exe`, **or** `Install.exe`, **or something similar, and double-click that file.**

The program's installer will walk you through the process of setting up your new software.

After you've installed the programs that you want, you can eject the CD. Carefully place it back in the plastic jacket of the book for safekeeping.

Using the CD with Linux or UNIX

To install the items from the CD to your hard drive, follow these steps:

1. **Log on as root.**

2. **Insert the CD into your computer's CD-ROM or DVD drive.**

3. **Mount the CD-ROM.**

4. **Examine the** `Readme.txt` **file on the CD.**

The `readme.txt` file contains information about the CD's programs and any last-minute instructions you may need in order to correctly install them.

5. **To install most programs, expand the GNU Zip (.gz) archive and run the install program.**

6. **Umount the CD-ROM.**

You can eject the CD now. Carefully place it back in the plastic jacket of the book for safekeeping.

7. **Log out.**

Using the CD with the Mac OS

To install the items from the CD to your hard drive, follow these steps:

1. **Insert the CD into your computer's CD-ROM or DVD drive.**

   In a moment, an icon representing the CD you just inserted appears on your Mac desktop. Chances are, the icon looks like a CD-ROM.

2. **Double-click the CD icon to show the CD's contents.**

3. **Double-click the file called** License.txt.

   This file contains the end-user license that you agree to by using the CD. When you are done reading the license, you can close the window that displayed the file.

4. **Double-click the Read Me First icon.**

   This text file contains information about the CD's programs and any last-minute instructions you need to know about installing the programs on the CD that we don't cover in this appendix.

   Most programs come with installers, making installation a point-and-click process.

5. **Open the program's folder on the CD, and double-click the icon with the words "Install" or "Installer," or sometimes "sea" (for self-extracting archive).**

6. **If you don't find an installer, just drag the program's folder from the CD window and drop it on your hard drive icon.**

   You can eject the CD after you've installed the programs that you want. Carefully place it back in the plastic jacket of the book for safekeeping.

What You'll Find

Here's a summary of the software on this CD arranged by category.

Shareware programs are fully functional, trial versions of copyrighted programs. If you like particular programs, register with their authors for a nominal fee and receive licenses, enhanced versions, and technical support. *Freeware programs* are copyrighted games, applications, and utilities that are free for personal use. Unlike shareware, these programs do not require a fee or provide technical -support. *GNU software* is governed by its own license, which is included inside the folder of the GNU product. See the GNU license for more details.

Trial, demo, or evaluation versions are usually limited either by time or functionality (such as being unable to save projects). Some trial versions are very sensitive to system date changes. If you alter your computer's date, the programs will "time out" and will no longer be functional.

Do you have to pay?

While some of the stuff on this CD-ROM is completely free, you may have to pay for some of the software if you decide to keep using it. Here's what all the technical lingo means:

✔ **Freeware:** A program that you can use forever at no cost.

✔ **Open source:** A program with underlying source code that's available to the licensee. It's usually a public collaboration to enhance the existing software and then share the modifications with other developers and users through the newly developed open source.

✔ **Shareware:** A program you can try for free for a short time, after which you must pay a small fee or stop using the program.

✔ **Trial version:** A program that you can try for free for a short time. If you like the program, you must purchase the commercial version.

Read each software's licensing agreement in its respective folder before installing it onto your computer.

Bonus chapters

The following chapters are in PDF format. Adobe Acrobat Reader is required to view them, and we've included a copy of it on the CD.

✔ **Sharing Files with NFS:** Sharing disk space and files is one of the most common reasons to link computers via a network. *NFS*, the Network File System, is a client/server environment that allows computers to share disk space and users to see their files from multiple computers without having to copy the files to those computers. You can mix and match all major operating systems for NFS clients and servers.

✔ **Using NIS to Share System Files across a Network:** NIS, the Network Information Service, allows Linux and UNIX systems to share system information. You may also occasionally see it used on Windows, especially when you mix Windows with Linux and UNIX on your intranet.

Browsers

A browser is the client software that you use to surf the Web on your organization's intranet or the World Wide Web on the Internet. Don't forget that you need an ISP (Internet Service Provider) or LAN connection in order to connect to the Internet.

On the CD, you'll find *Mozilla*, an open source browser for Linux, UNIX, Mac OS X, Mac OS 8.1-9.x and higher, and various Microsoft Windows flavors. Netscape bases its browser code on Mozilla.

Messaging and IP telephony tools

Messaging tools help you exchange information with other people via e-mail or Usenet news. You can use them on an intranet or the Internet. To use them on the Internet, you need an Internet connection, either from an ISP or a permanent LAN connection.

On the CD, you'll find ilChat Logger (ilSoftware). ilChat Logger automatically logs Instant Messaging on MSN Messenger, ICQ, and AIM clients. ilChat Logger also includes a viewer so that you can sort the log files by client program, the person you were chatting to, and the time of your chats.

Networking utilities and tools

The networking utilities and tools listed in this section are programs that help you access and manage your intranet or the Internet. To use the following programs on the Internet, you need an Internet connection, either from an ISP or a permanent LAN connection.

- **AdKiller Daemon** (InfoCrackes Software) runs on Windows 95/98/Me/NT/2000/XP and requires the Visual Basic 6.0 Runtime module. This program is a PopUp Killer that closes ad windows that open automatically while you're browsing.

- **Boson Wildcard Mask Checker and Decimal to IP Calculator 1.3** (networkingfiles.com) is a set of tools for checking the network IP address range created by a subnet mask and converting between formats for Windows 95, 98, Me, NT, 2000, and XP. Freeware.

- **FTP Voyager** (Rhino Software, Inc.) is a graphical FTP client for Windows 95, 98, Me, 2000, XP, and NT. Voyager supports SSL connections to encrypt logons to secure servers. Shareware.

- **GoodTech Telnet Servers** (GoodTech Systems) is for Windows 95, 98, Me, NT, 2000, and XP. The telnet servers for Windows 95, 98, Me, and XP allow so-called client operating systems to function as telnet servers. Telnet users can run a variety of character-based applications from the command line. These telnet servers accept any telnet connection from any client including Linux, UNIX, and Mac OS.

- **Handy Backup** (Novosoft, Inc.) is a backup program that runs on Windows 95/98/Me/NT 4.0/2000/XP. It lets you automatically back up data to various storage media, including networked devices and remote FTP servers. Handy Backup also provides secure backups with 128-bit encryption support.

✔ **IPrint2Fax** (Quicknet Technologies, Inc.) is a free PC-to-fax application for Windows. Using IPrint2Fax, you can send free faxes to single fax machines. You can also send faxes as virus-checked e-mail attachments to any e-mail recipient. Broadcasting faxes simultaneously to multiple fax machines incurs a per-minute charge. See `www.quicknet.net` for information on broadcast charges.

✔ **The IP Subnet Calculator** (Wildpackets Inc.) for Windows 95/98/NT/2000 is a freeware program that calculates IP addresses and subnets.

✔ **InterGate** (Vicomsoft) for Mac OS and Windows 95/98/NT is an Internet Gateway software router for connecting networks to the Internet. Intergate also speeds up Web browsing with a high-speed caching server.

✔ **NetSwitcher** (J. W. Hance) is a graphical program that lets you easily (without reconfiguring network settings) move your portable computer among different networks for Windows 95, 98, NT, and 2000. Shareware.

✔ **Serv-U FTP Server** (Rhino Software, Inc.) for Windows 95, 98, Me, 2000, XP, and NT uses SSL for transfers between a Serv-U server and secure clients, including FTP Voyager. You can set a wide range of permissions and acess control rules on archives if you replace the basic FTP server that comes with TCP/IP with Serv-U. Serv-U also logs all user commands so that system and network administrators can track user activities. Free personal edition.

✔ **WhoIs-IP** (Olivier Martyn - Vincent Marchetti) for Windows 95, 98, Me, NT, and 2000 includes a graphic interface to three WhoIs databases: ARIN (North America, South America, the Caribbean, sub-Saharan Africa); RIPE (Europe); APNIC (Asia-Pacific). WhoIs-IP enables you to input an FQDN or IP address for registered Internet domains and returns information about the owner of the domain, the registrar, and business and technical contacts for the domain. Freeware.

Reference information

✔ **"CERT FAQ, Techtips, Modules and Practices"** (CERT Coordination Center, The Software Engineering Institute, Carnegie Mellon University): This is a collection of useful documents from the Computer Emergency Response Team at Carnegie Mellon University. This collection includes "The CERT Coordination Center FAQ, CERT/CC Overview Incident and Vulnerability Trends, File Cabinets and Pig Latin: Guards for Information Assets, Buffer Overflows: What Are They and What Can I Do About Them?, Is There an Intruder in my Computer?, Internet — Friend or Foe?, Larry Rogers: Attack Scenarios: How to Get There from Here, Yesterday I Couldn't Spell Systems Administrator; Now I Am One!, E-mail — A Postcard Written in Pencil, Home Network Security, Intruder Detection Checklist, Using PGP to Verify Digital Signatures, and CERT Incident Note IN-2002-03 Social Engineering Attacks via IRC and Instant Messaging." In HTML format.

✔ **Entire collection of RFCs** (the IETF): Every RFC available at the time of publication. These are presented as text files stored in a compressed archive on the CD. Windows and Mac users will need a program capable of reading ".zip" formatted files. We've included a copy of WinACE, a popular tool for working with compressed archives.

Security applications

The security applications and tools listed in this section are programs that help you protect access to computers on your intranet both from internal users and from the Internet. To use the following programs across the Internet, you need an Internet connection, either from an ISP or a permanent LAN connection.

✔ **Entunnel (VanDyke Software, Inc.)** for Windows 95, 98, Me, NT 4.0, 2000, and XP provides SSH2 data-tunneling (port-forwarding) services when connected to an SSH2 server. The Secure Shell protocol provides inter-operability with SSH servers on different platforms.

✔ **ilSystem Wiper** (il Software) allows you to clear the history of your activites from you computer, including Internet Explorer history, temporary Internet files, and cookies. In addition to internetworking history, you can also clear the following:

- Windows list of recently used files
- Find File History
- Run Program History
- Recycle Bin
- Windows Media Player Recent Lists
- Information saved by P2P programs
- Microsoft Office Recent File Lists

✔ **SAINT** [The Security Administrator's Integrated Network Tool (SAINT)] from the SAINT Corporation is an open source program that tests the security of networked computers running Linux. It scans your Linux systems looking for security weaknesses. If SAINT finds any network vulnerabilities, it reports them and recommends ways to protect your data.

NOTE: This product requires a product key to install. To get a key, visit http://www.saintcorporation.com/products/download.html, click on "Download a Free Trial" and fill out the form. A trial key will be sent to your e-mail address.

✔ **SecureCRT** (VanDyke Software, Inc.) is a secure remote-access client for Windows 95, 98, NT, Me, 2000, and XP. SecureCRT supports authenticated and encrypted client connections to secure servers. It provides telnet, rlogin, and SSH functionality. You can also use SecureCRT for client access to non-secure servers.

- ✔ **SecureFX** (VanDyke Software, Inc.) provides a public-key assistant to make the initial transfer of a public key to a server both easy and secure. Instead of an administrator manually depositing your public keys on a server for you, you can use SecureFX to upload your own public key to a secure server. The public-key assistant is integrated into the Secure Shell protocol.

- ✔ **Secure Network Client & Server** (GoodTech Systems) for Windows 98/Me/NT/2000/XP is a client server system that keeps your data protected as it travels over an intranet or the Internet.

- ✔ **Secure Tunnel** (IP*Works!) incorporates SSL protocol functionality into any server. It provides encryption and authentication.

- ✔ **Serv-U FTP Server** (See the earlier section "Networking utilities and tools.")

Troubleshooting the CD

We tried our best to include programs that work on most computers with the minimum system requirements. Alas, your computer may differ, and some programs may not work properly for some reason.

The two likeliest problems are that you don't have enough memory (RAM) for the programs you want to use, or you have other programs running that are affecting installation or running of a program. If you get error messages like `Not enough memory` or `Setup cannot continue`, try one or more of these methods and then try using the software again:

1. **Turn off any anti-virus software that you have on your computer.**

   Installers sometimes mimic virus activity and may make your computer incorrectly believe that it is being infected by a virus. Don't forget to turn it back on again, later!

2. **Close all running programs.**

   The more programs you're running, the less memory is available to other programs. Installers also typically update files and programs; if you keep other programs running, installation may not work properly.

3. **In Windows, close the CD interface and run demos or installations directly from Windows Explorer.**

   The interface itself can tie up system memory, or even conflict with certain kinds of interactive demos. Use Windows Explorer to browse the files on the CD and launch installers or demos.

4. **Add memory.**

   (We've been uttering this mantra continuously since the day we bought our first PC.) This step may let you run more programs at the same time and faster. Fortunately, the price of memory continues to go lower and lower.

If you still have trouble installing the items from the CD, please call the Customer Service phone number at 800-762-2974 (outside the U.S.: 317-572-3993) or send e-mail to techsupdum@wiley.com. Wiley Publishing, Inc. will provide technical support only for installation and other general quality control items. For technical support on the applications themselves, consult the program's vendor or author.

Index

• **D** •

• *E* •

Wiley Publishing, Inc.
End-User License Agreement

READ THIS. You should carefully read these terms and conditions before opening the software packet(s) included with this book "Book". This is a license agreement "Agreement" between you and Wiley Publishing, Inc."WPI". By opening the accompanying software packet(s), you acknowledge that you have read and accept the following terms and conditions. If you do not agree and do not want to be bound by such terms and conditions, promptly return the Book and the unopened software packet(s) to the place you obtained them for a full refund.

1. **License Grant.** WPI grants to you (either an individual or entity) a nonexclusive license to use one copy of the enclosed software program(s) (collectively, the "Software" solely for your own personal or business purposes on a single computer (whether a standard computer or a workstation component of a multi-user network). The Software is in use on a computer when it is loaded into temporary memory (RAM) or installed into permanent memory (hard disk, CD-ROM, or other storage device). WPI reserves all rights not expressly granted herein.

2. **Ownership.** WPI is the owner of all right, title, and interest, including copyright, in and to the compilation of the Software recorded on the disk(s) or CD-ROM "Software Media". Copyright to the individual programs recorded on the Software Media is owned by the author or other authorized copyright owner of each program. Ownership of the Software and all proprietary rights relating thereto remain with WPI and its licensers.

3. **Restrictions On Use and Transfer.**

   (a) You may only (i) make one copy of the Software for backup or archival purposes, or (ii) transfer the Software to a single hard disk, provided that you keep the original for backup or archival purposes. You may not (i) rent or lease the Software, (ii) copy or reproduce the Software through a LAN or other network system or through any computer subscriber system or bulletin- board system, or (iii) modify, adapt, or create derivative works based on the Software.

   (b) You may not reverse engineer, decompile, or disassemble the Software. You may transfer the Software and user documentation on a permanent basis, provided that the transferee agrees to accept the terms and conditions of this Agreement and you retain no copies. If the Software is an update or has been updated, any transfer must include the most recent update and all prior versions.

4. **Restrictions on Use of Individual Programs.** You must follow the individual requirements and restrictions detailed for each individual program in the About the CD appendix of this Book. These limitations are also contained in the individual license agreements recorded on the Software Media. These limitations may include a requirement that after using the program for a specified period of time, the user must pay a registration fee or discontinue use. By opening the Software packet(s), you will be agreeing to abide by the licenses and restrictions for these individual programs that are detailed in the About the CD appendix and on the Software Media. None of the material on this Software Media or listed in this Book may ever be redistributed, in original or modified form, for commercial purposes.

GNU General Public License

Version 2, June 1991
Copyright © 1989, 1991 Free Software Foundation, Inc.
59 Temple Place - Suite 330, Boston, MA 02111-1307, USA

Preamble

The licenses for most software are designed to take away your freedom to share and change it. By contrast, the GNU General Public License is intended to guarantee your freedom to share and change free software—to make sure the software is free for all its users. This General Public License applies to most of the Free Software Foundation's software and to any other program whose authors commit to using it. (Some other Free Software Foundation software is covered by the GNU Library General Public License instead.) You can apply it to your programs, too.

When we speak of free software, we are referring to freedom, not price. Our General Public Licenses are designed to make sure that you have the freedom to distribute copies of free software (and charge for this service if you wish), that you receive source code or can get it if you want it, that you can change the software or use pieces of it in new free programs; and that you know you can do these things.

To protect your rights, we need to make restrictions that forbid anyone to deny you these rights or to ask you to surrender the rights. These restrictions translate to certain responsibilities for you if you distribute copies of the software, or if you modify it.

For example, if you distribute copies of such a program, whether gratis or for a fee, you must give the recipients all the rights that you have. You must make sure that they, too, receive or can get the source code. And you must show them these terms so they know their rights.

We protect your rights with two steps: (1) copyright the software, and (2) offer you this license which gives you legal permission to copy, distribute and/or modify the software.

Also, for each author's protection and ours, we want to make certain that everyone understands that there is no warranty for this free software. If the software is modified by someone else and passed on, we want its recipients to know that what they have is not the original, so that any problems introduced by others will not reflect on the original authors' reputations.

Finally, any free program is threatened constantly by software patents. We wish to avoid the danger that redistributors of a free program will individually obtain patent licenses, in effect making the program proprietary. To prevent this, we have made it clear that any patent must be licensed for everyone's free use or not licensed at all.

The precise terms and conditions for copying, distribution and modification follow.

Terms and Conditions for Copying, Distribution and Modification

0. This License applies to any program or other work which contains a notice placed by the copyright holder saying it may be distributed under the terms of this General Public License. The "Program", below, refers to any such program or work, and a "work based on the Program" means either the Program or any derivative work under copyright law: that is to say, a work containing the Program or a portion of it, either verbatim or with modifications and/or translated into another language. (Hereinafter, translation is included without limitation in the term "modification".) Each licensee is addressed as "you".

    Activities other than copying, distribution and modification are not covered by this License; they are outside its scope. The act of running the Program is not restricted, and the output from the Program is covered only if its contents constitute a work based on the Program (independent of having been made by running the Program). Whether that is true depends on what the Program does.

1. You may copy and distribute verbatim copies of the Program's source code as you receive it, in any medium, provided that you conspicuously and appropriately publish on each copy an appropriate copyright notice and disclaimer of warranty; keep intact all the notices that refer to this License and to the absence of any warranty; and give any other recipients of the Program a copy of this License along with the Program.

    You may charge a fee for the physical act of transferring a copy, and you may at your option offer warranty protection in exchange for a fee.

2. You may modify your copy or copies of the Program or any portion of it, thus forming a work based on the Program, and copy and distribute such modifications or work under the terms of Section 1 above, provided that you also meet all of these conditions:

    a) You must cause the modified files to carry prominent notices stating that you changed the files and the date of any change.

    b) You must cause any work that you distribute or publish, that in whole or in part contains or is derived from the Program or any part thereof, to be licensed as a whole at no charge to all third parties under the terms of this License.

    c) If the modified program normally reads commands interactively when run, you must cause it, when started running for such interactive use in the most ordinary way, to print or display an announcement including an appropriate copyright notice and a notice that there is no warranty (or else, saying that you provide a warranty) and that users may redistribute the program under these conditions, and telling the user how to view a copy of this License. (Exception: if the Program itself is interactive but does not normally print such an announcement, your work based on the Program is not required to print an announcement.)

    These requirements apply to the modified work as a whole. If identifiable sections of that work are not derived from the Program, and can be reasonably considered independent and separate works in themselves, then this License, and its terms, do not apply to those sections when you distribute them as separate works. But when you distribute the same sections as part of a whole which is a work based on the Program, the distribution of the whole must be on the terms of this License, whose permissions for other licensees extend to the entire whole, and thus to each and every part regardless of who wrote it.

Thus, it is not the intent of this section to claim rights or contest your rights to work written entirely by you; rather, the intent is to exercise the right to control the distribution of derivative or collective works based on the Program.

In addition, mere aggregation of another work not based on the Program with the Program (or with a work based on the Program) on a volume of a storage or distribution medium does not bring the other work under the scope of this License.

3. You may copy and distribute the Program (or a work based on it, under Section 2) in object code or executable form under the terms of Sections 1 and 2 above provided that you also do one of the following:

   a) Accompany it with the complete corresponding machine-readable source code, which must be distributed under the terms of Sections 1 and 2 above on a medium customarily used for software interchange; or,

   b) Accompany it with a written offer, valid for at least three years, to give any third party, for a charge no more than your cost of physically performing source distribution, a complete machine-readable copy of the corresponding source code, to be distributed under the terms of Sections 1 and 2 above on a medium customarily used for software interchange; or,

   c) Accompany it with the information you received as to the offer to distribute corresponding source code. (This alternative is allowed only for noncommercial distribution and only if you received the program in object code or executable form with such an offer, in accord with Subsection b above.)

The source code for a work means the preferred form of the work for making modifications to it. For an executable work, complete source code means all the source code for all modules it contains, plus any associated interface definition files, plus the scripts used to control compilation and installation of the executable. However, as a special exception, the source code distributed need not include anything that is normally distributed (in either source or binary form) with the major components (compiler, kernel, and so on) of the operating system on which the executable runs, unless that component itself accompanies the executable.

If distribution of executable or object code is made by offering access to copy from a designated place, then offering equivalent access to copy the source code from the same place counts as distribution of the source code, even though third parties are not compelled to copy the source along with the object code.

4. You may not copy, modify, sublicense, or distribute the Program except as expressly provided under this License. Any attempt otherwise to copy, modify, sublicense or distribute the Program is void, and will automatically terminate your rights under this License. However, parties who have received copies, or rights, from you under this License will not have their licenses terminated so long as such parties remain in full compliance.

5. You are not required to accept this License, since you have not signed it. However, nothing else grants you permission to modify or distribute the Program or its derivative works. These actions are prohibited by law if you do not accept this License. Therefore, by modifying or distributing the Program (or any work based on the Program), you indicate your acceptance of this License to do so, and all its terms and conditions for copying, distributing or modifying the Program or works based on it.

6. Each time you redistribute the Program (or any work based on the Program), the recipient automatically receives a license from the original licensor to copy, distribute or modify the Program subject to these terms and conditions. You may not impose any further restrictions on the recipients' exercise of the rights granted herein. You are not responsible for enforcing compliance by third parties to this License.

7. If, as a consequence of a court judgment or allegation of patent infringement or for any other reason (not limited to patent issues), conditions are imposed on you (whether by court order, agreement or otherwise) that contradict the conditions of this License, they do not excuse you from the conditions of this License. If you cannot distribute so as to satisfy simultaneously your obligations under this License and any other pertinent obligations, then as a consequence you may not distribute the Program at all. For example, if a patent license would not permit royalty-free redistribution of the Program by all those who receive copies directly or indirectly through you, then the only way you could satisfy both it and this License would be to refrain entirely from distribution of the Program.

    If any portion of this section is held invalid or unenforceable under any particular circumstance, the balance of the section is intended to apply and the section as a whole is intended to apply in other circumstances.

    It is not the purpose of this section to induce you to infringe any patents or other property right claims or to contest validity of any such claims; this section has the sole purpose of protecting the integrity of the free software distribution system, which is implemented by public license practices. Many people have made generous contributions to the wide range of software distributed through that system in reliance on consistent application of that system; it is up to the author/donor to decide if he or she is willing to distribute software through any other system and a licensee cannot impose that choice.

    This section is intended to make thoroughly clear what is believed to be a consequence of the rest of this License.

8. If the distribution and/or use of the Program is restricted in certain countries either by patents or by copyrighted interfaces, the original copyright holder who places the Program under this License may add an explicit geographical distribution limitation excluding those countries, so that distribution is permitted only in or among countries not thus excluded. In such case, this License incorporates the limitation as if written in the body of this License.

9. The Free Software Foundation may publish revised and/or new versions of the General Public License from time to time. Such new versions will be similar in spirit to the present version, but may differ in detail to address new problems or concerns.

    Each version is given a distinguishing version number. If the Program specifies a version number of this License which applies to it and "any later version", you have the option of following the terms and conditions either of that version or of any later version published by the Free Software Foundation. If the Program does not specify a version number of this License, you may choose any version ever published by the Free Software Foundation.

10. If you wish to incorporate parts of the Program into other free programs whose distribution conditions are different, write to the author to ask for permission. For software which is copyrighted by the Free Software Foundation, write to the Free Software Foundation; we sometimes make exceptions for this. Our decision will be guided by the two goals of preserving the free status of all derivatives of our free software and of promoting the sharing and reuse of software generally.

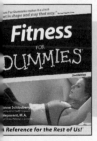

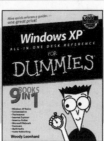